GREAT EXPECTATIONS

THE GRAPHIC NOVEL
Charles Dickens

ORIGINAL TEXT VERSION

Script Adaptation: Jen Green
Character Designs & Original Artwork: John Stokes
Colouring: Digikore Studios Ltd.
Colour Finishing: Jason Cardy
Lettering: Jim Campbell
Design & Layout: Jo Wheeler & Jenny Placentino

Editor in Chief: Clive Bryant

Great Expectations: The Graphic Novel
Original Text Version

Charles Dickens

First UK Edition

Published by: Classical Comics Ltd
Copyright ©2009 Classical Comics Ltd.

Acknowledgments: Every effort has been made to trace copyright holders of
material reproduced in this book. Any rights not acknowledged here will be
acknowledged in subsequent editions if notice is given to Classical Comics Ltd.

All enquiries should be addressed to:
Classical Comics Ltd.
PO Box 7280
Litchborough
Towcester
NN12 9AR
United Kingdom
Tel: 0845 812 3000

info@classicalcomics.com
www.classicalcomics.com

ISBN: 978-1-906332-09-9

Printed in the UK

This book is printed by 3P Direct Ltd. using biodegradable vegetable inks, on environmentally
friendly paper which is FSC (Forest Stewardship Council) certified (TT-COC-002291). This material
can be disposed of by recycling, incineration for energy recovery, composting and biodegradation.

The rights of Jen Green, John Stokes, Digikore Studios Ltd., Jason Cardy and Jim Campbell
to be identified as the artists of this work have been asserted in accordance with
the Copyright, Designs and Patents Act 1988 sections 77 and 78.

Contents

Dramatis Personæ

Young Pip
An orphan who lives with his sister and her husband

Adult Pip

Miss Havisham
An eccentric rich lady

Abel Magwitch
An escaped convict

Older Magwitch

Joe Gargery
Pip's brother-in-law

Mrs. Joe Gargery
Wife of Joe Gargery, and Pip's sister

Young Estella
Adopted daughter of Miss Havisham

Adult Estella

Young Biddy
Granddaughter to Mr. Wopsle's great aunt

Adult Biddy

Herbert Pocket
Son of Miss Havisham's cousin

4

Mr. Matthew Pocket
*Herbert's father
and Miss Havisham's cousin*

Sarah Pocket
Miss Havisham's cousin

Clara Barley
Fiancée to Herbert Pocket

Bentley Drummle
Student, taught by Matthew Pocket

Startop
Student, taught by Matthew Pocket

Mr. Jaggers
A lawyer from London

John Wemmick
Clerk to Mr. Jaggers

Aged Parent
Wemmick's father

Molly
Jaggers's housekeeper

Dolge Orlick
Works for Joe Gargery

Compeyson
A criminal

Mr. Pumblechook
Joe Gargery's uncle

Prologue

The year is 1812.

In the south-east corner of England, about thirty miles from the City of London, lies an area of marshland that separates the estuaries of the River Thames and the River Medway.

It's a cold, damp and misty area, home only to wildlife. There are a small number of villages nearby where a few countryside dwellings can be found, along with merchant traders, blacksmith's forges and public houses. There's also an old church that marks the end of life – before the desolate rough lands reach out towards the sea.

Far out from the shore lie floating prisons – converted warships called 'hulks' – that remove criminals from the overcrowded jails and keep them well away from society, while they await transportation to Australia and Tasmania. Murderers are hanged; but these ship-bound convicts are still considered dangerous enough to be banished from Britain for life.

This marshland is truly a bleak and barren place – the sort of place where someone could go unnoticed for a very long time; and where someone could stay hidden for as long as they wanted to hide...

Editor's Note:
The text that appears in this adaptation has been rigorously and diligently checked back to the original Dickens novel. Misspelled words (such as "pint" instead of "point", opposite) that were used to imply an accent in the speaker are reproduced in this adaptation, to remain true to the author's intentions.

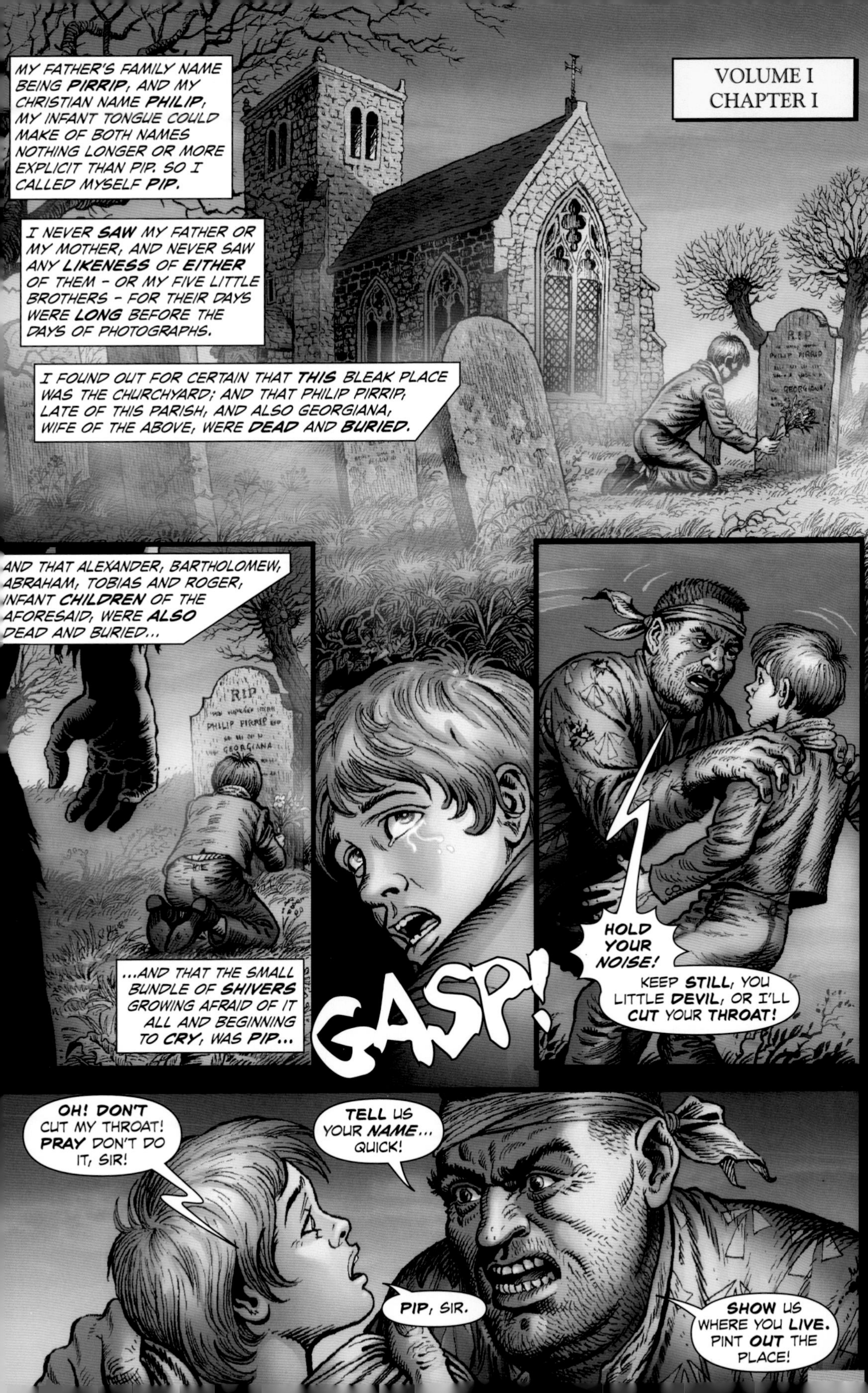
VOLUME I
CHAPTER I
MY FATHER'S FAMILY NAME BEING PIRRIP, AND MY CHRISTIAN NAME PHILIP, MY INFANT TONGUE COULD MAKE OF BOTH NAMES NOTHING LONGER OR MORE EXPLICIT THAN PIP. SO I CALLED MYSELF PIP.
I NEVER SAW MY FATHER OR MY MOTHER, AND NEVER SAW ANY LIKENESS OF EITHER OF THEM - OR MY FIVE LITTLE BROTHERS - FOR THEIR DAYS WERE LONG BEFORE THE DAYS OF PHOTOGRAPHS.
I FOUND OUT FOR CERTAIN THAT THIS BLEAK PLACE WAS THE CHURCHYARD; AND THAT PHILIP PIRRIP, LATE OF THIS PARISH, AND ALSO GEORGIANA, WIFE OF THE ABOVE, WERE DEAD AND BURIED.
AND THAT ALEXANDER, BARTHOLOMEW, ABRAHAM, TOBIAS AND ROGER, INFANT CHILDREN OF THE AFORESAID, WERE ALSO DEAD AND BURIED...
RIP
PHILIP PIRRIP
GEORGIANA
...AND THAT THE SMALL BUNDLE OF SHIVERS GROWING AFRAID OF IT ALL AND BEGINNING TO CRY, WAS PIP...
GASP!
HOLD YOUR NOISE!
KEEP STILL, YOU LITTLE DEVIL, OR I'LL CUT YOUR THROAT!
OH! DON'T CUT MY THROAT! PRAY DON'T DO IT, SIR!
TELL US YOUR NAME... QUICK!
PIP, SIR.
SHOW US WHERE YOU LIVE. PINT OUT THE PLACE!

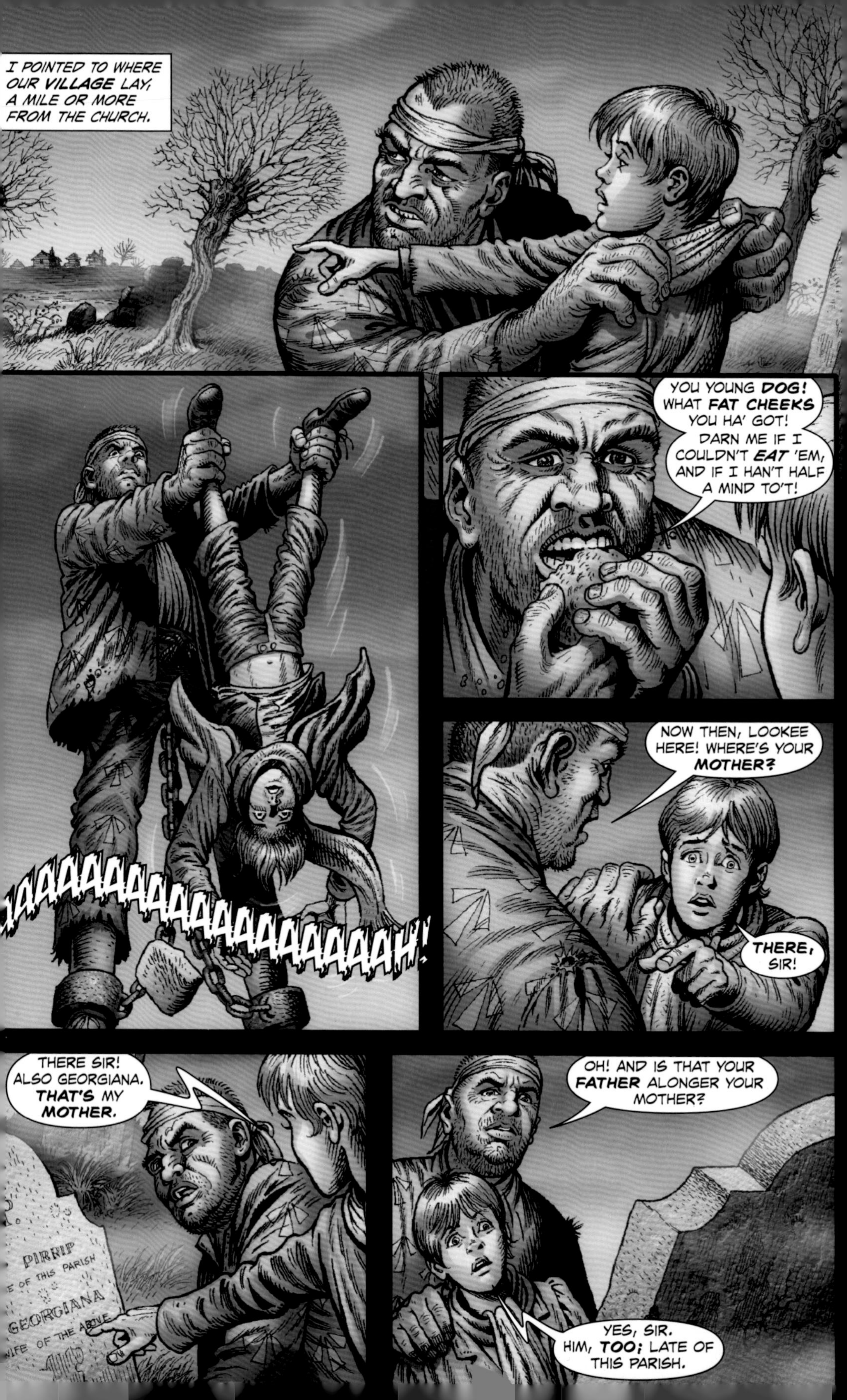
I POINTED TO WHERE OUR VILLAGE LAY, A MILE OR MORE FROM THE CHURCH.
YOU YOUNG DOG! WHAT FAT CHEEKS YOU HA' GOT! DARN ME IF I COULDN'T EAT 'EM, AND IF I HAN'T HALF A MIND TO'T!
AAAAAAAAAAAAAAAAAAAAAAAAAAH!
NOW THEN, LOOKEE HERE! WHERE'S YOUR MOTHER?
THERE, SIR!
THERE SIR! ALSO GEORGIANA. THAT'S MY MOTHER.
PIRRIP
GEORGIANA
OH! AND IS THAT YOUR FATHER ALONGER YOUR MOTHER?
YES, SIR. HIM, TOO; LATE OF THIS PARISH.

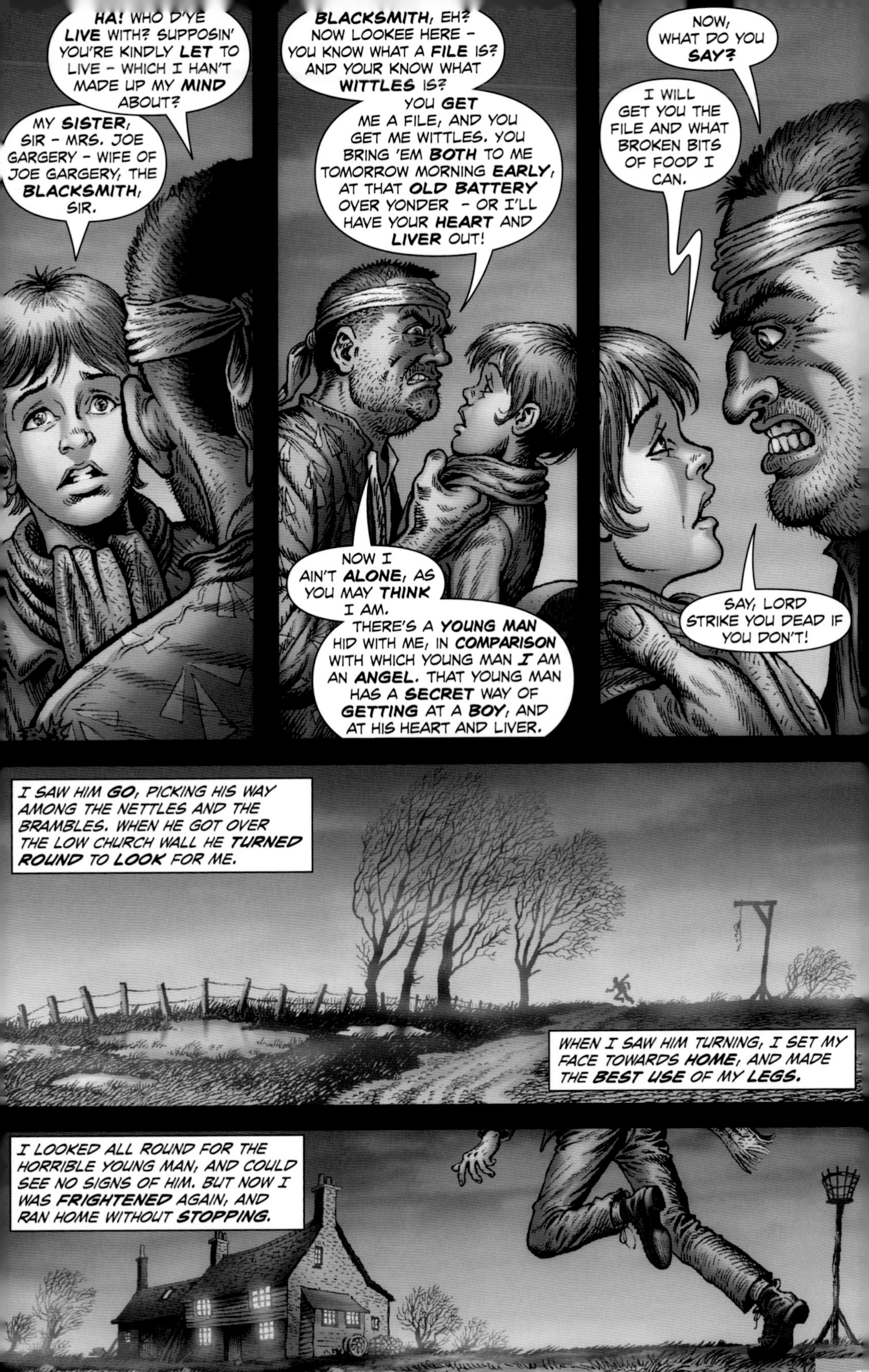
HA! WHO D'YE LIVE WITH? SUPPOSIN' YOU'RE KINDLY LET TO LIVE – WHICH I HAN'T MADE UP MY MIND ABOUT?
MY SISTER, SIR – MRS. JOE GARGERY – WIFE OF JOE GARGERY, THE BLACKSMITH, SIR.
BLACKSMITH, EH? NOW LOOKEE HERE – YOU KNOW WHAT A FILE IS? AND YOUR KNOW WHAT WITTLES IS?
YOU GET ME A FILE, AND YOU GET ME WITTLES. YOU BRING 'EM BOTH TO ME TOMORROW MORNING EARLY, AT THAT OLD BATTERY OVER YONDER – OR I'LL HAVE YOUR HEART AND LIVER OUT!
NOW I AIN'T ALONE, AS YOU MAY THINK I AM.
THERE'S A YOUNG MAN HID WITH ME, IN COMPARISON WITH WHICH YOUNG MAN I AM AN ANGEL. THAT YOUNG MAN HAS A SECRET WAY OF GETTING AT A BOY, AND AT HIS HEART AND LIVER.
NOW, WHAT DO YOU SAY?
I WILL GET YOU THE FILE AND WHAT BROKEN BITS OF FOOD I CAN.
SAY, LORD STRIKE YOU DEAD IF YOU DON'T!
I SAW HIM GO, PICKING HIS WAY AMONG THE NETTLES AND THE BRAMBLES. WHEN HE GOT OVER THE LOW CHURCH WALL HE TURNED ROUND TO LOOK FOR ME.
WHEN I SAW HIM TURNING, I SET MY FACE TOWARDS HOME, AND MADE THE BEST USE OF MY LEGS.
I LOOKED ALL ROUND FOR THE HORRIBLE YOUNG MAN, AND COULD SEE NO SIGNS OF HIM. BUT NOW I WAS FRIGHTENED AGAIN, AND RAN HOME WITHOUT STOPPING.

VOLUME I CHAPTER II

MY SISTER, MRS. JOE GARGERY, WAS MORE THAN TWENTY YEARS OLDER THAN I, AND HAD ESTABLISHED A GREAT **REPUTATION** BECAUSE SHE HAD BROUGHT ME UP "BY HAND."

JOE WAS ALONE IN THE KITCHEN. BEING FELLOW-SUFFERERS, HE IMPARTED A CONFIDENCE TO ME.

MRS. JOE HAS BEEN OUT A **DOZEN** TIMES, **LOOKING** FOR YOU, PIP. AND WHAT'S **WORSE**, SHE'S GOT **TICKLER** WITH HER!

SHE'S A **COMING**! GET BEHIND THE **DOOR**, OLD CHAP!

JOE GARGERY, THE BLACKSMITH, WAS A MILD, GOOD-NATURED, SWEET-TEMPERED, EASY-GOING, FOOLISH, DEAR FELLOW. HIS FORGE ADJOINED OUR HOUSE.

TICKLER WAS A WAX-ENDED PIECE OF CANE, **WORN** SMOOTH BY COLLISION WITH MY TICKLED **FRAME**.

WHERE HAVE YOU **BEEN**, YOU YOUNG MONKEY? **TELL** ME WHAT YOU'VE BEEN **DOING** TO WEAR ME AWAY WITH **FRET** AND **FRIGHT** AND **WORRIT**!

I HAVE ONLY BEEN TO THE CHURCHYARD.

CHURCHYARD! IF IT **WARN'T** FOR **ME** YOU'D HAVE BEEN TO THE CHURCHYARD **LONG AGO**, AND **STAYED** THERE.

THWACK THWACK

WHO BROUGHT YOU UP BY HAND?

YOU DID!

I'D NEVER DO IT **AGAIN**! I'VE NEVER HAD THIS APRON OF MINE OFF SINCE BORN YOU WERE.

IT'S **BAD** ENOUGH TO BE A **BLACKSMITH'S** WIFE (AND HIM A GARGERY) WITHOUT BEING YOUR **MOTHER**!

BOOOOOOMMM!!

HARK! WAS THAT **GREAT GUNS**, JOE?

THERE'S **ANOTHER CONVICT** OFF. THERE WAS A CONWICT OFF LAST NIGHT, AFTER SUNSET-GUN. AND THEY FIRED **WARNING** OF HIM.

AND NOW IT APPEARS THEY'RE FIRING WARNING OF **ANOTHER**!

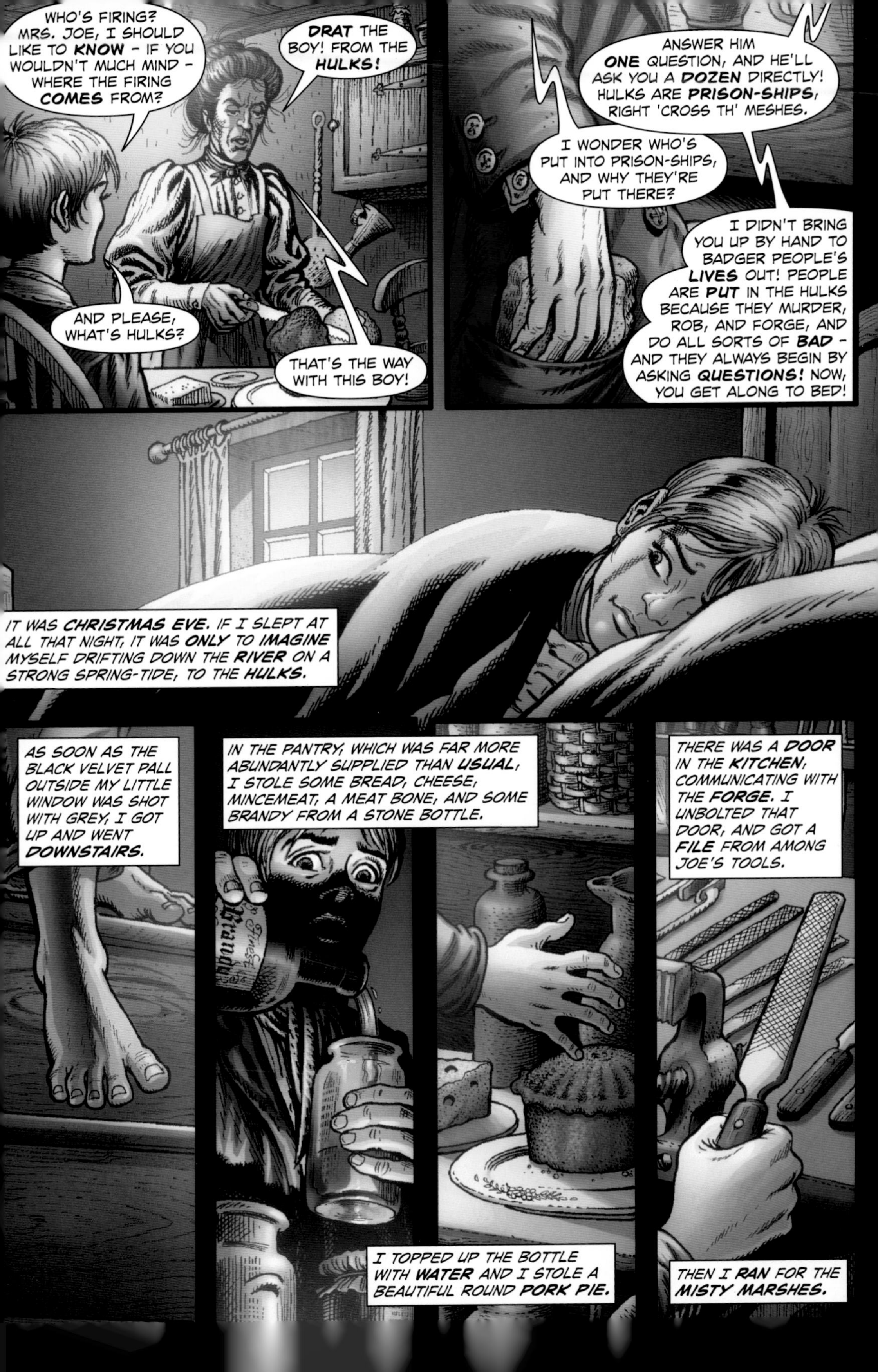
WHO'S FIRING? MRS. JOE, I SHOULD LIKE TO KNOW – IF YOU WOULDN'T MUCH MIND – WHERE THE FIRING COMES FROM?
DRAT THE BOY! FROM THE HULKS!
AND PLEASE, WHAT'S HULKS?
THAT'S THE WAY WITH THIS BOY!
ANSWER HIM ONE QUESTION, AND HE'LL ASK YOU A DOZEN DIRECTLY! HULKS ARE PRISON-SHIPS, RIGHT 'CROSS TH' MESHES.
I WONDER WHO'S PUT INTO PRISON-SHIPS, AND WHY THEY'RE PUT THERE?
I DIDN'T BRING YOU UP BY HAND TO BADGER PEOPLE'S LIVES OUT! PEOPLE ARE PUT IN THE HULKS BECAUSE THEY MURDER, ROB, AND FORGE, AND DO ALL SORTS OF BAD – AND THEY ALWAYS BEGIN BY ASKING QUESTIONS! NOW, YOU GET ALONG TO BED!
IT WAS CHRISTMAS EVE. IF I SLEPT AT ALL THAT NIGHT, IT WAS ONLY TO IMAGINE MYSELF DRIFTING DOWN THE RIVER ON A STRONG SPRING-TIDE, TO THE HULKS.
AS SOON AS THE BLACK VELVET PALL OUTSIDE MY LITTLE WINDOW WAS SHOT WITH GREY, I GOT UP AND WENT DOWNSTAIRS.
IN THE PANTRY, WHICH WAS FAR MORE ABUNDANTLY SUPPLIED THAN USUAL, I STOLE SOME BREAD, CHEESE, MINCEMEAT, A MEAT BONE, AND SOME BRANDY FROM A STONE BOTTLE.
I TOPPED UP THE BOTTLE WITH WATER AND I STOLE A BEAUTIFUL ROUND PORK PIE.
THERE WAS A DOOR IN THE KITCHEN, COMMUNICATING WITH THE FORGE. I UNBOLTED THAT DOOR, AND GOT A FILE FROM AMONG JOE'S TOOLS.
THEN I RAN FOR THE MISTY MARSHES.

VOLUME I
CHAPTER III

I KNEW MY WAY TO THE BATTERY; FOR I HAD BEEN THERE OF A SUNDAY WITH JOE. WE WOULD HAVE SUCH LARKS THERE!

I CROSSED A DITCH NEAR THE BATTERY, WHEN I SAW A MAN SITTING BEFORE ME, HEAVY WITH SLEEP. I WENT FORWARD SOFTLY AND TOUCHED HIM ON THE SHOULDER.

IT WAS **NOT** THE SAME MAN, BUT **ANOTHER** MAN!

IT'S THE **YOUNG MAN,** I THOUGHT, FEELING MY HEART **SHOOT** AS I **IDENTIFIED** HIM.

HE **STUMBLED** AND **RAN OFF.** I WAS SOON AT THE BATTERY AFTER THAT...

...AND THERE WAS THE **RIGHT** MAN, WAITING FOR ME. HE WAS AWFULLY COLD, TO BE SURE, AND LOOKED AWFULLY HUNGRY.

HE DID NOT TURN ME **UPSIDE DOWN** THIS TIME. I OPENED THE **BUNDLE** AND **EMPTIED** MY POCKETS.

I AM AFRAID YOU WON'T LEAVE ANY OF IT FOR **HIM.** THERE'S **NO MORE** TO BE GOT WHERE THAT CAME FROM.

THE YOUNG MAN THAT YOU SPOKE OF, THAT WAS *HID* WITH YOU.

HIM? WHO'S HIM?

HIM? HE DON'T WANT NO WITTLES!

HE *LOOKED* AS IF HE DID. JUST NOW, *YONDER*, OVER THERE. I FOUND HIM NODDING ASLEEP AND THOUGHT IT WAS *YOU*.

SHOW ME THE WAY HE WENT. I'LL PULL HIM DOWN, LIKE A *BLOODHOUND!* *CURSE* THIS IRON ON MY SORE LEG! GIVE US HOLD OF THE *FILE*, BOY.

I INDICATED IN WHAT *DIRECTION* THE MIST HAD SHROUDED THE *OTHER* MAN, AND HE LOOKED UP AT IT FOR AN INSTANCE.

BUT HE WAS DOWN ON THE RANK WET GRASS, FILING AT HIS IRON LIKE A *MADMAN.*

I WAS VERY MUCH *AFRAID* AGAIN. THE BEST THING I COULD DO WAS TO SLIP OFF.

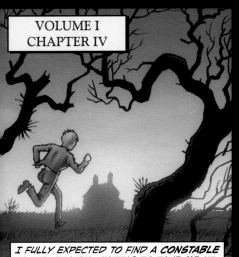

VOLUME I
CHAPTER IV

I FULLY EXPECTED TO FIND A *CONSTABLE* IN THE KITCHEN, WAITING TO TAKE ME UP. BUT NOT ONLY WAS THERE *NO* CONSTABLE, BUT NO *DISCOVERY* HAD YET BEEN MADE OF THE *ROBBERY.*

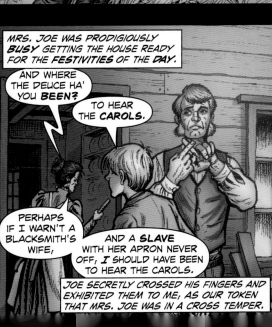

MRS. JOE WAS PRODIGIOUSLY *BUSY* GETTING THE HOUSE READY FOR THE *FESTIVITIES* OF THE *DAY.*

AND WHERE THE DEUCE HA' YOU *BEEN?*

TO HEAR THE *CAROLS.*

PERHAPS IF I WARN'T A BLACKSMITH'S WIFE,

AND A *SLAVE* WITH HER APRON NEVER OFF, *I* SHOULD HAVE BEEN TO HEAR THE CAROLS.

JOE SECRETLY CROSSED HIS FINGERS AND EXHIBITED THEM TO ME, AS OUR TOKEN THAT MRS. JOE WAS IN A CROSS TEMPER.

MR. WOPSLE, THE CLERK AT CHURCH, WAS TO DINE WITH US; AND MR. HUBBLE THE WHEELWRIGHT AND MRS. HUBBLE; AND UNCLE PUMBLECHOOK (JOE'S UNCLE), WHO WAS A WELL-TO-DO CORN CHANDLER.

AS THE COMPLIMENTS OF THE SEASON, I HAVE BROUGHT YOU, MUM, A BOTTLE OF SHERRY WINE; AND A BOTTLE OF PORT WINE.

OH, UN--CLE PUM-BLE--CHOOK! THIS IS KIND!

THIS GOOD COMPANY WOULD NEVER LEAVE ME ALONE. IT BEGAN THE MOMENT WE SAT DOWN TO DINNER AND MR. WOPSLE SAID GRACE.

...MAY WE BE TRULY GRATEFUL.

DO YOU HEAR THAT? BE GRATEFUL!

BE GRATEFUL, BOY, TO THEM WHICH BROUGHT YOU UP BY HAND.

HAVE A LITTLE BRANDY, UNCLE.

O HEAVENS! HE WILL FIND IT IS WEAK!

TAR!

UNCLE PUMBLECHOOK IMPERIOUSLY WAVED IT AWAY WITH HIS HAND. FOR THE TIME BEING, I WAS SAVED.

I BEGAN TO THINK I SHOULD GET OVER THE DAY; THEN MY SISTER SPOKE...

I HAD FILLED UP THE BOTTLE FROM THE TAR-WATER JUG, WITH WHICH MRS. JOE DOSED ME REGULARLY.

TAR! WHY, HOW EVER COULD TAR COME THERE?

TO FINISH WITH, YOU MUST TASTE A DELIGHTFUL PRESENT OF UNCLE PUMBLECHOOK'S! IT'S A SAVOURY PORK PIE.

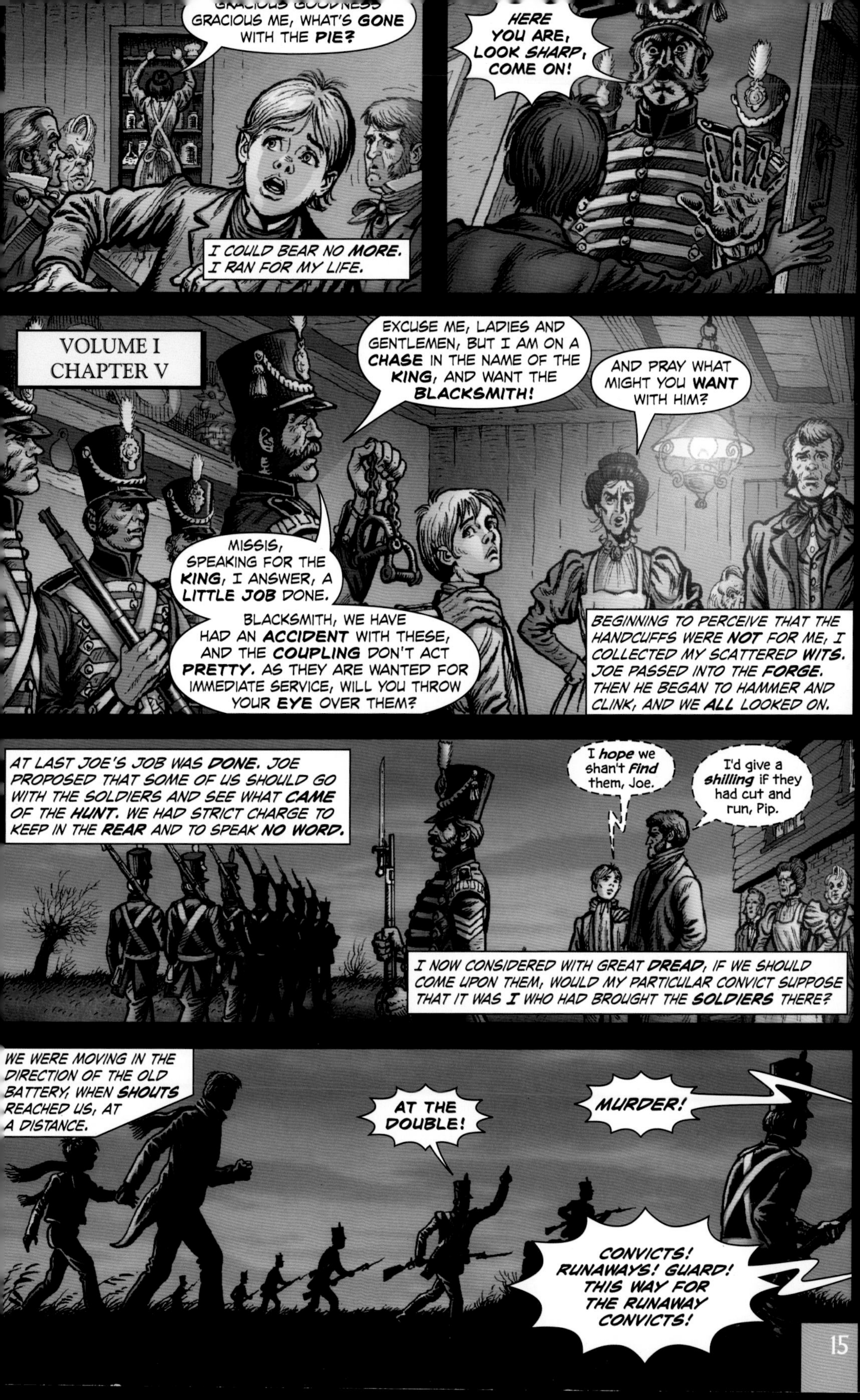
GRACIOUS GOODNESS GRACIOUS ME, WHAT'S GONE WITH THE PIE?
I COULD BEAR NO MORE. I RAN FOR MY LIFE.
HERE YOU ARE, LOOK SHARP, COME ON!
VOLUME I
CHAPTER V
EXCUSE ME, LADIES AND GENTLEMEN, BUT I AM ON A CHASE IN THE NAME OF THE KING, AND WANT THE BLACKSMITH!
AND PRAY WHAT MIGHT YOU WANT WITH HIM?
MISSIS, SPEAKING FOR THE KING, I ANSWER, A LITTLE JOB DONE.
BLACKSMITH, WE HAVE HAD AN ACCIDENT WITH THESE, AND THE COUPLING DON'T ACT PRETTY. AS THEY ARE WANTED FOR IMMEDIATE SERVICE, WILL YOU THROW YOUR EYE OVER THEM?
BEGINNING TO PERCEIVE THAT THE HANDCUFFS WERE NOT FOR ME, I COLLECTED MY SCATTERED WITS. JOE PASSED INTO THE FORGE. THEN HE BEGAN TO HAMMER AND CLINK, AND WE ALL LOOKED ON.
AT LAST JOE'S JOB WAS DONE. JOE PROPOSED THAT SOME OF US SHOULD GO WITH THE SOLDIERS AND SEE WHAT CAME OF THE HUNT. WE HAD STRICT CHARGE TO KEEP IN THE REAR AND TO SPEAK NO WORD.
I hope we shan't find them, Joe.
I'd give a shilling if they had cut and run, Pip.
I NOW CONSIDERED WITH GREAT DREAD, IF WE SHOULD COME UPON THEM, WOULD MY PARTICULAR CONVICT SUPPOSE THAT IT WAS I WHO HAD BROUGHT THE SOLDIERS THERE?
WE WERE MOVING IN THE DIRECTION OF THE OLD BATTERY, WHEN SHOUTS REACHED US, AT A DISTANCE.
AT THE DOUBLE!
MURDER!
CONVICTS! RUNAWAYS! GUARD! THIS WAY FOR THE RUNAWAY CONVICTS!

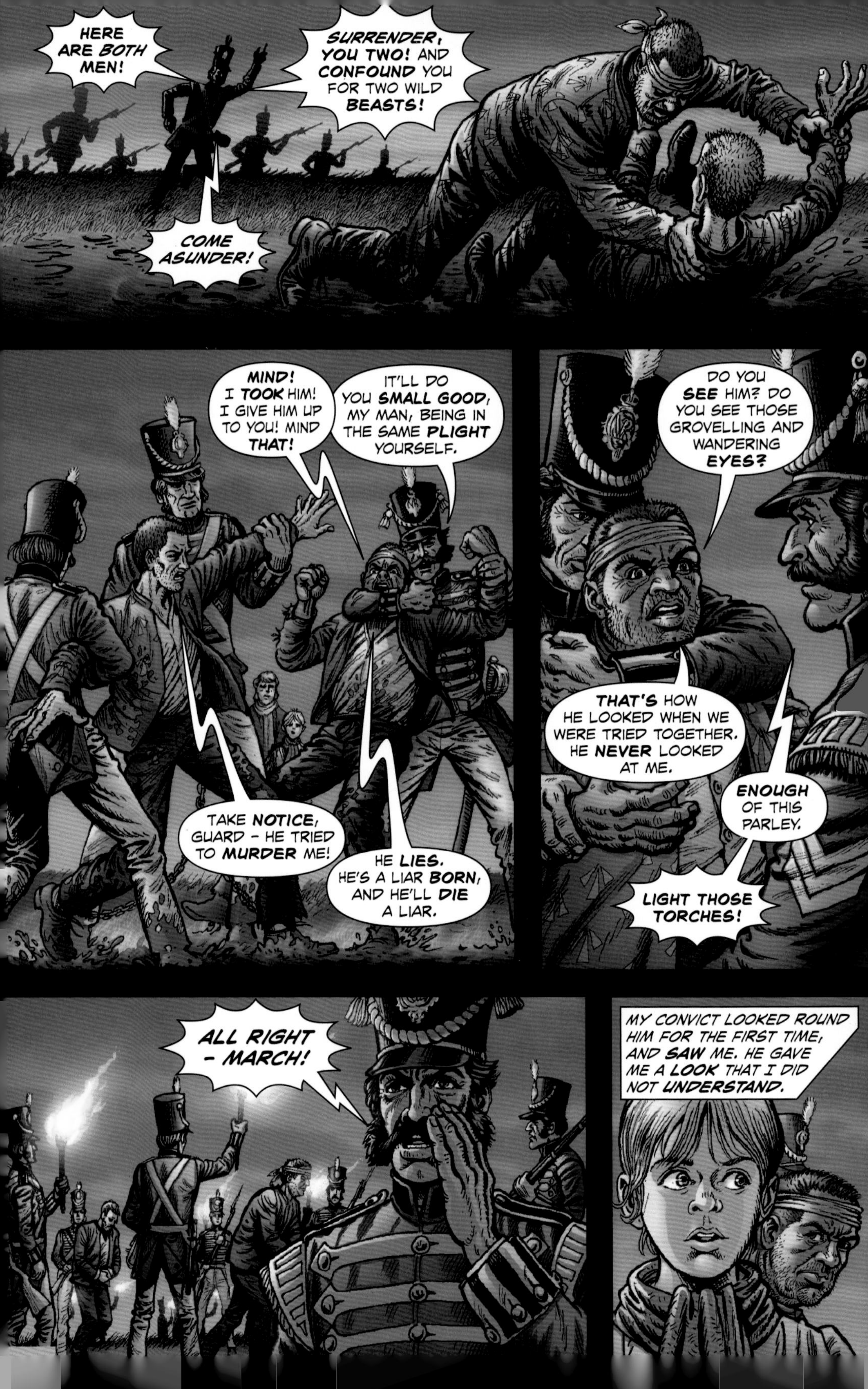
HERE ARE BOTH MEN!
SURRENDER, YOU TWO! AND CONFOUND YOU FOR TWO WILD BEASTS!
COME ASUNDER!
MIND! I TOOK HIM! I GIVE HIM UP TO YOU! MIND THAT!
IT'LL DO YOU SMALL GOOD, MY MAN, BEING IN THE SAME PLIGHT YOURSELF.
TAKE NOTICE, GUARD - HE TRIED TO MURDER ME!
HE LIES. HE'S A LIAR BORN, AND HE'LL DIE A LIAR.
DO YOU SEE HIM? DO YOU SEE THOSE GROVELLING AND WANDERING EYES?
THAT'S HOW HE LOOKED WHEN WE WERE TRIED TOGETHER. HE NEVER LOOKED AT ME.
ENOUGH OF THIS PARLEY.
LIGHT THOSE TORCHES!
ALL RIGHT - MARCH!
MY CONVICT LOOKED ROUND HIM FOR THE FIRST TIME, AND SAW ME. HE GAVE ME A LOOK THAT I DID NOT UNDERSTAND.

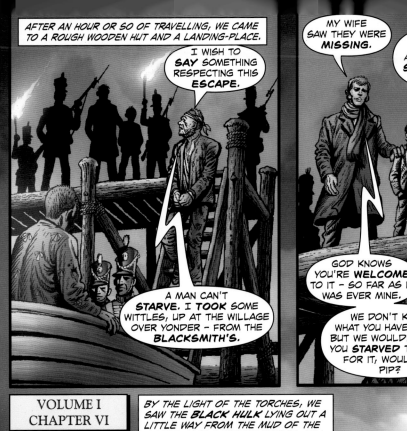

AFTER AN HOUR OR SO OF TRAVELLING, WE CAME TO A ROUGH WOODEN HUT AND A LANDING-PLACE.

I WISH TO **SAY** SOMETHING RESPECTING THIS **ESCAPE**.

A MAN CAN'T **STARVE**. I **TOOK** SOME WITTLES, UP AT THE WILLAGE OVER YONDER – FROM THE **BLACKSMITH'S**.

MY WIFE SAW THEY WERE **MISSING**.

SO **YOU'RE** THE BLACKSMITH, ARE YOU? THEN I'M **SORRY** TO SAY, I'VE EAT YOUR **PIE**.

GOD KNOWS YOU'RE **WELCOME** TO IT – SO FAR AS IT WAS EVER MINE.

WE DON'T KNOW WHAT YOU HAVE **DONE**, BUT WE WOULDN'T HAVE YOU **STARVED** TO DEATH FOR IT, WOULD US, PIP?

VOLUME I
CHAPTER VI

BY THE LIGHT OF THE TORCHES, WE SAW THE **BLACK HULK** LYING OUT A LITTLE WAY FROM THE MUD OF THE SHORE, LIKE A WICKED NOAH'S ARK.

WE SAW HIM TAKEN UP THE SIDE AND DISAPPEAR. THEN THE ENDS OF THE TORCHES WERE FLUNG **HISSING** INTO THE WATER, AND WENT OUT, AS IF IT WERE **ALL OVER** WITH HIM.

I HAD BEEN EXONERATED, BUT IT DID NOT **IMPEL** ME TO FRANK DISCLOSURE FOR **FEAR** OF LOSING JOE'S **CONFIDENCE**.

MR. WOPSLE'S GREAT-AUNT KEPT AN EVENING SCHOOL IN THE VILLAGE. SHE WAS A *RIDICULOUS* OLD WOMAN, WHO USED TO GO TO SLEEP FROM SIX TO SEVEN EVERY EVENING, IN THE SOCIETY OF YOUTH WHO PAID TWO PENCE PER WEEK, FOR THE OPPORTUNITY OF SEEING HER DO IT.

MORE BY THE HELP OF BIDDY THAN MR. WOPSLE'S GREAT-AUNT, I STRUGGLED THROUGH THE ALPHABET. *BIDDY* WAS MR. WOPSLE'S GREAT-AUNT'S GRANDDAUGHTER. SHE WAS AN *ORPHAN* LIKE *MYSELF*; LIKE ME, TOO, SHE HAD BEEN BROUGHT UP BY HAND.

ONE NIGHT I WAS SITTING IN THE CHIMNEY CORNER WITH MY SLATE, EXPENDING *GREAT* EFFORTS ON THE PRODUCTION OF A LETTER TO JOE.

Mi deer Jo i ope u r kn write well i ope i shal son b habell 4 2 teedge u jo an then we shall b so glodd an wenn m prengtd 2 u Jo wot larx an bleve me inf xn Pip

I SAY, PIP, OLD CHAP! WHY, HERE'S A J, AND A J-O, JOE. *ASTONISHING!* YOU *ARE* A SCHOLAR.

LIKE STEAM, JOE'S EDUCATION WAS YET IN ITS INFANCY. I OFFERED TO TEACH HIM MORE LETTERS.

NOW, WHEN YOU TAKE ME IN HAND IN MY LEARNING, PIP (AND I TELL YOU BEFOREHAND I AM *AWFUL* DULL), MRS. JOE MUSTN'T SEE TOO MUCH OF WHAT WE'RE *UP* TO.

SHE WOULD *NOT* BE OVER PARTIAL TO MY BEING A *SCHOLAR*, FOR FEAR AS I MIGHT *RISE*. LIKE A SORT OF *REBEL*, DON'T YOU SEE?

DON'T *DENY* THAT YOUR SISTER DROPS DOWN UPON US *HEAVY*. WHY DON'T I *RISE?* WELL, YOUR SISTER'S A MASTER-MIND. AND I *AIN'T* A MASTER-MIND.

LAST OF ALL, PIP, I WISH THERE *WARN'T* NO *TICKLER* FOR YOU, OLD CHAP; I WISH I COULD TAKE IT ALL ON MYSELF;

HOWEVER, HERE'S THE DUTCH CLOCK A WORKING HIMSELF UP TO STRIKE *EIGHT* OF 'EM, AND SHE'S NOT HOME YET.

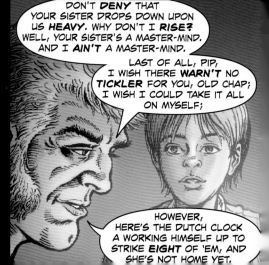

HERE COMES THE MARE, *RINGING* LIKE A *PEAL* OF BELLS!

NOW IF THIS BOY AIN'T *GRATEFUL* THIS NIGHT, HE NEVER *WILL* BE! IT'S ONLY TO BE HOPED THAT HE WON'T BE *POMPEYED*. BUT I HAVE MY *FEARS*.

?

SHE AIN'T IN THAT LINE, MUM. SHE KNOWS *BETTER*.

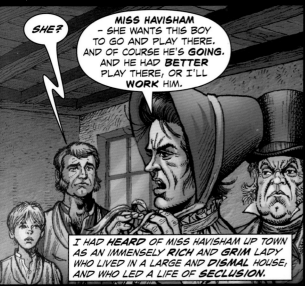

SHE?

MISS HAVISHAM — SHE WANTS THIS BOY TO GO AND PLAY THERE. AND OF COURSE HE'S *GOING*. AND HE HAD *BETTER* PLAY THERE, OR I'LL *WORK* HIM.

I HAD *HEARD* OF MISS HAVISHAM UP TOWN AS AN *IMMENSELY* RICH AND *GRIM* LADY WHO LIVED IN A LARGE AND *DISMAL* HOUSE, AND WHO LED A LIFE OF *SECLUSION*.

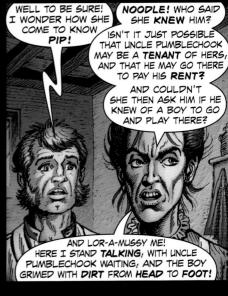

WELL TO BE SURE! I WONDER HOW SHE COME TO KNOW *PIP*!

NOODLE! WHO SAID SHE *KNEW* HIM? ISN'T IT JUST POSSIBLE THAT UNCLE PUMBLECHOOK MAY BE A *TENANT* OF HERS, AND THAT HE MAY GO THERE TO PAY HIS *RENT*?

AND COULDN'T SHE THEN ASK HIM IF HE KNEW OF A BOY TO GO AND PLAY THERE?

AND LOR-A-MUSSY ME! HERE I STAND *TALKING*, WITH UNCLE PUMBLECHOOK WAITING, AND THE BOY GRIMED WITH *DIRT* FROM *HEAD* TO *FOOT*!

SPLOOSH

BOY, BE FOREVER *GRATEFUL* TO ALL FRIENDS, BUT ESPECIALLY UNTO THEM WHICH BROUGHT YOU UP BY HAND!

I WAS THEN *DELIVERED* OVER TO MR. PUMBLECHOOK.

GOD BLESS YOU, PIP, OLD CHAP!

THE NEXT MORNING, MR. PUMBLECHOOK AND I BREAKFASTED AND AT TEN O'CLOCK WE STARTED FOR MISS HAVISHAM'S.

WITHIN A QUARTER OF AN HOUR WE CAME TO THE HOUSE. AFTER RINGING THE BELL, WE *WAITED* AT THE GATE.

THIS IS PIP.

THIS IS *PIP*, IS IT? COME *IN*, PIP.

DON'T *LOITER*, BOY.

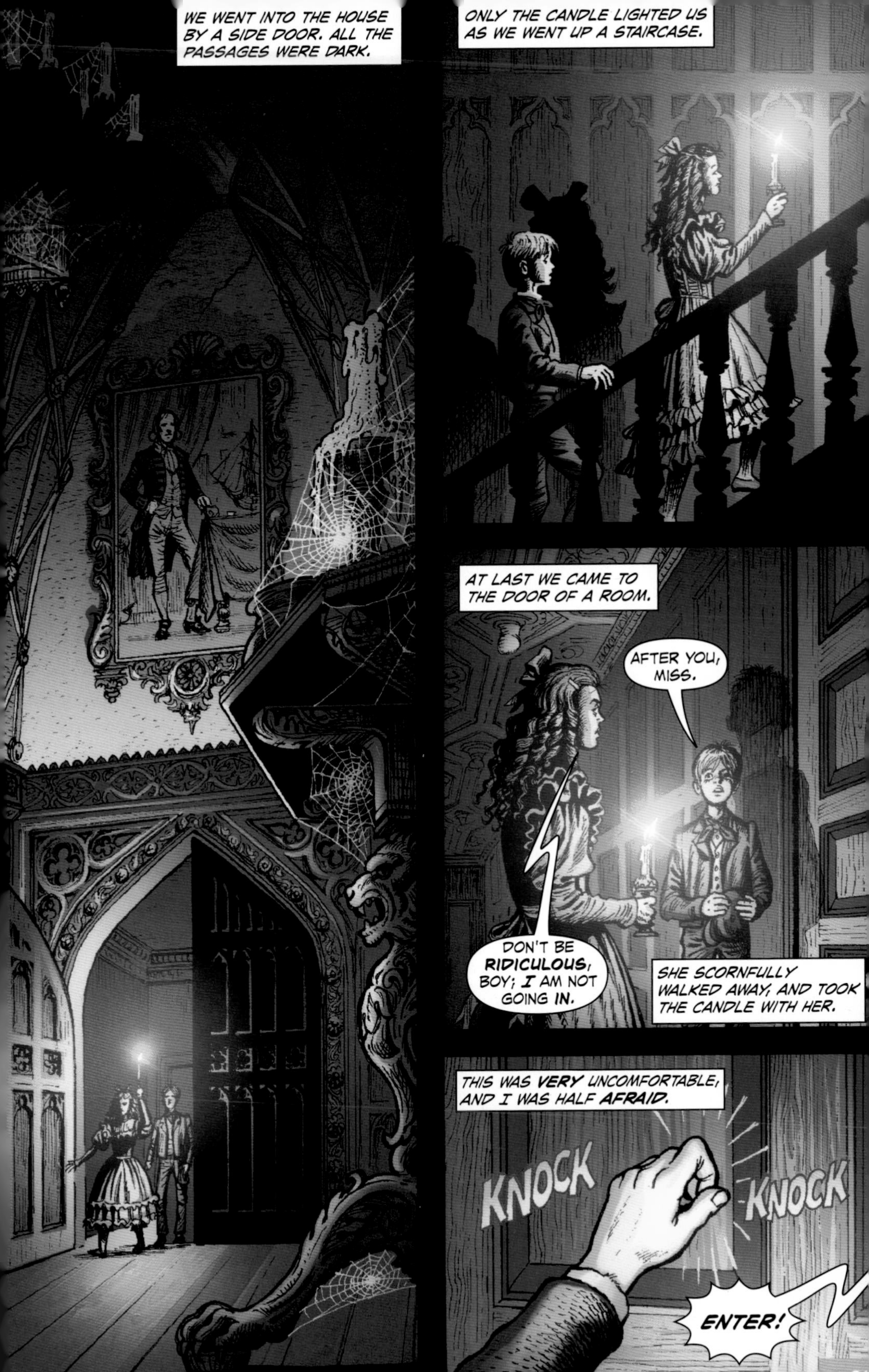
WE WENT INTO THE HOUSE BY A SIDE DOOR. ALL THE PASSAGES WERE DARK.
ONLY THE CANDLE LIGHTED US AS WE WENT UP A STAIRCASE.
AT LAST WE CAME TO THE DOOR OF A ROOM.
AFTER YOU, MISS.
DON'T BE RIDICULOUS, BOY; I AM NOT GOING IN.
SHE SCORNFULLY WALKED AWAY, AND TOOK THE CANDLE WITH HER.
THIS WAS VERY UNCOMFORTABLE, AND I WAS HALF AFRAID.
KNOCK
KNOCK
ENTER!

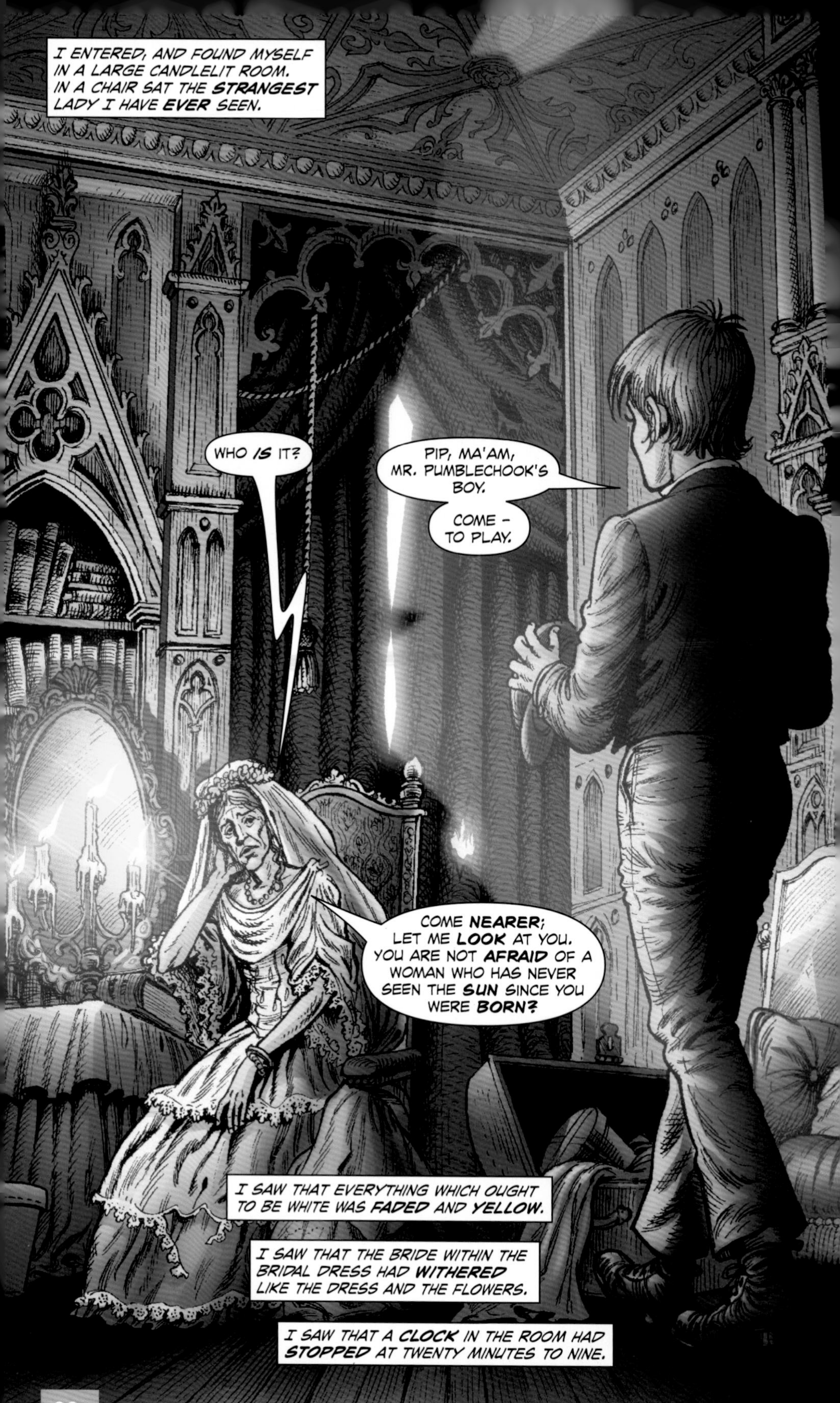
I ENTERED, AND FOUND MYSELF IN A LARGE CANDLELIT ROOM. IN A CHAIR SAT THE STRANGEST LADY I HAVE EVER SEEN.
WHO IS IT?
PIP, MA'AM, MR. PUMBLECHOOK'S BOY.
COME - TO PLAY.
COME NEARER; LET ME LOOK AT YOU. YOU ARE NOT AFRAID OF A WOMAN WHO HAS NEVER SEEN THE SUN SINCE YOU WERE BORN?
I SAW THAT EVERYTHING WHICH OUGHT TO BE WHITE WAS FADED AND YELLOW.
I SAW THAT THE BRIDE WITHIN THE BRIDAL DRESS HAD WITHERED LIKE THE DRESS AND THE FLOWERS.
I SAW THAT A CLOCK IN THE ROOM HAD STOPPED AT TWENTY MINUTES TO NINE.

DO YOU KNOW WHAT I TOUCH **HERE**?

YES, MA'AM — YOUR **HEART**.

BROKEN!

I SOMETIMES HAVE SICK **FANCIES**. AND I HAVE A SICK FANCY THAT I WANT TO SEE SOME **PLAY**.

THERE, THERE! PLAY, PLAY, **PLAY!**

ARE YOU SULLEN AND OBSTINATE?

NO, MA'AM, I AM VERY **SORRY** I CAN'T PLAY JUST NOW.

I WOULD DO IT IF I **COULD**; BUT IT'S SO NEW HERE, AND SO **STRANGE**, AND FINE, AND **MELANCHOLY**....

So **new** to him, so **old** to me; so **strange** to him, so **familiar** to me. So **melancholy** to **both** of us!

CALL **ESTELLA**. YOU CAN DO THAT AT THE DOOR.

ESTELLA !!!

ESTELLA ANSWERED AT LAST, AND HER **LIGHT** CAME ALONG THE DARK PASSAGE LIKE A **STAR**.

MISS HAVISHAM BECKONED HER CLOSE, TOOK UP A JEWEL FROM THE TABLE, AND TRIED ITS EFFECT AGAINST HER **PRETTY** BROWN HAIR.

YOUR **OWN**, ONE DAY, MY DEAR, AND YOU WILL USE IT **WELL**.

LET ME SEE YOU PLAY **CARDS** WITH THIS **BOY**.

WITH **THIS** BOY? WHY, HE IS A COMMON **LABOURING** BOY!

WHAT DO YOU **PLAY**, BOY?

NOTHING BUT BEGGAR MY NEIGHBOUR, MISS.

BEGGAR HIM.

SO WE SAT DOWN TO CARDS.

MISS HAVISHAM SAT **CORPSE-LIKE** AS WE PLAYED AT CARDS. ESTELLA COMPLAINED BEFORE THE FIRST **GAME** WAS OUT.

HE CALLS THE KNAVES JACKS, THIS BOY! AND WHAT **COARSE HANDS** HE HAS! AND WHAT **THICK BOOTS!**

I HAD NEVER THOUGHT OF BEING **ASHAMED** OF MY **HANDS** BEFORE. BUT HER CONTEMPT FOR ME WAS SO **STRONG**, THAT IT BECAME **INFECTIOUS**, AND I **CAUGHT** IT.

23

ESTELLA WON THE GAME, AND I DEALT. I MISDEALT, AND SHE DENOUNCED ME FOR A STUPID, CLUMSY LABOURING-BOY.

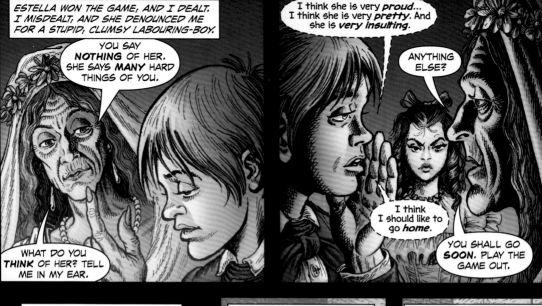

YOU SAY **NOTHING** OF HER. SHE SAYS **MANY** HARD THINGS OF YOU.

WHAT DO YOU **THINK** OF HER? TELL ME IN MY EAR.

I think she is very **proud**... I think she is very **pretty**. And she is **very insulting**.

ANYTHING ELSE?

I think I should like to go **home**.

YOU SHALL GO **SOON**. PLAY THE GAME OUT.

I PLAYED THE GAME TO AN **END** WITH ESTELLA, AND SHE **BEGGARED** ME. SHE THREW THE CARDS DOWN ON THE TABLE AS IF SHE **DESPISED** THEM.

WHEN SHALL I HAVE YOU HERE AGAIN? LET ME THINK.

COME AGAIN AFTER **SIX DAYS**.

ESTELLA, TAKE HIM DOWN. LET HIM HAVE SOMETHING TO EAT, AND LET HIM LOOK ABOUT HIM WHILE HE EATS.

I FOLLOWED THE CANDLE DOWN, AS I HAD FOLLOWED THE CANDLE UP. AS ESTELLA OPENED THE SIDE ENTRANCE, THE RUSH OF THE DAYLIGHT QUITE **CONFOUNDED** ME.

YOU ARE TO WAIT HERE, YOU BOY.

SHE DISAPPEARED AND CLOSED THE DOOR. ALONE IN THE COURT-YARD, I LOOKED AT MY COARSE HANDS AND MY COMMON BOOTS. THEY HAD NEVER TROUBLED ME BEFORE, BUT THEY TROUBLED ME NOW, AS VULGAR APPENDAGES.

SHE CAME BACK, WITH SOME BREAD AND MEAT AND A LITTLE MUG OF BEER. SHE GAVE IT TO ME WITHOUT LOOKING AT ME, AS IF I WERE A DOG IN DISGRACE.

I WAS SO HUMILIATED AND HURT THAT I HAD TO HOLD BACK MY TEARS.

BUT WHEN SHE WAS **GONE**, I **HID** MY FACE AND **CRIED**.

I GOT RID OF MY **INJURED FEELINGS** FOR THE TIME, AND AFTER THE FOOD AND DRINK I WAS SOON IN SPIRITS TO LOOK ABOUT ME.

I ENTERED A GARDEN, OVERGROWN WITH TANGLED WEEDS, AND THERE FOUND AN OLD BREWERY; TO BE SURE, IT WAS A **DESERTED** PLACE.

AS I TURNED MY EYES TOWARDS A GREAT WOODEN BEAM, I SAW A FIGURE HANGING BY THE NECK.

AND THE FACE WAS **MISS HAVISHAM'S**.

MY **TERROR** WAS **GREATEST** WHEN I FOUND NO FIGURE THERE.

GASP!

THE FROSTY LIGHT OF THE CHEERFUL SKY BROUGHT ME ROUND. I SAW **ESTELLA** APPROACHING WITH THE KEYS, TO LET ME OUT.

BREWE

WHY DON'T YOU **CRY?**

BECAUSE I DON'T **WANT** TO.

YOU **DO.** YOU HAVE BEEN CRYING TILL YOU ARE HALF-BLIND, AND YOU ARE NEAR CRYING **AGAIN** NOW.

HA, HA, HA!

SHE **LOCKED** THE GATE UPON ME. I SET OFF ON THE FOUR-MILE WALK TO OUR FORGE, PONDERING ALL I HAD SEEN, AND **DEEPLY REVOLVING** THAT MY **HANDS** WERE COARSE, MY **BOOTS** WERE **THICK,** AND THAT I WAS A **COMMON** LABOURING-BOY.

25

WHEN I REACHED HOME, MR. PUMBLECHOOK WAS THERE. JOE WAS BUSY IN THE FORGE. MY SISTER WAS **VERY** CURIOUS TO KNOW ALL ABOUT MISS HAVISHAM'S, AND ASKED A NUMBER OF **QUESTIONS**. I FELT CONVINCED THAT IF I **DESCRIBED** MISS HAVISHAM'S AS MY EYES HAD SEEN IT, I SHOULD **NOT** BE UNDERSTOOD.

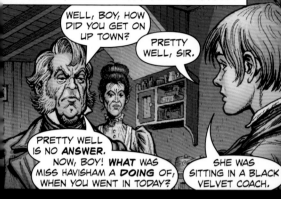

WELL, BOY, HOW DID YOU GET ON UP TOWN?

PRETTY WELL, SIR.

PRETTY WELL IS NO **ANSWER**. NOW, BOY! **WHAT** WAS MISS HAVISHAM A **DOING** OF, WHEN YOU WENT IN TODAY?

SHE WAS SITTING IN A BLACK VELVET COACH.

MISS ESTELLA – THAT'S HER **NIECE**, I THINK – HANDED HER IN **CAKE** AND **WINE** AT THE COACH-WINDOW, ON A **GOLD** PLATE. WE **ALL** HAD CAKE AND WINE ON GOLD PLATES. THERE WERE FOUR IMMENSE DOGS. AND THEY FOUGHT FOR VEAL-CUTLETS OUT OF A SILVER BASKET.

IN A BLACK VELVET COACH? CAN THIS BE **POSSIBLE**, UNCLE? WHAT CAN THE BOY MEAN?

MY OPINION, MUM, IS, IT'S A SEDAN-CHAIR. SHE'S **FLIGHTY**, YOU KNOW – QUITE FLIGHTY ENOUGH TO PASS HER DAYS IN A SEDAN-CHAIR.

WHEN JOE CAME IN FROM HIS WORK, MY SISTER RELATED MY PRETENDED EXPERIENCES. NOW, WHEN I SAW JOE OPEN HIS EYES IN HELPLESS AMAZEMENT, I WAS OVERTAKEN BY **PENITENCE**.

MRS. JOE AND MR. PUMBLECHOOK SAT DEBATING WHAT RESULTS WOULD COME FROM MISS HAVISHAM'S **FAVOUR**. THEY HAD NO DOUBT THAT MISS HAVISHAM WOULD "**DO SOMETHING**" FOR ME.

AFTER MR. PUMBLECHOOK HAD DRIVEN OFF, I STOLE INTO THE FORGE TO JOE.

JOE, I SHOULD LIKE TO **TELL** YOU SOMETHING. YOU REMEMBER ALL THAT ABOUT MISS HAVISHAM'S?

IT'S A TERRIBLE THING, BUT IT AIN'T **TRUE**. IT'S **LIES**, JOE.

NOT **ALL** OF IT? PIP, OLD CHAP!

I SAY! THAT'S **AWFUL**! WHAT **POSSESSED** YOU?

THEN I TOLD JOE THAT I FELT VERY **MISERABLE**, AND HOW I WISHED I WAS NOT **COMMON**, AND THE LIES HAD COME OF IT SOMEHOW.

LIES IS **LIES**. HOWSEVER THEY COME, THEY DIDN'T OUGHT TO COME. AND AS TO BEING COMMON, I DON'T MAKE IT OUT. YOU ARE ONCOMMON IN SOME THINGS. YOU'RE ONCOMMON **SMALL**. LIKEWISE YOU'RE A ONCOMMON **SCHOLAR**.

NO, I AM IGNORANT AND **BACKWARD**, JOE.

WELL, PIP, BE IT SO OR BE IT SON'T, YOU MUST BE A COMMON SCHOLAR **AFORE** YOU CAN BE A ONCOMMON ONE! THE KING **CAN'T** WRITE HIS ACTS OF PARLIAMENT, WITHOUT HAVING BEGUN, WHEN HE WAS A PRINCE, WITH THE **ALPHABET**.

THERE WAS SOME **HOPE** IN THIS PIECE OF WISDOM.

THE IDEA OCCURRED TO ME THAT THE **BEST** STEP I COULD TAKE TOWARDS MAKING MYSELF UNCOMMON WAS TO GET OUT OF BIDDY **EVERYTHING** SHE KNEW. I MENTIONED TO HER THAT I HAD A PARTICULAR **REASON** FOR WISHING TO **GET ON** IN LIFE.

I TOLD BIDDY THAT I SHOULD FEEL VERY MUCH OBLIGED TO HER IF SHE WOULD IMPART **ALL** HER LEARNING TO ME. BIDDY, WHO WAS THE MOST **OBLIGING** OF GIRLS, IMMEDIATELY SAID SHE **WOULD**, AND INDEED BEGAN TO CARRY OUT HER PROMISE WITHIN FIVE MINUTES.

THERE WAS A PUBLIC-HOUSE IN THE VILLAGE, AND JOE LIKED SOMETIMES TO SMOKE HIS PIPE THERE. I HAD RECEIVED **STRICT** ORDERS FROM MY SISTER TO CALL FOR HIM AT THE THREE JOLLY BARGEMEN ON MY WAY FROM SCHOOL, AND BRING HIM **HOME**.

I FOUND HIM IN THE COMMON ROOM, SMOKING HIS PIPE WITH MR. WOPSLE AND A **STRANGER**.

THE MOMENT JOE GREETED ME, THE STRANGER TURNED HIS HEAD AND **LOOKED** AT ME. HE WAS A SECRET-LOOKING MAN WHOM I HAD NEVER SEEN BEFORE. HE LOOKED HARD AT ME, NODDED, AND MADE ROOM ON THE SETTLE BESIDE HIM.

I WAS USED TO SIT BESIDE JOE, SO I FELL INTO THE SPACE BESIDE HIM. THE STRANGE MAN, AFTER GLANCING AT JOE, AND SEEING THAT HIS ATTENTION WAS ENGAGED, NODDED TO ME AGAIN, AND THEN RUBBED HIS **LEG** IN A VERY **ODD** WAY.

YOU WAS SAYING THAT YOU WAS A **BLACKSMITH?** WHAT'LL YOU DRINK, MR.-- GARGERY, IS IT?

AT MY EXPENSE?

I WOULDN'T WISH TO BE STIFF COMPANY! **RUM!**

THREE RUMS! GLASSES ROUND!

I AM NOT ACQUAINTED WITH THIS COUNTRY, GENTLEMEN, BUT IT SEEMS A **SOLITARY** COUNTRY TOWARDS THE RIVER.

THE STRANGER LOOKED AT ME **AGAIN** – STILL COCKING HIS EYE, AS IF HE WERE TAKING AIM AT ME WITH HIS INVISIBLE **GUN**.

MOST MARSHES **IS** SOLITARY. NONE BUT A RUNAWAY **CONVICT** NOW AND THEN. AND WE DON'T FIND THEM, **EASY.** EH, MR. WOPSLE?

SEEMS YOU HAVE BEEN **OUT** AFTER SUCH?

ONCE.

HE'S A **LIKELY** YOUNG PARCEL OF BONES THAT.

WHAT IS IT YOU CALL HIM?

PIP.

HE STIRRED HIS RUM WITH A **FILE**.

HE DID THIS SO THAT **NOBODY** BUT **I** SAW THE FILE.

I KNEW IT TO BE JOE'S FILE, AND **I KNEW** THAT HE KNEW MY CONVICT, THE MOMENT I **SAW** THE INSTRUMENT.

HE PROCEEDED IN TAKING LITTLE NOTICE OF ME. AFTER HALF AN HOUR, JOE GOT UP TO GO.

STOP HALF A MOMENT, MR. GARGERY. I THINK I'VE GOT A BRIGHT NEW **SHILLING** IN MY POCKET, AND IF I HAVE, THE BOY SHALL **HAVE** IT.

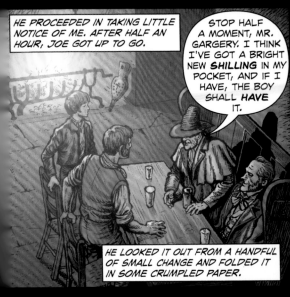

HE LOOKED IT OUT FROM A HANDFUL OF SMALL CHANGE AND FOLDED IT IN SOME CRUMPLED PAPER.

YOURS! MIND! YOUR OWN.

THANK YOU.

JOE AND I SAID OUR "GOODNIGHT"S AND WALKED HOME.

MY SISTER WAS NOT IN A VERY BAD TEMPER WHEN WE PRESENTED OURSELVES IN THE KITCHEN, SO JOE TOLD HER ABOUT THE BRIGHT SHILLING.

A **BAD** UN, I'LL BE BOUND, OR HE WOULDN'T HAVE GIVEN IT TO THE **BOY!** LET'S LOOK AT IT.

BUT WHAT'S **THIS?** TWO ONE-POUND NOTES?

JOE RAN BACK WITH THEM TO THE JOLLY BARGEMEN; BUT THE MAN WAS **GONE**. JOE LEFT WORD THERE ABOUT THE NOTES, AND MY SISTER SEALED THEM IN A TEAPOT IN THE STATE PARLOUR. THERE THEY **REMAINED**, A **NIGHTMARE** TO ME, MANY A NIGHT AND DAY.

AT THE APPOINTED TIME I RETURNED TO MISS HAVISHAM'S. MY RING AT THE GATE BROUGHT ESTELLA, WHO LED ME TO QUITE **ANOTHER** PART OF THE HOUSE.

YOU ARE TO COME THIS WAY TODAY.

SHE LED ME ALONG DARK PASSAGES, AND OUT ACROSS A SMALL PAVED COURT-YARD, TO A DETACHED DWELLING-HOUSE. WE ENTERED A **GLOOMY** ROOM. THERE WAS SOME COMPANY IN THE ROOM, THREE LADIES AND A GENTLEMAN.

MY COMING **STOPPED** THE CONVERSATION, AND THE OTHER OCCUPANTS **LOOKED** AT ME.

YOU ARE TO GO AND STAND THERE, BOY, TILL YOU ARE **WANTED.**

THE THREE LADIES AND GENTLEMAN ALL HAD A **LISTLESS** AND **DREARY** AIR OF WAITING SOMEBODY'S **PLEASURE.**

POOR **DEAR** SOUL! MATTHEW IS NOBODY'S ENEMY BUT HIS **OWN**!

WE ARE TO LOVE OUR NEIGHBOUR.

POOR SOUL! HE IS SO VERY **STRANGE**!

DING A LING

NOW, BOY!

AS WE WERE GOING WITH OUR CANDLE ALONG THE DARK PASSAGE, ESTELLA **STOPPED** ALL OF A SUDDEN, AND FACED ME.

AM I **PRETTY**?

YES, I THINK YOU ARE **VERY** PRETTY.

AM I INSULTING?

NOT SO MUCH AS YOU WERE **LAST** TIME.

SMACK!

NOW, YOU LITTLE COARSE **MONSTER**, WHAT DO YOU THINK OF ME **NOW?**

I **SHALL** NOT TELL YOU.

WHICH WAS A FALSE DECLARATION AS **EVER** WAS MADE, FOR I WAS INWARDLY CRYING FOR HER THEN.

WHY DON'T YOU **CRY** AGAIN YOU LITTLE WRETCH?

BECAUSE I'LL **NEVER** CRY FOR YOU **AGAIN.**

AS WE WERE MAKING OUR WAY **UP** STAIRS, WE MET A GENTLEMAN GROPING HIS WAY **DOWN.**

WHOM HAVE WE HERE? BOY OF THE NEIGHBOURHOOD, HEY? HOW DO **YOU** COME **HERE?**

MISS HAVISHAM SENT FOR ME, SIR.

WELL! BEHAVE YOURSELF. I HAVE A PRETTY LARGE EXPERIENCE OF BOYS; AND YOU'RE A **BAD** SET OF FELLOWS. MIND YOU BEHAVE YOURSELF!

WITH THOSE WORDS, HE RELEASED ME. I WAS **GLAD**, FOR HIS HAND SMELT OF SCENTED SOAP. HE WENT HIS WAY DOWN STAIRS.

WE WERE SOON IN MISS HAVISHAM'S ROOM. ESTELLA LEFT ME STANDING NEAR THE DOOR.

ARE YOU READY TO **PLAY?**

I DON'T THINK I **AM**, MA'AM.

THEN ARE YOU WILLING TO **WORK?**

I AM QUITE WILLING.

THEN GO INTO THAT OPPOSITE ROOM, AND **WAIT** THERE TILL I COME.

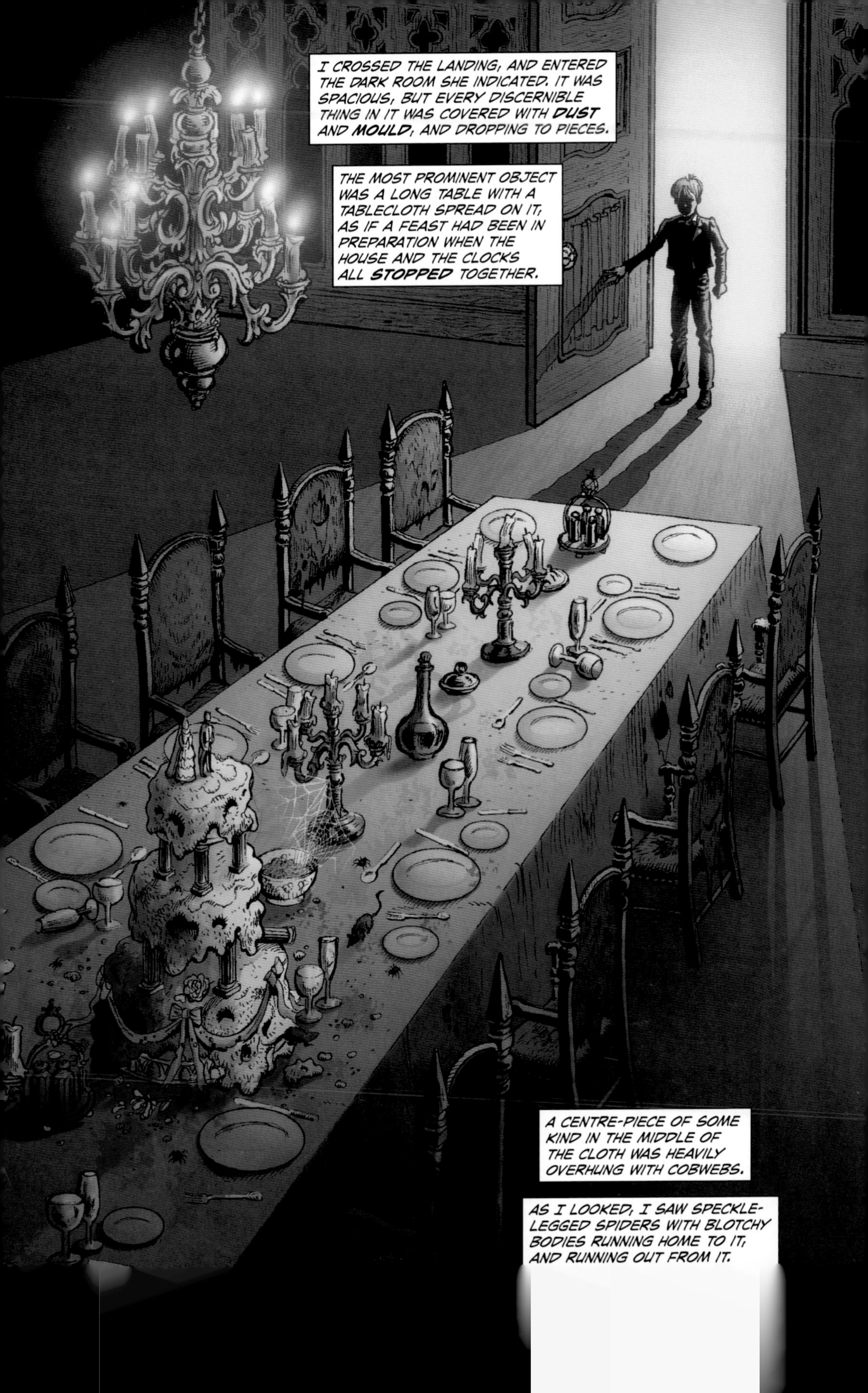
I CROSSED THE LANDING, AND ENTERED THE DARK ROOM SHE INDICATED. IT WAS SPACIOUS, BUT EVERY DISCERNIBLE THING IN IT WAS COVERED WITH DUST AND MOULD, AND DROPPING TO PIECES.
THE MOST PROMINENT OBJECT WAS A LONG TABLE WITH A TABLECLOTH SPREAD ON IT, AS IF A FEAST HAD BEEN IN PREPARATION WHEN THE HOUSE AND THE CLOCKS ALL STOPPED TOGETHER.
A CENTRE-PIECE OF SOME KIND IN THE MIDDLE OF THE CLOTH WAS HEAVILY OVERHUNG WITH COBWEBS.
AS I LOOKED, I SAW SPECKLE-LEGGED SPIDERS WITH BLOTCHY BODIES RUNNING HOME TO IT, AND RUNNING OUT FROM IT.

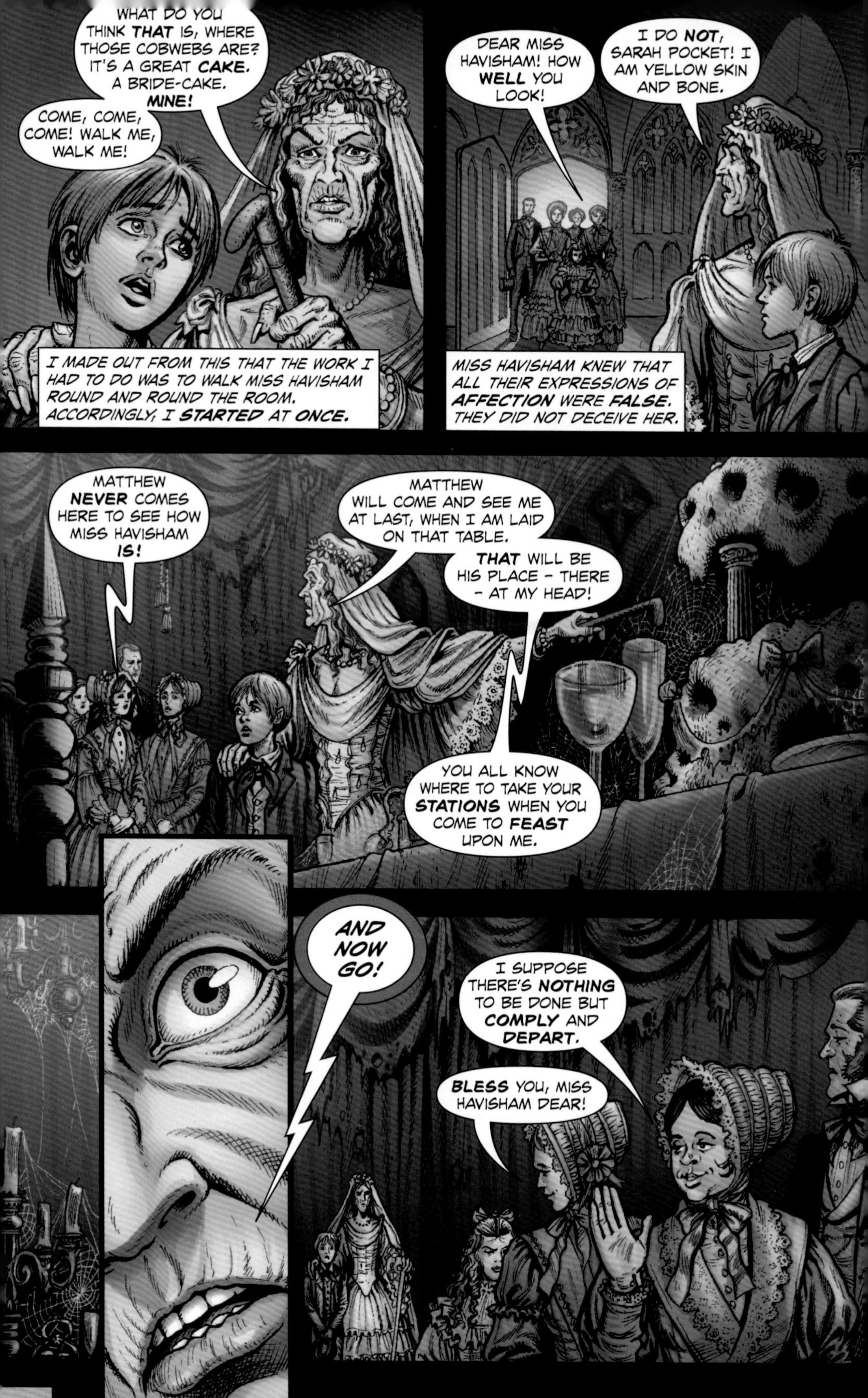
WHAT DO YOU THINK THAT IS, WHERE THOSE COBWEBS ARE? IT'S A GREAT CAKE. A BRIDE-CAKE. MINE!
COME, COME, COME! WALK ME, WALK ME!
I MADE OUT FROM THIS THAT THE WORK I HAD TO DO WAS TO WALK MISS HAVISHAM ROUND AND ROUND THE ROOM. ACCORDINGLY, I STARTED AT ONCE.
DEAR MISS HAVISHAM! HOW WELL YOU LOOK!
I DO NOT, SARAH POCKET! I AM YELLOW SKIN AND BONE.
MISS HAVISHAM KNEW THAT ALL THEIR EXPRESSIONS OF AFFECTION WERE FALSE. THEY DID NOT DECEIVE HER.
MATTHEW NEVER COMES HERE TO SEE HOW MISS HAVISHAM IS!
MATTHEW WILL COME AND SEE ME AT LAST, WHEN I AM LAID ON THAT TABLE.
THAT WILL BE HIS PLACE - THERE - AT MY HEAD!
YOU ALL KNOW WHERE TO TAKE YOUR STATIONS WHEN YOU COME TO FEAST UPON ME.
AND NOW GO!
I SUPPOSE THERE'S NOTHING TO BE DONE BUT COMPLY AND DEPART.
BLESS YOU, MISS HAVISHAM DEAR!

THIS IS MY BIRTHDAY, PIP.

I DON'T SUFFER THOSE WHO WERE HERE JUST NOW TO **SPEAK** OF IT. ON THIS DAY OF THE YEAR, LONG BEFORE YOU WERE BORN, THIS HEAP OF DECAY WAS BROUGHT HERE.

IT AND I HAVE WORN AWAY **TOGETHER**. THE MICE HAVE GNAWED AT IT, AND SHARPER TEETH THAN TEETH OF **MICE** HAVE **GNAWED** AT **ME**.

SHE STOOD LOOKING AT THE TABLE, AND I REMAINED QUIET.

AT LENGTH, ESTELLA RETURNED, AND A DAY WAS APPOINTED FOR MY RETURN. THEN I WAS TAKEN DOWN INTO THE YARD TO BE **FED** IN THE FORMER DOG-LIKE MANNER.

THERE, TOO, I WAS AGAIN LEFT TO WANDER ABOUT AS I LIKED.

AFTER A STROLL AROUND THE GARDEN, WHICH WAS QUITE A **WILDERNESS**, I FOUND MYSELF BACK BY THE DISMAL HOUSE IN WHICH I HAD WAITED EARLIER. BELIEVING THAT THE HOUSE WAS NOW EMPTY, I LOOKED IN AT A WINDOW...

...AND SAW A PALE YOUNG GENTLEMAN, WHO QUICKLY **DISAPPEARED**...

...AND **REAPPEARED** BESIDE ME. HE HAD BEEN AT HIS BOOKS WHEN HE FOUND ME **STARING** AT HIM.

HALLOA, YOUNG FELLOW! WHO LET **YOU** IN AND GAVE YOU **LEAVE** TO **PROWL** ABOUT?

MISS ESTELLA.

COME AND FIGHT!

WHAT COULD I DO BUT **FOLLOW** HIM? HIS MANNER WAS SO **FINAL**, AND I WAS SO **ASTONISHED**, THAT I FOLLOWED WHERE HE LED.

AARRGH!

33

DOOFFF!

THWUMMPP!

AT LAST HE GOT A BAD FALL. HE WENT ON HIS **KNEES** TO HIS **SPONGE** AND THREW IT UP.

≷GASP≷ THAT MEANS ≷GASP≷ YOU HAVE **WON**.

CAN I HELP YOU?

NO THANKEE. ≷GASP≷ GOOD AFTERNOON.

AFTER DRESSING, I WISHED HIM A GOOD AFTERNOON IN RETURN. WHEN I GOT INTO THE COURT-YARD, I FOUND ESTELLA **WAITING**.

THERE WAS A BRIGHT **FLUSH** UPON HER FACE, AS THOUGH SOMETHING HAD HAPPENED TO **DELIGHT** HER.

COME HERE! YOU MAY **KISS** ME, IF YOU LIKE.

I KISSED HER CHEEK AS SHE TURNED IT TO ME.

BUT I FELT THAT THE KISS WAS GIVEN TO THE COARSE **COMMON** BOY AS A PIECE OF **MONEY** MIGHT HAVE BEEN.

VOLUME I
CHAPTER XII

THE MORE I THOUGHT OF THE FIGHT, THE MORE CERTAIN IT APPEARED THAT *SOMETHING* WOULD BE DONE TO ME.

FOR SOME DAYS, I EVEN KEPT CLOSE AT HOME, AND LOOKED OUT AT THE KITCHEN DOOR WITH THE GREATEST *CAUTION* AND TREPIDATION BEFORE GOING ON AN ERRAND, LEST THE OFFICERS OF THE *COUNTY JAIL* SHOULD *POUNCE* UPON ME.

WHEN THE DAY CAME ROUND FOR MY *RETURN* TO THE SCENE OF THE DEED OF VIOLENCE, MY *TERRORS* REACHED THEIR *HEIGHT*.

HOWEVER, GO TO MISS HAVISHAM'S I *MUST*, AND GO I *DID*.

AND *BEHOLD!* NOTHING CAME OF THE LATE STRUGGLE. IT WAS NOT ALLUDED TO IN ANY WAY, AND NO PALE YOUNG GENTLEMAN WAS TO BE DISCOVERED ON THE PREMISES.

I ENTERED, THAT SAME DAY, ON A REGULAR OCCUPATION OF PUSHING MISS HAVISHAM ROUND HER OWN ROOM, AND ACROSS THE LANDING, AND ROUND THE OTHER ROOM.

OVER AND OVER AND OVER AGAIN, WE WOULD MAKE THESE JOURNEYS, AND SOMETIMES THEY WOULD LAST AS LONG AS THREE HOURS AT A STRETCH.

Does she grow *prettier* and *prettier* Pip?

Yes.

I SHOULD RETURN EVERY ALTERNATE DAY AT NOON FOR THESE PURPOSES, OVER A PERIOD OF AT LEAST *EIGHT* OR *TEN* MONTHS.

ESTELLA WAS ALWAYS ABOUT, BUT NEVER TOLD ME I MIGHT KISS HER AGAIN. SOMETIMES SHE WOULD COLDLY *TOLERATE* ME. SOMETIMES SHE WOULD *CONDESCEND* TO ME.

SOMETIMES SHE WOULD BE QUITE *FAMILIAR* WITH ME. SOMETIMES SHE WOULD TELL ME *ENERGETICALLY* THAT SHE *HATED* ME.

Break their *hearts* my pride and hope, break their hearts and have *no mercy!*

I REPOSED CONFIDENCE IN NO ONE BUT **BIDDY**; BUT, I TOLD POOR BIDDY **EVERYTHING**. WHY IT CAME NATURAL TO ME TO DO SO, AND WHY BIDDY HAD A DEEP **CONCERN** IN EVERYTHING I TOLD HER, I DID NOT KNOW **THEN**.

THOUGH I THINK I KNOW **NOW**.

MEANWHILE, COUNCILS WENT ON IN THE KITCHEN AT HOME. THAT ASS, PUMBLECHOOK, USED OFTEN TO COME OVER FOR THE PURPOSE OF DISCUSSING MY **PROSPECTS** WITH MY SISTER.

NOW, MUM, **HERE** IS THE BOY WHICH YOU BROUGHT UP BY HAND.

HOLD UP YOUR HEAD, BOY, AND BE FOR EVER **GRATEFUL** UNTO THEM WHICH DID SO.

WE WENT ON IN THIS WAY FOR A LONG TIME...

...AND IT SEEMED **LIKELY** THAT WE SHOULD **CONTINUE** TO GO ON IN THIS WAY; WHEN, ONE DAY, MISS HAVISHAM **STOPPED SHORT** AS SHE AND I WERE WALKING.

YOU ARE GROWING **TALL**, PIP!

TELL ME THE NAME AGAIN OF THAT **BLACKSMITH** OF YOURS – THE MASTER YOU WERE TO BE APPRENTICED TO?

JOE GARGERY, MA'AM.

YOU HAD BETTER BE APPRENTICED AT **ONCE**. WOULD GARGERY COME HERE WITH YOU, AND BRING YOUR INDENTURES, DO YOU THINK?

HE WOULD TAKE IT AS AN **HONOUR** TO BE ASKED.

WHEN I GOT HOME AT NIGHT, AND DELIVERED THIS MESSAGE, MY SISTER WENT ON THE **RAMPAGE** IN AN ALARMING DEGREE, BECAUSE THE MESSAGE WAS NOT FOR **HER**, BUT **JOE**.

AM I DOOR MATS UNDER YOUR **FEET**?

WHAT **COMPANY** AM **I FIT** FOR THEN?

ON THE NEXT DAY BUT ONE, JOE ARRAYED HIMSELF IN HIS SUNDAY CLOTHES TO ACCOMPANY ME TO MISS HAVISHAM'S. THE FORGE WAS SHUT UP FOR THE DAY.

MY SISTER DECLARED HER INTENTION OF GOING TO TOWN WITH US, AND BEING LEFT AT UNCLE PUMBLECHOOK'S.

AT MISS HAVISHAM'S HOUSE, ESTELLA OPENED THE GATE AS USUAL. SHE TOOK **NO NOTICE** OF **EITHER** OF US, BUT LED US THE WAY THAT I KNEW SO WELL.

YOU ARE **BOTH** TO GO IN.

THROUGHOUT THE INTERVIEW, JOE **PERSISTED** IN ADDRESSING **ME** INSTEAD OF MISS HAVISHAM...

YOU HAVE **REARED** THE BOY, WITH THE INTENTION OF TAKING HIM FOR YOUR **APPRENTICE**; IS THAT SO, MR. GARGERY?

AS YOU AND ME WERE EVER **FRIENDS**, IF YOU HAD EVER MADE **OBJECTIONS** TO THE BUSINESS, THEY WOULD HAVE BEEN **ATTENDED** TO.

HAVE YOU BROUGHT HIS INDENTURES **WITH** YOU?

WELL, **PIP**, YOU YOURSELF SEE ME PUT 'EM IN MY 'AT.

YOU EXPECTED NO **PREMIUM** WITH THE BOY?

PIP, WHICH I MEANTERSAY; YOU KNOW THE ANSWER TO BE FULL WELL NO, PIP.

PIP HAS EARNED A PREMIUM **HERE**, AND HERE IT IS. THERE ARE FIVE-AND-TWENTY GUINEAS IN THIS BAG. GIVE IT TO YOUR **MASTER**, PIP.

THIS IS WERY **LIBERAL** ON YOUR PART, PIP --

-- AND IT IS AS SUCH RECEIVED AND GRATEFUL WELCOME; THOUGH NEVER LOOKED FOR. AND NOW, OLD CHAP, MAY YOU AND ME DO OUR **DUTY**, BOTH ON US, BY ONE AND ANOTHER!

GOODBYE, PIP! LET THEM OUT, ESTELLA.

AM I TO COME **AGAIN**, MISS HAVISHAM?

NO. **GARGERY** IS YOUR **MASTER** NOW.

WHAT'S HAPPENED TO YOU?

MISS HAVISHAM MADE IT WERY PARTICK'LER THAT WE SHOULD GIVE HER COMPLIMENTS TO MRS. J. GARGERY--

MUCH GOOD THEY'LL DO ME! AND WHAT DID SHE GIVE YOUNG RANTIPOLE HERE?

SHE GIV' HIM NOTHING.

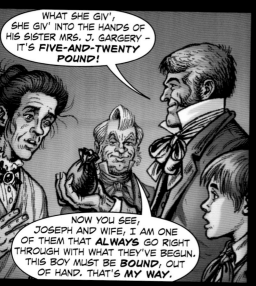

WHAT SHE GIV', SHE GIV' INTO THE HANDS OF HIS SISTER MRS. J. GARGERY – IT'S FIVE-AND-TWENTY POUND!

NOW YOU SEE, JOSEPH AND WIFE, I AM ONE OF THEM THAT ALWAYS GO RIGHT THROUGH WITH WHAT THEY'VE BEGUN. THIS BOY MUST BE BOUND, OUT OF HAND. THAT'S MY WAY.

THE JUSTICES WERE SITTING IN THE TOWN HALL NEAR AT HAND, AND WE AT ONCE WENT OVER TO HAVE ME BOUND APPRENTICE TO JOE IN THE MAGISTERIAL PRESENCE.

What's he done?

He's a young 'un, too, but looks bad don't he?

TOWN HALL

MY SISTER BECAME SO EXCITED, THAT NOTHING WOULD SERVE HER BUT WE MUST HAVE A DINNER AT THE BLUE BOAR; A MOST MELANCHOLY DAY I PASSED.

THE SWINDLING PUMBLECHOOK TOOK THE TOP OF THE TABLE AND, WHEN HE ADDRESSED THEM ON THE SUBJECT OF MY BEING BOUND, HE PLACED ME ON A CHAIR BESIDE HIM.

THEY WOULDN'T LET ME GO TO SLEEP. WHENEVER THEY SAW ME DROPPING OFF, THEY WOKE ME UP AND TOLD ME TO ENJOY MYSELF.

WHEN I FINALLY GOT INTO MY LITTLE BEDROOM I WAS TRULY WRETCHED, AND HAD A STRONG CONVICTION THAT I SHOULD NEVER LIKE JOE'S TRADE.

I HAD LIKED IT ONCE, BUT ONCE WAS NOT NOW.

IT IS A MOST **MISERABLE** THING TO FEEL **ASHAMED** OF HOME. I CAN TESTIFY. HOME HAD NEVER BEEN A VERY **PLEASANT** PLACE TO ME, BECAUSE OF MY SISTER'S **TEMPER**. BUT JOE HAD **SANCTIFIED** IT, AND I HAD **BELIEVED** IN IT.

VOLUME I
CHAPTER XIV

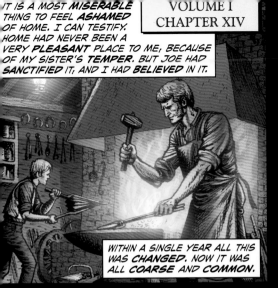

WITHIN A SINGLE YEAR ALL THIS WAS **CHANGED**. NOW IT WAS ALL **COARSE** AND **COMMON**.

I USED TO STAND ABOUT THE CHURCHYARD ON SUNDAY EVENINGS, COMPARING MY **OWN** PERSPECTIVE WITH THE FLAT, LOW MARSH VIEW. **WHAT I WANTED, WHO CAN SAY?**

WHAT I **DREADED** WAS, THAT IN SOME UNLUCKY HOUR I, BEING AT MY **GRIMIEST** AND **COMMONEST**, SHOULD LOOK UP AND SEE **ESTELLA** LOOKING IN AT THE FORGE. SHE WOULD FIND ME WITH A BLACK **FACE** AND **HANDS**, AND WOULD **DESPISE** ME.

VOLUME I
CHAPTER XV

AS I WAS GETTING TOO BIG FOR MR. WOPSLE'S GREAT-AUNT'S ROOM, MY EDUCATION UNDER THAT FEMALE **TERMINATED**.

NOT, HOWEVER, UNTIL BIDDY HAD IMPARTED TO ME EVERYTHING SHE **KNEW**. WHATEVER I ACQUIRED BY WAY OF EDUCATION FROM BIDDY, I TRIED TO IMPART TO **JOE**.

THIS STATEMENT SOUNDS WELL, BUT I DID IT TO MAKE JOE LESS IGNORANT AND COMMON, THAT HE MIGHT BE **WORTHIER** OF MY SOCIETY AND LESS OPEN TO ESTELLA'S **REPROACH**.

JOE, DON'T YOU THINK I **OUGHT** TO MAKE MISS HAVISHAM A **VISIT?**

WELL, PIP, WHAT **FOR?**

HERE AM I, GETTING ON IN THE FIRST YEAR OF MY TIME, AND I HAVE NEVER **THANKED** MISS HAVISHAM, OR SHOWN THAT I **REMEMBER** HER.

AS WE ARE RATHER SLACK JUST NOW, IF YOU WOULD GIVE ME A HALF-HOLIDAY TO-MORROW, I THINK I WOULD **GO** UP-TOWN AND MAKE A CALL ON MISS **EST**... HAVISHAM.

WHICH HER NAME **AIN'T** ESTAVISHAM, PIP, UNLESS SHE HAVE BEEN RECHRIS'ENED.

I **KNOW**, JOE, IT WAS A **SLIP** OF MINE. WHAT DO YOU THINK OF IT, JOE?

JOE THOUGHT **WELL** ENOUGH OF IT. BUT, HE WAS PARTICULAR IN STIPULATING THAT IF I WERE **NOT** RECEIVED WITH **CORDIALITY**, THIS TRIP SHOULD HAVE **NO SUCCESSOR**. BY THESE CONDITIONS I PROMISED TO **ABIDE**.

JOE KEPT A JOURNEYMAN AT WEEKLY WAGES WHOSE NAME WAS **DOLGE ORLICK**. HE WAS A FELLOW OF **OBSTINATE** DISPOSITION; AND ALWAYS SLOUCHING. THIS MOROSE JOURNEYMAN HAD NO LIKING FOR ME. WHEN I BECAME JOE'S 'PRENTICE, ORLICK WAS PERHAPS **CONFIRMED** IN THE SUSPICION THAT I SHOULD **DISPLACE** HIM.

NOW MASTER, SURE YOU'RE NOT A-GOING TO FAVOUR ONLY **ONE** OF US. IF YOUNG PIP HAS A HALF-HOLIDAY, DO AS MUCH FOR OLD **ORLICK**.

WHY, WHAT'LL **YOU** DO WITH A HALF-HOLIDAY, IF YOU GET IT?

WHAT'LL I DO WITH IT! I'LL DO AS **MUCH** WITH IT AS **HIM**.

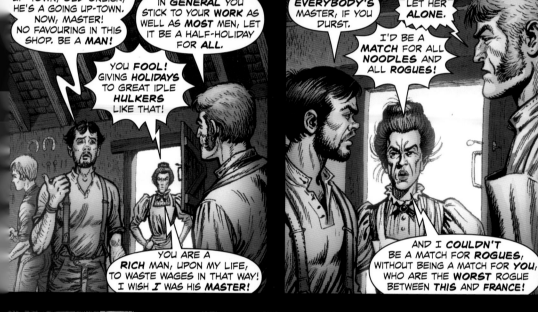

IF YOUNG PIP'S A GOING UP-TOWN, OLD ORLICK, HE'S A GOING UP-TOWN. NOW, MASTER! NO FAVOURING IN THIS SHOP. BE A **MAN**!

THEN, AS IN **GENERAL** YOU STICK TO YOUR **WORK** AS WELL AS **MOST** MEN, LET IT BE A HALF-HOLIDAY FOR **ALL**.

YOU **FOOL**! GIVING **HOLIDAYS** TO GREAT IDLE **HULKERS** LIKE THAT!

YOU ARE A **RICH** MAN, UPON MY LIFE, TO WASTE WAGES IN THAT WAY! I WISH **I** WAS HIS **MASTER**!

YOU'D BE **EVERYBODY'S** MASTER, IF YOU DURST.

LET HER **ALONE**.

I'D BE A **MATCH** FOR ALL **NOODLES** AND ALL **ROGUES**!

AND I **COULDN'T** BE A MATCH FOR **ROGUES**, WITHOUT BEING A MATCH FOR **YOU**, WHO ARE THE **WORST** ROGUE BETWEEN **THIS** AND **FRANCE**!

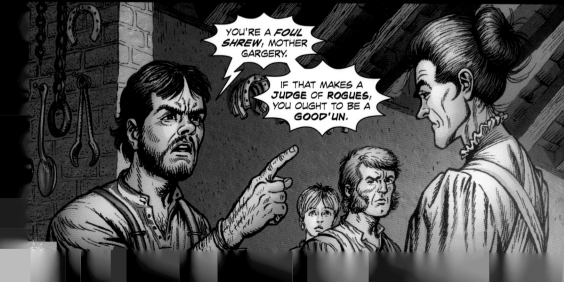

YOU'RE A **FOUL SHREW**, MOTHER GARGERY.

IF THAT MAKES A **JUDGE** OF **ROGUES**, YOU OUGHT TO BE A **GOOD'UN**.

THWAAKK!

JOE PICKED UP MY SISTER WHO HAD DROPPED **INSENSIBLE** TO THE FLOOR. SHE WAS CARRIED INTO THE HOUSE TO **REVIVE**.
I WENT UP-STAIRS TO DRESS MYSELF.

WHEN I CAME DOWN AGAIN, I FOUND JOE AND ORLICK SWEEPING UP, WITHOUT **ANY TRACES** OF DISCOMPOSURE.

WITH WHAT **ABSURD** EMOTIONS I FOUND MYSELF AGAIN GOING TO MISS HAVISHAM'S, MATTERS **LITTLE**.

MISS SARAH POCKET LET ME IN, AND BROUGHT THE MESSAGE THAT I WAS TO "COME UP". EVERYTHING WAS **UNCHANGED**, AND MISS HAVISHAM WAS **ALONE**. THERE WAS NO **ESTELLA**.

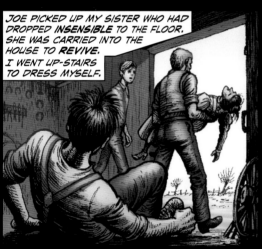

YOU ARE LOOKING ROUND FOR **ESTELLA**?

I H-H-HOPE THAT SHE IS W-W-WELL.

ABROAD, EDUCATING FOR A **LADY**. **FAR** OUT OF REACH. DO YOU FEEL THAT YOU HAVE **LOST** HER? Heh-heh-heh...

I WAS AT A **LOSS** WHAT TO SAY. SHE SPARED ME THE TROUBLE OF CONSIDERING, BY **DISMISSING** ME.

WHEN THE GATE WAS CLOSED ON ME, I FELT MORE THAN EVER **DISSATISFIED** WITH MY **HOME** AND WITH MY **TRADE** AND WITH **EVERYTHING**.

I WAS LOITERING ALONG THE HIGH STREET WHEN I MET WITH MR. WOPSLE, WHO **INSISTED** ON MY ACCOMPANYING HIM TO SEE UNCLE PUMBLECHOOK. IT WAS A **VERY** DARK NIGHT BY THE TIME WE SET OUT ON THE WALK HOME.

HALLOA! ORLICK, THERE?

AH! I WAS STANDING BY, A MINUTE, ON THE **CHANCE** OF COMPANY.

THE **GUNS** IS GOING AGAIN. THERE'S SOME **JAIL-BIRDS** FLOWN FROM THE **HULKS.**

WE CAME TO THE VILLAGE BY WAY OF THE JOLLY BARGEMEN, WHICH WE WERE SURPRISED TO FIND IN A STATE OF **COMMOTION.** MR. WOPSLE DROPPED IN TO ASK WHAT WAS THE MATTER BUT CAME RUNNING OUT IN A GREAT **HURRY.**

THERE'S SOMETHING **WRONG** UP AT YOUR PLACE, PIP!

THE HOUSE SEEMS TO HAVE BEEN **VIOLENTLY** ENTERED WHEN JOE WAS OUT.

SOMEBODY HAS BEEN **ATTACKED** AND **HURT.**

RUN ALL!

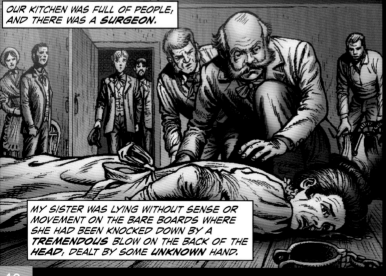

OUR KITCHEN WAS FULL OF PEOPLE, AND THERE WAS A **SURGEON.**

MY SISTER WAS LYING WITHOUT SENSE OR MOVEMENT ON THE BARE BOARDS WHERE SHE HAD BEEN KNOCKED DOWN BY A **TREMENDOUS** BLOW ON THE BACK OF THE **HEAD**, DEALT BY SOME **UNKNOWN** HAND.

ON THE GROUND BESIDE HER WAS A **LEG-IRON** WHICH HAD BEEN FILED ASUNDER SOME TIME AGO.

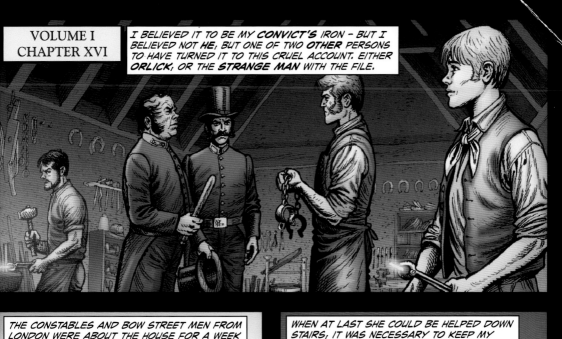

VOLUME I CHAPTER XVI

I BELIEVED IT TO BE MY **CONVICT'S** IRON – BUT I BELIEVED NOT **HE**, BUT ONE OF TWO **OTHER** PERSONS TO HAVE TURNED IT TO THIS CRUEL ACCOUNT. EITHER **ORLICK**, OR THE **STRANGE MAN** WITH THE FILE.

THE CONSTABLES AND BOW STREET MEN FROM LONDON WERE ABOUT THE HOUSE FOR A WEEK OR TWO. THEY STOOD ABOUT THE DOOR OF THE JOLLY BARGEMEN WITH KNOWING LOOKS.

THEY HAD A MYSTERIOUS MANNER OF TAKING THEIR DRINK, THAT WAS ALMOST AS GOOD AS TAKING THE CULPRIT. BUT NOT QUITE, FOR THEY NEVER DID IT.

LONG AFTER THESE POWERS HAD **DISPERSED**, MY SISTER LAY ILL IN BED. HER **SIGHT** WAS DISTURBED, HER **HEARING** IMPAIRED, HER **MEMORY** ALSO; AND HER SPEECH WAS **UNINTELLIGIBLE**.

WHEN AT LAST SHE COULD BE HELPED DOWN STAIRS, IT WAS NECESSARY TO KEEP MY SLATE BY HER, THAT SHE MIGHT INDICATE IN **WRITING** WHAT SHE COULD NOT IN **SPEECH**.

HOWEVER, HER **TEMPER** WAS GREATLY **IMPROVED**, AND SHE WAS **PATIENT**.

WE WERE AT A LOSS TO FIND A SUITABLE ATTENDANT FOR HER, UNTIL MR. WOPSLE'S GREAT-AUNT DIED, AND **BIDDY** BECAME A PART OF OUR **HOUSEHOLD**.

SHE QUICKLY BECAME A **BLESSING** TO US, AND ABOVE ALL, TO JOE, WHO WAS SADLY CUT UP.

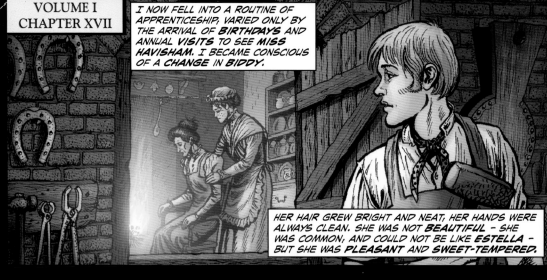

I NOW FELL INTO A ROUTINE OF APPRENTICESHIP, VARIED ONLY BY THE ARRIVAL OF **BIRTHDAYS** AND ANNUAL **VISITS** TO SEE **MISS HAVISHAM.** I BECAME CONSCIOUS OF A **CHANGE** IN **BIDDY.**

HER HAIR GREW BRIGHT AND NEAT, HER HANDS WERE ALWAYS CLEAN. SHE WAS NOT **BEAUTIFUL** – SHE WAS COMMON, AND COULD NOT BE LIKE **ESTELLA** – BUT SHE WAS **PLEASANT** AND **SWEET-TEMPERED.**

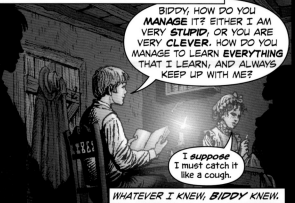

BIDDY HAD NOT BEEN WITH US MORE THAN A YEAR WHEN I OBSERVED ONE EVENING THAT SHE HAD CURIOUSLY THOUGHTFUL **EYES,** THAT WERE VERY **PRETTY.** I WAS BEGINNING TO BE RATHER **VAIN** OF MY **KNOWLEDGE** AT THE TIME.

BIDDY, HOW DO YOU **MANAGE** IT? EITHER I AM VERY **STUPID,** OR YOU ARE VERY **CLEVER.** HOW DO YOU MANAGE TO LEARN **EVERYTHING** THAT I LEARN, AND ALWAYS KEEP UP WITH ME?

I *suppose* I MUST CATCH IT LIKE A COUGH.

WHATEVER I KNEW, **BIDDY** KNEW.

BIDDY, YOU ARE ONE OF THOSE WHO MAKE THE **MOST** OF EVERY CHANCE. YOU NEVER HAD A CHANCE **BEFORE** YOU CAME **HERE,** AND SEE HOW **IMPROVED** YOU ARE!

I WAS **YOUR** FIRST TEACHER THOUGH; WASN'T I?

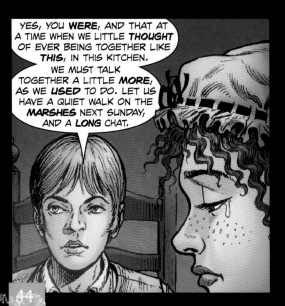

YES, YOU **WERE,** AND THAT AT A TIME WHEN WE LITTLE **THOUGHT** OF EVER BEING TOGETHER LIKE **THIS,** IN THIS KITCHEN. WE MUST TALK TOGETHER A LITTLE **MORE,** AS WE **USED** TO DO. LET US HAVE A QUIET WALK ON THE **MARSHES** NEXT SUNDAY, AND A **LONG** CHAT.

THAT SUNDAY AFTERNOON, WHILE JOE UNDERTOOK THE CARE OF MY SISTER, BIDDY AND I WENT OUT **TOGETHER.** I RESOLVED THAT IT WAS A GOOD TIME FOR TAKING BIDDY INTO MY **CONFIDENCE.**

BIDDY, I WANT TO BE A **GENTLEMAN.**

YOU KNOW BEST, PIP; BUT DON'T YOU THINK YOU ARE **HAPPIER** AS YOU **ARE?**

BIDDY, I AM NOT AT ALL HAPPY AS I AM. I AM *DISGUSTED* WITH MY CALLING AND WITH MY *LIFE*. I HAVE NEVER TAKEN TO *EITHER*.

I NEVER SHALL BE *COMFORTABLE*, OR *ANYTHING* BUT MISERABLE, UNLESS I CAN LEAD A VERY *DIFFERENT* SORT OF LIFE.

THAT'S A PITY!

IF I COULD HAVE SETTLED DOWN AT THE FORGE, JOE AND I MIGHT HAVE BECOME *PARTNERS*, AND I MIGHT EVEN HAVE GROWN UP TO KEEP COMPANY WITH *YOU*.

I SHOULD HAVE BEEN *GOOD ENOUGH* FOR YOU; SHOULDN'T I, BIDDY?

YES; I AM NOT OVER-PARTICULAR.

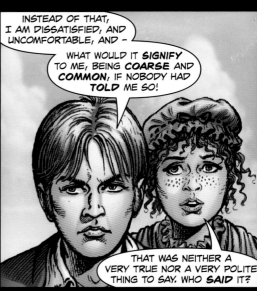

INSTEAD OF THAT, I AM DISSATISFIED, AND UNCOMFORTABLE, AND –

WHAT WOULD IT *SIGNIFY* TO ME, BEING *COARSE* AND *COMMON*, IF NOBODY HAD *TOLD* ME SO!

THAT WAS NEITHER A VERY TRUE NOR A VERY POLITE THING TO SAY. WHO *SAID* IT?

THE BEAUTIFUL YOUNG LADY AT MISS HAVISHAM'S, AND SHE'S MORE BEAUTIFUL THAN ANYBODY *EVER* WAS, AND I ADMIRE HER *DREADFULLY*, AND I WANT TO BE A GENTLEMAN ON *HER* ACCOUNT.

DO YOU WANT TO BE A GENTLEMAN TO *SPITE* HER, OR TO *GAIN* HER *OVER*?

EXACTLY WHAT I MYSELF HAD WONDERED *MANY* TIMES.

45

I AM **GLAD** OF ONE THING, AND THAT IS, THAT YOU HAVE FELT YOU COULD GIVE ME YOUR **CONFIDENCE.**

BIDDY, I SHALL **ALWAYS** TELL YOU **EVERYTHING!**

TILL YOU'RE A **GENTLEMAN.**

YOU KNOW I **NEVER** SHALL BE, SO THAT'S **ALWAYS.**

WE WALKED A LITTLE **FARTHER**, AND **TALKED** A GOOD DEAL. I BEGAN TO THINK IT WOULD BE VERY GOOD FOR ME IF I COULD GET ESTELLA **OUT** OF MY HEAD.

I SURELY KNEW THAT IF **ESTELLA** WERE BESIDE ME NOW INSTEAD OF BIDDY, SHE WOULD MAKE ME **MISERABLE.** BIDDY WAS **NEVER** INSULTING OR CAPRICIOUS. HOW COULD IT BE, THAT I DID NOT **LIKE** HER MUCH THE **BETTER** OF THE **TWO?**

BIDDY, I WISH YOU COULD PUT ME **RIGHT.**

I WISH I COULD!

IF I COULD ONLY GET MYSELF TO FALL IN **LOVE** WITH **YOU.**

YOU DON'T MIND MY SPEAKING SO **OPENLY** TO SUCH AN OLD ACQUAINTANCE?

OH DEAR, NOT AT **ALL!** DON'T MIND ME.

IF I COULD **ONLY** GET MYSELF TO DO IT, THAT WOULD BE THE **THING** FOR ME.

BUT YOU **NEVER** **WILL**, YOU SEE.

IN MY **HEART** I BELIEVED HER TO BE **RIGHT.**

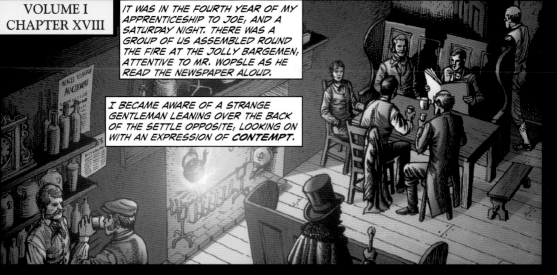

IT WAS IN THE FOURTH YEAR OF MY APPRENTICESHIP TO JOE, AND A SATURDAY NIGHT. THERE WAS A GROUP OF US ASSEMBLED ROUND THE FIRE AT THE JOLLY BARGEMEN, ATTENTIVE TO MR. WOPSLE AS HE READ THE NEWSPAPER ALOUD.

I BECAME AWARE OF A STRANGE GENTLEMAN LEANING OVER THE BACK OF THE SETTLE OPPOSITE, LOOKING ON WITH AN EXPRESSION OF **CONTEMPT**.

THE STRANGE GENTLEMAN WENT AND STOOD BY THE FIRE. HE DID NOT RECOGNISE **ME**, BUT I RECOGNISED **HIM** AS THE GENTLEMAN I HAD MET ON THE STAIRS, ON MY SECOND VISIT TO MISS HAVISHAM.

FROM INFORMATION I HAVE RECEIVED, I HAVE REASON TO BELIEVE THERE IS A **BLACKSMITH** AMONG YOU, BY NAME JOSEPH – OR JOE – GARGERY. WHICH IS THE MAN?

HERE IS THE MAN.

YOU HAVE AN APPRENTICE, COMMONLY KNOWN AS **PIP**? IS HE **HERE**?

I AM HERE!

I WISH TO HAVE A **PRIVATE** CONFERENCE WITH YOU TWO. IT WILL TAKE A LITTLE TIME. PERHAPS WE HAD BETTER GO TO YOUR PLACE OF **RESIDENCE**.

AMIDST A **WONDERING SILENCE**, WE WALKED OUT OF THE JOLLY BARGEMEN, AND IN A **WONDERING SILENCE** WALKED **HOME**.

MY NAME IS JAGGERS, AND I AM A **LAWYER** IN **LONDON**. I AM PRETTY WELL KNOWN. I HAVE **UNUSUAL** BUSINESS TO TRANSACT WITH YOU, WHICH IS NOT OF **MY** ORIGINATING.

IF MY ADVICE HAD BEEN **ASKED**, I SHOULD NOT HAVE BEEN HERE. IT WAS **NOT** ASKED, AND YOU SEE ME HERE. WHAT I HAVE TO DO AS THE CONFIDENTIAL AGENT OF **ANOTHER**, I DO.

NO LESS, NO MORE.

NOW, JOSEPH GARGERY; I AM THE **BEARER** OF AN OFFER TO **RELIEVE** YOU OF THIS YOUNG FELLOW YOUR APPRENTICE.

YOU WOULD NOT OBJECT TO CANCEL HIS INDENTURES AT HIS **REQUEST** AND FOR HIS **GOOD?** YOU WOULD WANT NOTHING FOR SO DOING?

LORD FORBID THAT I SHOULD WANT **ANYTHING** FOR NOT STANDING IN PIP'S WAY.

VERY WELL. THE COMMUNICATION I HAVE GOT TO MAKE IS, THAT HE HAS

GREAT EXPECTATIONS.

I AM INSTRUCTED TO COMMUNICATE TO HIM, THAT HE WILL COME INTO A **HANDSOME** PROPERTY.

FURTHER, THAT IT IS THE DESIRE OF THE PRESENT POSSESSOR OF THAT PROPERTY, THAT HE BE IMMEDIATELY **REMOVED** FROM HIS PRESENT SPHERE OF LIFE, AND BE BROUGHT UP AS A **GENTLEMAN** - IN A WORD, AS A YOUNG FELLOW OF *GREAT EXPECTATIONS.*

MY DREAM IS OUT - MISS HAVISHAM IS GOING TO MAKE MY **FORTUNE** ON A **GRAND SCALE.**

NOW, MR. PIP. YOU ARE TO UNDERSTAND, FIRST, THAT IT IS THE REQUEST OF THE PERSON FROM WHOM I TAKE MY INSTRUCTIONS THAT YOU **ALWAYS** BEAR THE NAME OF **PIP.**

YOU HAVE NO **OBJECTION** TO YOUR GREAT EXPECTATIONS BEING ENCUMBERED WITH THAT **EASY** CONDITION?

N...N...N...NO.

I SHOULD THINK **NOT!**

MY HEART WAS BEATING SO *FAST* THAT I COULD SCARCELY STAMMER.

YOU ARE TO UNDERSTAND, SECONDLY, THAT THE **NAME** OF THE PERSON WHO IS YOUR LIBERAL BENEFACTOR REMAINS A PROFOUND **SECRET,** UNTIL THE PERSON **CHOOSES** TO **REVEAL** IT AT FIRST HAND.

WHEN THAT INTENTION MAY BE CARRIED OUT, I CANNOT SAY; IT MAY BE **YEARS** HENCE.

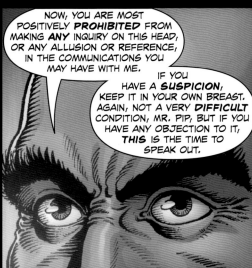

NOW, YOU ARE MOST POSITIVELY **PROHIBITED** FROM MAKING **ANY** INQUIRY ON THIS HEAD, OR ANY ALLUSION OR REFERENCE, IN THE COMMUNICATIONS YOU MAY HAVE WITH ME.

IF YOU HAVE A **SUSPICION,** KEEP IT IN YOUR OWN BREAST. AGAIN, NOT A VERY **DIFFICULT** CONDITION, MR. PIP, BUT IF YOU HAVE ANY OBJECTION TO IT, **THIS** IS THE TIME TO SPEAK OUT.

N...N...N...NO.

WE COME NEXT, TO THE **DETAILS** OF ARRANGEMENT. YOU ARE NOT ENDOWED WITH EXPECTATIONS **ONLY.** THERE IS ALREADY LODGED IN MY HANDS A SUM OF **MONEY** AMPLY SUFFICIENT FOR YOUR SUITABLE EDUCATION AND MAINTENANCE.

YOU WILL PLEASE CONSIDER ME YOUR **GUARDIAN.** IT IS CONSIDERED THAT YOU MUST BE BETTER **EDUCATED,** IN ACCORDANCE WITH YOUR ALTERED POSITION.

I HAVE **ALWAYS** LONGED FOR IT.

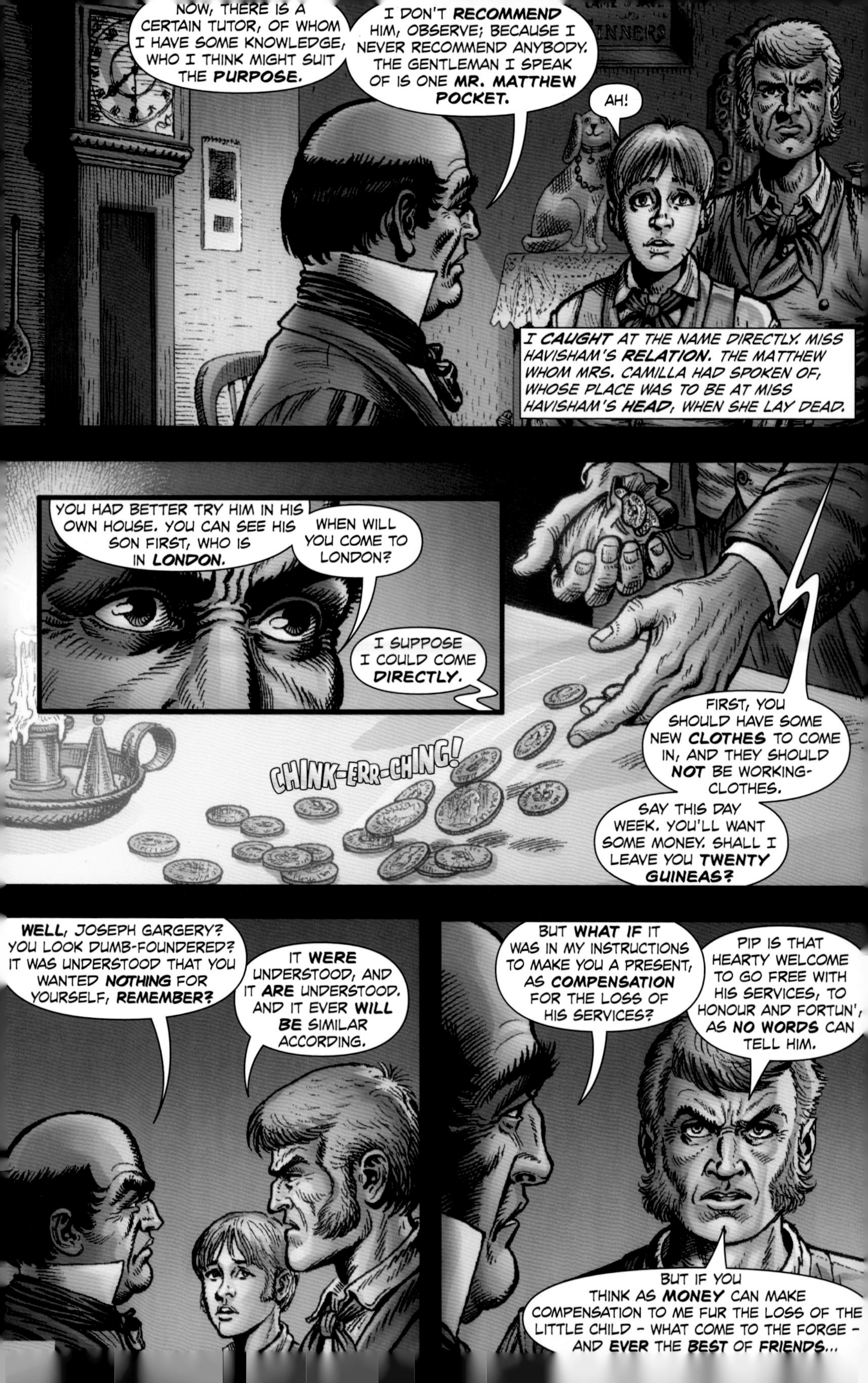

NOW, THERE IS A CERTAIN TUTOR, OF WHOM I HAVE SOME KNOWLEDGE, WHO I THINK MIGHT SUIT THE **PURPOSE.**
I DON'T **RECOMMEND** HIM, OBSERVE; BECAUSE I NEVER RECOMMEND ANYBODY. THE GENTLEMAN I SPEAK OF IS ONE **MR. MATTHEW POCKET.**
AH!
*I **CAUGHT** AT THE NAME DIRECTLY. MISS HAVISHAM'S **RELATION.** THE MATTHEW WHOM MRS. CAMILLA HAD SPOKEN OF, WHOSE PLACE WAS TO BE AT MISS HAVISHAM'S **HEAD**, WHEN SHE LAY DEAD.*
YOU HAD BETTER TRY HIM IN HIS OWN HOUSE. YOU CAN SEE HIS SON FIRST, WHO IS IN **LONDON.**
WHEN WILL YOU COME TO LONDON?
I SUPPOSE I COULD COME **DIRECTLY.**
CHINK-ERR-CHING!
FIRST, YOU SHOULD HAVE SOME NEW **CLOTHES** TO COME IN, AND THEY SHOULD **NOT** BE WORKING-CLOTHES.
SAY THIS DAY WEEK. YOU'LL WANT SOME MONEY. SHALL I LEAVE YOU **TWENTY GUINEAS?**
WELL, JOSEPH GARGERY? YOU LOOK DUMB-FOUNDERED? IT WAS UNDERSTOOD THAT YOU WANTED **NOTHING** FOR YOURSELF, **REMEMBER?**
IT **WERE** UNDERSTOOD, AND IT **ARE** UNDERSTOOD. AND IT EVER **WILL BE** SIMILAR ACCORDING.
BUT **WHAT IF** IT WAS IN MY INSTRUCTIONS TO MAKE YOU A PRESENT, AS **COMPENSATION** FOR THE LOSS OF HIS SERVICES?
PIP IS THAT HEARTY WELCOME TO GO FREE WITH HIS SERVICES, TO HONOUR AND FORTUN', AS **NO WORDS** CAN TELL HIM.
BUT IF YOU THINK AS **MONEY** CAN MAKE COMPENSATION TO ME FUR THE LOSS OF THE LITTLE CHILD – WHAT COME TO THE FORGE – AND **EVER** THE **BEST** OF **FRIENDS**...

JOE'S VOICE DIED AWAY, AND HIS BROAD CHEST *HEAVED.* I *BEGGED* HIM TO BE COMFORTED.

NOW, JOSEPH GARGERY, I WARN YOU THIS IS YOUR *LAST* CHANCE.

IF YOU MEAN TO TAKE A *PRESENT* THAT I HAVE IT IN CHARGE TO MAKE YOU, SPEAK OUT, AND YOU SHALL *HAVE* IT.

IF ON THE *CONTRARY* YOU MEAN TO SAY --

WHICH I *MEANTERSAY,* THAT IF YOU COME INTO MY PLACE BULL-BAITING AND BADGERING ME, *COME OUT!*

WHICH I *MEANTERSAY* AS SECH IF YOU'RE A MAN, *COME ON!*

I DREW JOE AWAY, AND HE IMMEDIATELY BECAME PLACABLE.

WELL, MR. PIP, I THINK THE SOONER YOU *LEAVE* HERE – AS YOU ARE TO BE A *GENTLEMAN* – THE *BETTER.*

LET IT STAND FOR THIS DAY *WEEK,* AND YOU SHALL RECEIVE MY PRINTED *ADDRESS* IN THE MEANTIME.

I THINK HE WOULD HAVE GONE ON, BUT FOR HIS SEEMING TO THINK JOE *DANGEROUS* AND GOING OFF.

SOMETHING CAME INTO MY HEAD WHICH INDUCED ME TO RUN *AFTER* HIM.

I BEG YOUR PARDON, MR. JAGGERS. I WISH TO KEEP TO YOUR *DIRECTIONS;* SO I THOUGHT I HAD BETTER ASK.

WOULD THERE BE ANY *OBJECTION* TO MY TAKING LEAVE OF ANY ONE I KNOW, ABOUT HERE, BEFORE I GO AWAY? I DON'T MEAN IN THE VILLAGE ONLY, BUT UP-TOWN?

NO – NO OBJECTION.

THANK YOU, SIR.

I RAN HOME AGAIN.

JOE, HAVE YOU TOLD *BIDDY?*

NO, PIP. WHICH I LEFT IT TO YOURSELF, PIP.

I WOULD RATHER *YOU* TOLD, JOE.

PIP'S A **GENTLEMAN** OF FORTUN' THEN. AND GOD **BLESS** HIM IN IT!

OH! CONGRATULATIONS!

I IMPRESSED BIDDY AND JOE WITH THE OBLIGATION TO SAY NOTHING ABOUT THE **MAKER** OF MY FORTUNE.

IT WOULD ALL COME OUT IN GOOD TIME, I OBSERVED; AND IN THE MEANWHILE **NOTHING** WAS TO BE SAID, SAVE THAT I HAD COME INTO **GREAT EXPECTATIONS** FROM A MYSTERIOUS **PATRON.**

I'LL BE VERY **PARTICULAR.**

AY, AY, I'LL BE EKERVALLY **PARTICKLER,** PIP.

INFINITE PAINS WERE THEN TAKEN BY BIDDY TO CONVEY TO MY SISTER SOME IDEA OF WHAT HAD HAPPENED.

PIP...

...PROPERTY

I DOUBTED THOSE WORDS HAD ANY **MEANING** IN THEM FOR HER.

THAT NIGHT, AS I PUT THE WINDOW OPEN, I SAW JOE COME SLOWLY FORTH, AND TAKE A TURN IN THE AIR. BIDDY BROUGHT HIM HIS PIPE. HE NEVER SMOKED SO **LATE,** AND IT SEEMED TO HINT HE WANTED **COMFORTING.**

I KNEW THAT THEY TALKED OF **ME,** FOR I HEARD MY **NAME** MENTIONED IN AN ENDEARING TONE BY BOTH OF THEM MORE THAN ONCE.

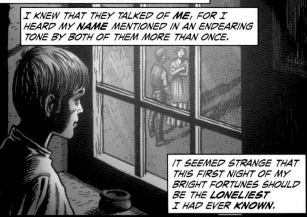

IT SEEMED STRANGE THAT THIS FIRST NIGHT OF MY BRIGHT FORTUNES SHOULD BE THE **LONELIEST** I HAD EVER **KNOWN.**

I CREPT INTO BED; AND IT WAS AN **UNEASY** BED NOW, AND I NEVER SLEPT THE OLD SOUND SLEEP IN IT ANY MORE.

THE NEXT MORNING, AFTER BREAKFAST, JOE BROUGHT OUT MY **INDENTURES** FROM THE PRESS IN THE BEST PARLOUR. WE PUT THEM IN THE **FIRE**, AND I FELT THAT I WAS **FREE**.

VOLUME I
CHAPTER XIX

AFTER CHURCH, AND AN EARLY DINNER, I STROLLED OUT **ALONE**.

AS I PASSED THE CHURCH, I THOUGHT, WITH SOMETHING ALLIED TO **SHAME**, OF MY COMPANIONSHIP WITH THE **FUGITIVE** WHOM I HAD ONCE SEEN LIMPING AMONG THOSE GRAVES. MY COMFORT WAS, THAT IT HAPPENED A **LONG** TIME AGO, AND THAT HE HAD DOUBTLESS BEEN TRANSPORTED A LONG WAY OFF, AND WAS **DEAD** TO ME.

I MADE MY **EXULTANT** WAY TO THE OLD BATTERY, AND, LYING DOWN THERE TO CONSIDER THE QUESTION WHETHER MISS HAVISHAM **INTENDED** ME FOR **ESTELLA**, FELL ASLEEP.

WHEN I AWOKE, I WAS MUCH **SURPRISED** TO FIND JOE SITTING BESIDE ME.

AS BEING THE **LAST** TIME, PIP, I THOUGHT I'D **FOLLER**.

I'M VERY **GLAD** YOU DID SO. YOU KNOW, I'D **ALWAYS** WANTED TO BE A **GENTLEMAN**.

HAVE YOU THOUGH? **ASTONISHING!**

IT'S A PITY NOW, JOE, THAT YOU DID NOT GET ON A LITTLE **MORE** WHEN WE HAD OUR **LESSONS** HERE; ISN'T IT?

WELL, I DON'T KNOW. I'M SO AWFUL **DULL**. I'M ONLY MASTER OF MY OWN TRADE. IT WERE ALWAYS A **PITY** AS I WAS SO AWFUL DULL.

AFTER TEA, I TOOK BIDDY INTO OUR LITTLE GARDEN; AND SAID I HAD A **FAVOUR** TO ASK OF HER.

AND IT IS, BIDDY, THAT YOU WILL NOT OMIT **ANY** OPPORTUNITY OF **HELPING** JOE ON, A LITTLE. JOE IS A DEAR **GOOD** FELLOW – BUT HE IS RATHER **BACKWARD** IN SOME THINGS. FOR INSTANCE, IN HIS **LEARNING** AND HIS **MANNERS.**

OH! WON'T HIS MANNERS **DO** THEN?

BUT IF I WERE TO **REMOVE** JOE INTO A **HIGHER** SPHERE, AS I **HOPE** TO, WHEN I **FULLY** COME INTO MY **PROPERTY...**

HE MAY BE TOO **PROUD** TO LET ANY ONE TAKE HIM OUT OF A PLACE THAT HE IS COMPETENT TO FILL, AND FILLS **WELL** AND WITH **RESPECT.**

NOW, BIDDY, I AM **VERY SORRY** TO SEE THIS IN YOU.

YOU ARE **ENVIOUS** AND **GRUDGING.** YOU ARE DISSATISFIED ON ACCOUNT OF MY **RISE** IN FORTUNE, AND CAN'T HELP SHOWING IT.

IF YOU HAVE THE HEART TO **THINK** SO; **SAY** SO. SAY SO OVER AND OVER AGAIN, IF YOU HAVE THE **HEART** TO THINK SO!

IF **YOU** HAVE THE HEART TO **BE** SO, YOU MEAN, BIDDY.

DON'T PUT IT OFF UPON **ME!** I AM VERY SORRY TO SEE IT, IT'S A – A **BAD** SIDE OF **HUMAN NATURE.**

I DID **INTEND** TO **ASK** YOU TO USE ANY LITTLE OPPORTUNITIES YOU MIGHT HAVE **AFTER** I WAS GONE, OF **IMPROVING** DEAR JOE. BUT AFTER THIS, I **ASK** YOU **NOTHING.**

I EXTENDED MY CLEMENCY TO BIDDY, AND WE DROPPED THE SUBJECT. I WENT INTO TOWN EARLY, AND PRESENTED MYSELF BEFORE MR. TRABB, THE TAILOR, TO BE MEASURED FOR A **FASHIONABLE** SUIT OF CLOTHES.

AFTER THIS, I WENT TO THE **HATTER'S**, AND THE **BOOTMAKER'S**, AND THE **HOSIER'S**.

WHEN I HAD ORDERED EVERYTHING I WANTED, I DIRECTED MY STEPS TOWARDS **PUMBLECHOOK'S**.

MY DEAR FRIEND, I GIVE YOU **JOY** OF YOUR GOOD FORTUNE! WELL DESERVED, WELL **DESERVED!**

TO THINK THAT **I** SHOULD HAVE BEEN THE HUMBLE **INSTRUMENT** OF LEADING UP TO THIS, IS A **PROUD** REWARD!

...AND YOUR **SISTER**, WHICH HAD THE HONOUR OF BRINGING YOU UP BY HAND!

WE'LL DRINK HER **HEALTH.**

REMEMBER THAT **NOTHING** IS TO BE **EVER** SAID OR HINTED ON THAT POINT.

BUT MY DEAR YOUNG FRIEND, YOU MUST BE **HUNGRY**, YOU MUST BE **EXHAUSTED.**

AH! THAT'S THE WAY YOU **KNOW** THE **NOBLE** MINDED! EVER FORGIVING AND EVER AFFABLE.

I HAD MY NEW CLOTHES DELIVERED TO MR. PUMBLECHOOK'S ON FRIDAY MORNING. FROM THERE, I WENT ON TO VISIT MISS HAVISHAM. **SARAH POCKET** CAME TO THE GATE.

YOU? GOOD GRACIOUS! WHAT DO YOU **WANT?**

I AM GOING TO **LONDON**, MISS POCKET, AND WANT TO SAY **GOODBYE** TO MISS HAVISHAM.

SHE TOOK ME UP, **STARING** AT ME ALL THE WAY.

DON'T **GO**, SARAH.

WELL, PIP?

I START FOR LONDON **TOMORROW**, MISS HAVISHAM, AND I THOUGHT YOU WOULD KINDLY NOT MIND MY TAKING **LEAVE** OF YOU.

MISS HAVISHAM MADE HER CRUTCH STICK PLAY ROUND ME, AS IF SHE WERE A **FAIRY GODMOTHER** WHO HAD **CHANGED** ME.

I HAVE COME INTO **SUCH** GOOD **FORTUNE** SINCE I SAW YOU LAST, MISS HAVISHAM. AND I AM SO **GRATEFUL** FOR IT, MISS HAVISHAM!

I HAVE SEEN MR. JAGGERS. I HAVE **HEARD** ABOUT IT, PIP.

WELL! YOU HAVE A **PROMISING** CAREER BEFORE YOU. BE GOOD – **DESERVE** IT – ABIDE BY MR. JAGGERS'S INSTRUCTIONS.

GOOD-BY, PIP! – YOU WILL **ALWAYS** KEEP THE NAME OF PIP, YOU KNOW.

ON THIS LAST EVENING, I DRESSED MYSELF OUT IN MY NEW CLOTHES FOR JOE AND BIDDY; AND SAT IN MY SPLENDOUR UNTIL BEDTIME. WE HAD A HOT SUPPER ON THE OCCASION. WE WERE ALL VERY **LOW**, AND NONE THE HIGHER FOR **PRETENDING** TO BE IN SPIRITS.

I WAS TO **LEAVE** OUR VILLAGE AT FIVE IN THE MORNING, AND HAD TOLD JOE THAT I WISHED TO WALK AWAY **ALONE**.

AFTER A HURRIED BREAKFAST, I TOOK UP MY LITTLE PORTMANTEAU AND WALKED OUT.

HOOROAR!

I WALKED AWAY AT A GOOD PACE, THINKING IT WAS **EASIER** TO GO THAN I HAD SUPPOSED.

BUT THE VILLAGE WAS VERY **PEACEFUL**, AND I HAD BEEN SO INNOCENT AND LITTLE THERE, AND ALL BEYOND WAS SO UNKNOWN AND GREAT, THAT IN A MOMENT I BROKE INTO **TEARS**.

I WAS BETTER AFTER I HAD CRIED – MORE SORRY, MORE **AWARE** OF MY OWN **INGRATITUDE**.

IT WAS NOW TOO **FAR** TO GO BACK. THE MISTS HAD ALL SOLEMNLY RISEN NOW...

...AND THE WORLD LAY SPREAD **BEFORE** ME.

VOLUME II
CHAPTER I

THE JOURNEY FROM OUR TOWN TO THE METROPOLIS WAS OF ABOUT FIVE HOURS. IT WAS A LITTLE PAST MIDDAY WHEN THE STAGE REACHED **CHEAPSIDE**, LONDON.

I WAS SCARED BY THE **IMMENSITY** OF LONDON. I THINK I MIGHT HAVE HAD SOME FAINT DOUBTS WHETHER IT WAS NOT RATHER **UGLY**, CROOKED, NARROW, AND **DIRTY**.

57

MR. JAGGERS HAD SENT ME HIS ADDRESS; IT WAS **LITTLE BRITAIN**; AND HE HAD WRITTEN AFTER IT ON HIS CARD, "JUST OUT OF SMITHFIELD, CLOSE BY THE COACH-OFFICE." A HACKNEY-COACHMAN PACKED ME UP IN HIS COACH, WHICH SOON STOPPED IN A **GLOOMY** STREET.

JAGGERS & CO

IS MR. JAGGERS AT HOME?

HE IS **NOT**. HE IS IN **COURT** AT PRESENT.

AM I ADDRESSING MR. PIP?

YES.

MR. JAGGERS LEFT WORD, WOULD YOU **WAIT** IN HIS ROOM? HE COULDN'T SAY HOW **LONG** HE MIGHT BE, HAVING A CASE ON. BUT HIS TIME BEING **VALUABLE**, THAT HE WON'T BE LONGER THAN HE CAN HELP.

MR. JAGGERS'S ROOM WAS A MOST **DISMAL** PLACE. THERE WERE TWO DREADFUL CASTS, OF FACES PECULIARLY **SWOLLEN**. I WONDERED WHETHER THEY WERE OF MR. JAGGERS'S **FAMILY**.

I SAT **WAITING**, UNTIL I REALLY COULD NOT **BEAR** THE TWO CASTS. I GOT UP AND TOLD THE CLERK THAT I WOULD TAKE A TURN IN THE AIR.

I TURNED INTO A STREET WHERE I SAW THE GREAT DOME OF SAINT PAUL'S BULGING FROM BEHIND A GRIM STONE BUILDING WHICH A BYSTANDER SAID WAS **NEWGATE PRISON**.

I SAW THE YARD WHERE THE **GALLOWS** WAS KEPT, AND WHERE PEOPLE WERE PUBLICLY WHIPPED. FOUR CONVICTS WERE TO COME OUT OF DEBTORS' DOOR TO BE **HANGED** THE DAY AFTER TOMORROW.

THIS GAVE ME A **SICKENING** IDEA OF LONDON.

RETURNING TO LITTLE BRITAIN, I BECAME AWARE THAT *OTHER* PEOPLE WERE WAITING ABOUT FOR MR. JAGGERS, AS WELL AS I. AT LENGTH I SAW MR. JAGGERS COMING ACROSS THE ROAD TOWARDS ME.

JAGGERS & CO

ALL THE OTHERS WHO WERE WAITING SAW HIM AT THE SAME TIME, AND THERE WAS QUITE A *RUSH* AT HIM.

NOW, I HAVE NOTHING TO *SAY* TO YOU. I WANT TO KNOW NO *MORE* THAN I KNOW.

AS TO THE *RESULT*, I TOLD YOU FROM THE FIRST IT WAS A TOSS-UP. HAVE YOU *PAID* WEMMICK?

YES, SIR.

WHAT ABOUT MY *BILL*, SIR?

NOW, I TELL YOU ONCE FOR ALL. IF *YOU* DON'T KNOW THAT YOUR BILL'S IN *GOOD* HANDS, *I* KNOW IT.

IF YOU COME HERE *BOTHERING* ME, I'LL MAKE AN *EXAMPLE* OF *BOTH* YOUR BILL AND *YOU*, AND LET HIM SLIP THROUGH MY FINGERS. HAVE YOU *PAID* WEMMICK?

OH *YES*, SIR! EVERY FARDEN.

MY GUARDIAN TOOK ME INTO HIS ROOM. WHILE HE LUNCHED, HE INFORMED ME WHAT ARRANGEMENTS HE HAD *MADE* FOR ME.

I WAS TO GO TO "BARNARD'S INN", TO YOUNG MR. POCKET'S ROOMS; I WAS TO REMAIN WITH YOUNG MR. POCKET UNTIL MONDAY, AND THEN GO WITH HIM TO HIS FATHER'S HOUSE, THAT I MIGHT TRY HOW I LIKED IT.

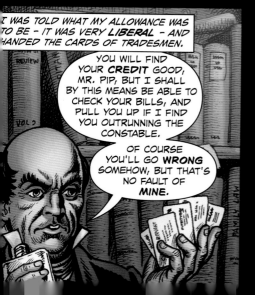

I WAS TOLD WHAT MY ALLOWANCE WAS TO BE – IT WAS VERY *LIBERAL* – AND HANDED THE CARDS OF TRADESMEN.

YOU WILL FIND YOUR *CREDIT* GOOD, MR. PIP, BUT I SHALL BY THIS MEANS BE ABLE TO CHECK YOUR BILLS, AND PULL YOU UP IF I FIND YOU OUTRUNNING THE CONSTABLE.

OF COURSE YOU'LL GO *WRONG* SOMEHOW, BUT THAT'S NO FAULT OF *MINE*.

I THEN FOUND THAT *WEMMICK*, THE CLERK, SHOULD WALK ROUND WITH ME.

I TELL YOU IT'S *NO USE*; HE WON'T HAVE A *WORD* TO SAY TO ONE OF YOU.

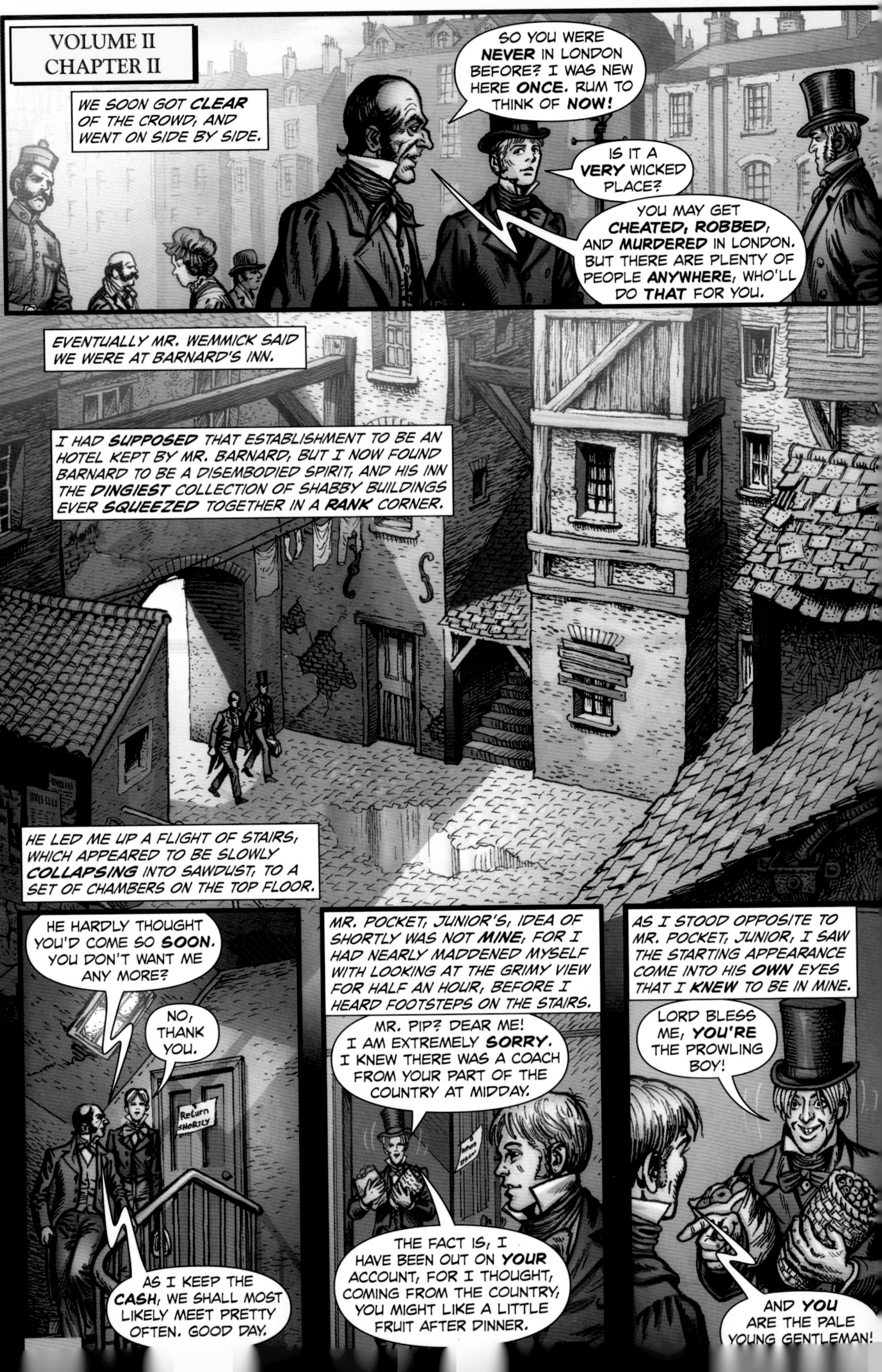
VOLUME II
CHAPTER II
WE SOON GOT CLEAR OF THE CROWD; AND WENT ON SIDE BY SIDE.
SO YOU WERE NEVER IN LONDON BEFORE? I WAS NEW HERE ONCE. RUM TO THINK OF NOW!
IS IT A VERY WICKED PLACE?
YOU MAY GET CHEATED, ROBBED, AND MURDERED IN LONDON. BUT THERE ARE PLENTY OF PEOPLE ANYWHERE, WHO'LL DO THAT FOR YOU.
EVENTUALLY MR. WEMMICK SAID WE WERE AT BARNARD'S INN.
I HAD SUPPOSED THAT ESTABLISHMENT TO BE AN HOTEL KEPT BY MR. BARNARD, BUT I NOW FOUND BARNARD TO BE A DISEMBODIED SPIRIT, AND HIS INN THE DINGIEST COLLECTION OF SHABBY BUILDINGS EVER SQUEEZED TOGETHER IN A RANK CORNER.
HE LED ME UP A FLIGHT OF STAIRS, WHICH APPEARED TO BE SLOWLY COLLAPSING INTO SAWDUST, TO A SET OF CHAMBERS ON THE TOP FLOOR.
HE HARDLY THOUGHT YOU'D COME SO SOON. YOU DON'T WANT ME ANY MORE?
NO, THANK YOU.
Return SHORTLY
AS I KEEP THE CASH, WE SHALL MOST LIKELY MEET PRETTY OFTEN. GOOD DAY.
MR. POCKET, JUNIOR'S, IDEA OF SHORTLY WAS NOT MINE, FOR I HAD NEARLY MADDENED MYSELF WITH LOOKING AT THE GRIMY VIEW FOR HALF AN HOUR, BEFORE I HEARD FOOTSTEPS ON THE STAIRS.
MR. PIP? DEAR ME! I AM EXTREMELY SORRY. I KNEW THERE WAS A COACH FROM YOUR PART OF THE COUNTRY AT MIDDAY.
THE FACT IS, I HAVE BEEN OUT ON YOUR ACCOUNT, FOR I THOUGHT, COMING FROM THE COUNTRY, YOU MIGHT LIKE A LITTLE FRUIT AFTER DINNER.
AS I STOOD OPPOSITE TO MR. POCKET, JUNIOR, I SAW THE STARTING APPEARANCE COME INTO HIS OWN EYES THAT I KNEW TO BE IN MINE.
LORD BLESS ME, YOU'RE THE PROWLING BOY!
AND YOU ARE THE PALE YOUNG GENTLEMAN!

THE IDEA OF ITS BEING **YOU**!

THE IDEA OF ITS BEING YOU! – WELL! IT'S ALL OVER NOW, I HOPE, AND IT WILL BE **MAGNANIMOUS** IN YOU IF YOU'LL **FORGIVE** ME FOR HAVING KNOCKED YOU ABOUT SO.

I DERIVED FROM THIS SPEECH THAT MR. HERBERT POCKET STILL RATHER CONFOUNDED HIS INTENTION WITH HIS EXECUTION.

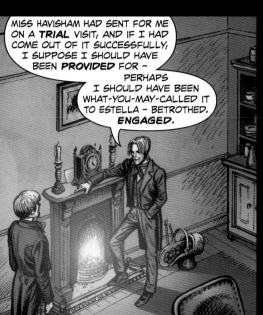

MISS HAVISHAM HAD SENT FOR ME ON A **TRIAL** VISIT, AND IF I HAD COME OUT OF IT SUCCESSFULLY, I SUPPOSE I SHOULD HAVE BEEN **PROVIDED** FOR –

PERHAPS I SHOULD HAVE BEEN WHAT-YOU-MAY-CALLED IT TO ESTELLA – BETROTHED. **ENGAGED**.

HOW DID YOU BEAR YOUR DISAPPOINTMENT?

POOH! SHE'S A **TARTAR**.

MISS HAVISHAM?

I MEANT **ESTELLA**. THAT GIRL'S **HARD** AND **HAUGHTY** AND **CAPRICIOUS** TO THE LAST DEGREE. SHE HAS BEEN BROUGHT UP BY MISS HAVISHAM TO WREAK **REVENGE** ON ALL THE MALE SEX.

WHAT RELATION IS SHE TO MISS HAVISHAM?

NONE, ONLY **ADOPTED**.

WHY **SHOULD** SHE WREAK REVENGE?

LORD, MR. PIP! DON'T YOU **KNOW**? DEAR ME! IT'S QUITE A STORY, AND SHALL BE SAVED TILL DINNER-TIME.

MR. JAGGERS IS YOUR **GUARDIAN**, I UNDERSTAND? YOU KNOW HE IS MISS HAVISHAM'S **SOLICITOR**, AND HAS HER CONFIDENCE WHEN NOBODY ELSE HAS?

HE WAS SO OBLIGING AS TO SUGGEST MY **FATHER** FOR YOUR TUTOR. MY FATHER IS MISS HAVISHAM'S COUSIN; NOT THAT THAT IMPLIES FAMILIAR INTERCOURSE BETWEEN THEM, FOR HE IS A **BAD** COURTIER AND WILL NOT PROPITIATE HER.

AS HE WAS SO COMMUNICATIVE, I TOLD HIM MY SMALL STORY, AND LAID STRESS ON MY BEING **FORBIDDEN** TO INQUIRE WHO MY BENEFACTOR WAS.

AS I HAVE BEEN BROUGHT UP A BLACKSMITH IN A COUNTRY PLACE, AND KNOW VERY LITTLE OF THE WAYS OF **POLITENESS**, I WOULD TAKE IT AS A KINDNESS IF YOU WOULD GIVE ME A HINT WHENEVER YOU SEE ME GOING WRONG.

WITH **PLEASURE.**

WILL YOU DO ME THE FAVOUR TO CALL ME BY MY CHRISTIAN NAME, HERBERT?

THANK YOU. MY CHRISTIAN NAME IS PHILIP.

I DON'T **TAKE** TO PHILIP. I TELL YOU WHAT I SHOULD LIKE – WE ARE SO **HARMONIOUS**, AND YOU HAVE BEEN A BLACKSMITH – WOULD YOU MIND **HANDEL** FOR A FAMILIAR NAME?

THERE'S A **CHARMING** PIECE OF MUSIC BY HANDEL, CALLED THE HARMONIOUS BLACKSMITH.

I SHOULD LIKE IT **VERY** MUCH.

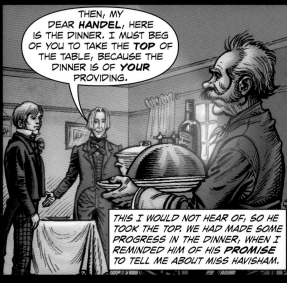

THEN, MY DEAR **HANDEL**, HERE IS THE DINNER. I MUST BEG OF YOU TO TAKE THE **TOP** OF THE TABLE, BECAUSE THE DINNER IS OF **YOUR** PROVIDING.

THIS I WOULD NOT HEAR OF, SO HE TOOK THE TOP. WE HAD MADE SOME PROGRESS IN THE DINNER, WHEN I REMINDED HIM OF HIS **PROMISE** TO TELL ME ABOUT MISS HAVISHAM.

MISS HAVISHAM, YOU MUST KNOW, WAS A **SPOILT** CHILD. HER MOTHER **DIED** WHEN SHE WAS A BABY, AND HER FATHER DENIED HER **NOTHING.**

HER FATHER WAS A COUNTRY GENTLEMAN DOWN IN **YOUR** PART OF THE WORLD, AND WAS A BREWER.

MR. HAVISHAM WAS VERY **RICH** AND VERY **PROUD.** SO WAS HIS **DAUGHTER.**

MISS HAVISHAM WAS AN **ONLY** CHILD?

NO, SHE HAD A **HALF-BROTHER.** HER FATHER PRIVATELY MARRIED AGAIN – HIS **COOK,** I RATHER THINK. IN THE COURSE OF TIME SHE DIED, AND THEN THE SON BECAME A PART OF THE **FAMILY.**

AS HE GREW UP, HE TURNED OUT RIOTOUS AND UNDUTIFUL. HIS FATHER **DISINHERITED** HIM, BUT LATER **SOFTENED,** AND LEFT HIM WELL OFF, THOUGH NOT NEARLY SO WELL OFF AS MISS HAVISHAM.

SHE WAS NOW AN **HEIRESS,** AND LOOKED AFTER AS A GREAT MATCH.

HER HALF-BROTHER **WASTED** HIS AMPLE MEANS. THERE WERE STRONG DIFFERENCES BETWEEN THEM, AND IT IS SUSPECTED THAT HE CHERISHED A DEEP **GRUDGE** AGAINST HER.

THERE **APPEARED** UPON THE SCENE – SAY AT THE RACES OR THE PUBLIC BALLS, OR ANYWHERE ELSE YOU LIKE – A CERTAIN **MAN,** WHO MADE **LOVE** TO MISS HAVISHAM. ALL THIS HAPPENED FIVE-AND-TWENTY YEARS AGO. HE WAS A **SHOWY** MAN.

HE **PURSUED** MISS HAVISHAM, AND PROFESSED TO BE **DEVOTED** TO HER. AND SHE FELL PASSIONATELY IN **LOVE** WITH HIM. HE PRACTISED ON HER AFFECTION, AND GOT GREAT SUMS OF **MONEY** FROM HER.

MY FATHER **WARNED** HER THAT SHE WAS DOING **TOO MUCH** FOR THIS MAN, AND WAS PLACING HERSELF TOO UNRESERVEDLY IN HIS POWER.

SHE TOOK THE FIRST OPPORTUNITY OF **ANGRILY** ORDERING MY FATHER **OUT** OF THE HOUSE, AND MY FATHER HAS NEVER SEEN HER **SINCE.**

SHE WAS TOO **HAUGHTY** AND TOO MUCH IN **LOVE** TO BE **ADVISED** BY ANYONE.

THE **MARRIAGE DAY** WAS FIXED, THE WEDDING **DRESSES** WERE BOUGHT, THE WEDDING **TOUR** WAS PLANNED OUT, THE WEDDING **GUESTS** WERE INVITED.

THE **DAY** CAME, BUT **NOT** THE BRIDEGROOM. HE WROTE HER A **LETTER** --

WHICH SHE RECEIVED WHEN SHE WAS **DRESSING?** AT TWENTY MINUTES TO NINE?

THE HOUR AND MINUTE AT WHICH SHE AFTERWARDS **STOPPED** THE CLOCKS.

THE LETTER **HEARTLESSLY** BROKE THE MARRIAGE OFF.

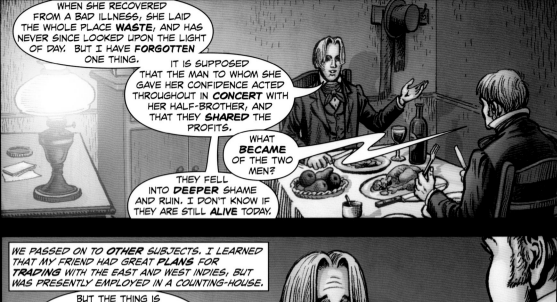

WHEN SHE RECOVERED FROM A BAD ILLNESS, SHE LAID THE WHOLE PLACE **WASTE**, AND HAS NEVER SINCE LOOKED UPON THE LIGHT OF DAY. BUT I HAVE **FORGOTTEN** ONE THING.

IT IS SUPPOSED THAT THE MAN TO WHOM SHE GAVE HER CONFIDENCE ACTED THROUGHOUT IN **CONCERT** WITH HER HALF-BROTHER, AND THAT THEY **SHARED** THE PROFITS.

WHAT **BECAME** OF THE TWO MEN?

THEY FELL INTO **DEEPER** SHAME AND RUIN. I DON'T KNOW IF THEY ARE STILL **ALIVE** TODAY.

WE PASSED ON TO **OTHER** SUBJECTS. I LEARNED THAT MY FRIEND HAD GREAT **PLANS** FOR **TRADING** WITH THE EAST AND WEST INDIES, BUT WAS PRESENTLY EMPLOYED IN A COUNTING-HOUSE.

BUT THE THING IS THAT YOU LOOK ABOUT YOU. **THEN** THE TIME COMES WHEN YOU SEE YOUR **OPENING**. AND YOU GO IN AND YOU **SWOOP** UPON IT AND YOU MAKE YOUR **CAPITAL**, AND THEN **THERE** YOU ARE!

WHEN YOU HAVE ONCE MADE YOUR CAPITAL, YOU HAVE **NOTHING** TO DO BUT **EMPLOY** IT.

IN THE COMPANY OF ONE WHO HAD **ALREADY** MADE HIS FORTUNE IN HIS OWN **MIND**, IT SEEMED MANY MONTHS SINCE I HAD LEFT JOE AND BIDDY.

ON THE MONDAY MORNING, HERBERT WENT TO THE COUNTING-HOUSE TO **LOOK ABOUT** HIM, AND I BORE HIM COMPANY.

AFTER LUNCH, WE TOOK COACH FOR **HAMMERSMITH**, WHERE MR. MATTHEW POCKET LIVED. WE WALKED TO HIS HOUSE AND WE PASSED DIRECT INTO A LITTLE GARDEN OVERLOOKING THE RIVER, WHERE MR. POCKET'S **CHILDREN** WERE PLAYING ABOUT.

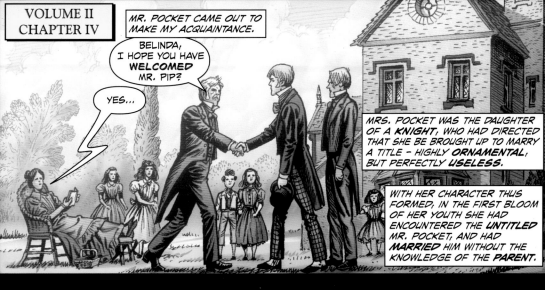

MR. POCKET CAME OUT TO MAKE MY ACQUAINTANCE.

BELINDA, I HOPE YOU HAVE **WELCOMED** MR. PIP?

YES...

MRS. POCKET WAS THE DAUGHTER OF A **KNIGHT**, WHO HAD DIRECTED THAT SHE BE BROUGHT UP TO MARRY A TITLE – HIGHLY **ORNAMENTAL**, BUT PERFECTLY **USELESS**.

WITH HER CHARACTER THUS FORMED, IN THE FIRST BLOOM OF HER YOUTH SHE HAD ENCOUNTERED THE **UNTITLED** MR. POCKET, AND HAD **MARRIED** HIM WITHOUT THE KNOWLEDGE OF THE **PARENT**.

MR. POCKET TOOK ME INTO THE HOUSE AND SHOWED ME MY ROOM, WHICH WAS A **PLEASANT** ONE. HE THEN KNOCKED AT THE DOORS OF TWO OTHER SIMILAR ROOMS, AND INTRODUCED ME TO THEIR OCCUPANTS, BY NAME **DRUMMLE** AND **STARTOP**.

BOTH MR. AND MRS. POCKET HAD SUCH A NOTICEABLE AIR OF BEING IN SOMEBODY ELSE'S **HANDS**, THAT I WONDERED WHO **REALLY** WAS IN POSSESSION OF THE HOUSE AND LET THEM LIVE THERE. AT DINNER I FOUND THIS UNKNOWN POWER TO BE THE **SERVANTS**.

MR. AND MRS. POCKET HAD A **TOADY** NEIGHBOUR; A WIDOW LADY WHO AGREED WITH EVERYBODY ACCORDING TO CIRCUMSTANCES. THIS LADY'S NAME WAS MRS. COILER, AND I HAD THE **HONOUR** OF TAKING HER DOWN TO DINNER.

THE PAGE CAME IN WITH THE ANNOUNCEMENT OF A DOMESTIC AFFLICTION: THE COOK HAD MISLAID THE BEEF. TO MY **AMAZEMENT**, I SAW MR. POCKET RELIEVE HIS MIND THROUGH AN **EXTRAORDINARY** PERFORMANCE. HE PUT HIS HANDS INTO HIS DISTURBED HAIR, AND APPEARED TO TRY TO **LIFT** HIMSELF UP BY IT.

HIS PERFORMANCE MADE **NO** IMPRESSION ON ANYBODY ELSE, AND I SOON BECAME AS **FAMILIAR** WITH IT AS THE REST.

AFTER DINNER, AND A ROW ON THE RIVER, I THINK WE **SHOULD** ALL HAVE ENJOYED OURSELVES, BUT FOR A RATHER **DISAGREEABLE** DOMESTIC OCCURRENCE. THE COOK WAS LYING **DRUNK** ON THE KITCHEN FLOOR.

AM I, GRANDPAPA'S GRANDDAUGHTER, TO BE **NOTHING** IN THE HOUSE? BESIDES, THE COOK HAS SAID THAT SHE FELT I WAS BORN TO BE A **DUCHESS**.

GOOD NIGHT, MR. PIP!!!

AFTER TWO OR THREE DAYS, MR. POCKET AND I HAD A LONG TALK. MR. JAGGERS HAD TOLD HIM THAT I WAS NOT DESIGNED FOR ANY **PROFESSION**, AND THAT I SHOULD BE WELL ENOUGH EDUCATED IF I COULD "HOLD MY OWN" WITH THE **AVERAGE** YOUNG MAN IN **PROSPEROUS** CIRCUMSTANCES.

HE **ADVISED** MY ATTENDING CERTAIN PLACES IN LONDON FOR THE ACQUISITION OF CERTAIN RUDIMENTS. HE WOULD ACT AS EXPLAINER AND DIRECTOR OF ALL MY **STUDIES**.

IT OCCURRED TO ME THAT IF I COULD **RETAIN** MY BEDROOM IN BARNARD'S INN, MY LIFE WOULD BE AGREEABLY VARIED, WHILE MY MANNERS WOULD BE **NONE** THE **WORSE** FOR HERBERT'S SOCIETY. MR. POCKET DID NOT OBJECT TO THIS ARRANGEMENT, BUT **URGED** THAT IT MUST BE SUBMITTED TO MY **GUARDIAN**.

I THEREFORE WENT TO LITTLE BRITAIN AND IMPARTED MY **WISH** TO MR. JAGGERS.

IF I COULD **BUY** THE FURNITURE NOW HIRED FOR ME, AND ONE OR TWO **OTHER** LITTLE THINGS, I SHOULD BE QUITE AT **HOME** THERE.

GO IT! I TOLD YOU YOU'D GET ON. WELL! HOW **MUCH** MONEY DO YOU **WANT?**

HOW MUCH? **FIFTY** POUNDS?

OH, NOT **NEARLY** SO MUCH.

FIVE POUNDS?

OH, MORE THAN **THAT**.

MORE THAN THAT, EH? COME! LET'S GET AT IT.

TWICE FIVE; WILL THAT DO? **FOUR** TIMES FIVE; WILL **THAT** DO?

I THINK THAT WILL DO HANDSOMELY.

WEMMICK! TAKE MR. PIP'S WRITTEN ORDER, AND PAY HIM TWENTY POUNDS.

MR. JAGGERS HAPPENED TO GO OUT AND WEMMICK WAS BRISK AND TALKATIVE.

I HARDLY KNOW WHAT TO **MAKE** OF MR. JAGGERS'S MANNER.

TELL HIM THAT, AND HE'LL TAKE IT AS A **COMPLIMENT**. HE DON'T MEAN THAT YOU SHOULD KNOW WHAT TO MAKE OF IT.

OH – IT'S NOT PERSONAL; IT'S **PROFESSIONAL**. ALWAYS SEEMS TO ME, AS IF HE HAD SET A **MAN-TRAP** AND WAS WATCHING IT.

SUDDENLY – *CLICK* – YOU'RE CAUGHT!

PRAY, WHOSE **LIKENESSES** ARE THOSE?

THESE? THESE ARE TWO **CELEBRATED** ONES. FAMOUS CLIENTS THAT GOT US A WORLD OF CREDIT.

THIS CHAP MURDERED HIS MASTER. THE CAST WAS MADE IN **NEWGATE**, DIRECTLY AFTER HE WAS TAKEN **DOWN**.

YOU HAD A **PARTICULAR** FANCY FOR ME, HADN'T YOU, OLD ARTFUL? HAD IT MADE FOR ME, EXPRESS!

DID THAT OTHER CREATURE COME TO THE **SAME** END? HE HAS THE SAME **LOOK**.

YES, HE CAME TO THE SAME END. HE FORGED **WILLS**, THIS BLADE DID, IF HE DIDN'T ALSO PUT THE SUPPOSED TESTATORS TO **SLEEP** TOO. HE SENT OUT TO **BUY** THIS FOR ME, ONLY THE DAY BEFORE.

ARE ALL YOUR PERSONAL JEWELLERY DERIVED FROM **LIKE** SOURCES?

OH YES, THESE ARE **ALL** GIFTS OF **THAT** KIND. ONE BRINGS ANOTHER, THAT'S THE WAY OF IT. I ALWAYS TAKE 'EM.

AFTER ALL, THEY'RE **PROPERTY** AND **PORTABLE**.

MY GUIDING-STAR ALWAYS IS, "GET HOLD OF PORTABLE PROPERTY".

IF AT ANY TIME WHEN YOU HAVE NOTHING **BETTER** TO DO, AND WOULDN'T MIND COMING OVER TO SEE ME AT WALWORTH, I COULD OFFER YOU A BED, AND CONSIDER IT AN **HONOUR**.

I HAVE TWO OR THREE **CURIOSITIES** YOU MIGHT LIKE TO LOOK OVER.

I SHOULD BE **DELIGHTED** TO ACCEPT YOUR **HOSPITALITY**.

HAVE YOU **DINED** WITH MR. JAGGERS YET?

NOT YET.

WHEN YOU **DO**, LOOK AT HIS **HOUSEKEEPER**. YOU'LL SEE A WILD BEAST TAMED. KEEP YOUR EYE ON IT.

67

SPENDING MY TIME WITH DRUMMLE, STARTOP AND MY INTIMATE COMPANION, HERBERT, I HAD NOT SEEN MR. WEMMICK FOR SOME **WEEKS**. I THOUGHT I WOULD WRITE HIM A NOTE AND **PROPOSE** TO GO HOME WITH HIM ON A CERTAIN EVENING. HE REPLIED THAT IT WOULD GIVE HIM MUCH **PLEASURE**, AND HE WOULD EXPECT ME AT THE OFFICE AT SIX O'CLOCK.

YOU DON'T **OBJECT** TO AN **AGED PARENT**, I HOPE? BECAUSE I HAVE GOT AN AGED PARENT AT MY PLACE.

NOT AT **ALL**.

SO, YOU HAVEN'T DINED WITH MR. JAGGERS YET? I EXPECT YOU'LL HAVE AN INVITATION **TO-MORROW**.

HE'S GOING TO ASK YOUR **PALS**, TOO.

THREE OF 'EM; AIN'T THERE? HE'S GOING TO ASK THE WHOLE GANG.

EVENTUALLY MR. WEMMICK GAVE ME TO UNDERSTAND THAT WE HAD ARRIVED IN THE DISTRICT OF WALWORTH.

MY **OWN** DOING. LOOKS PRETTY; DON'T IT? THAT'S A **REAL** FLAGSTAFF, YOU SEE, AND ON SUNDAYS I RUN UP A REAL **FLAG**.

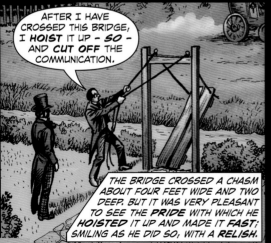

AFTER I HAVE CROSSED THIS BRIDGE, I **HOIST** IT UP – **SO** – AND **CUT OFF** THE COMMUNICATION.

THE BRIDGE CROSSED A CHASM ABOUT FOUR FEET WIDE AND TWO DEEP. BUT IT WAS VERY PLEASANT TO SEE THE **PRIDE** WITH WHICH HE **HOISTED** IT UP AND MADE IT **FAST**; SMILING AS HE DID SO, WITH A **RELISH**.

AT NINE O'CLOCK EVERY NIGHT, GREENWICH TIME, THE GUN FIRES. THERE HE IS, YOU SEE! AND WHEN YOU **HEAR** HIM **GO**, I THINK YOU'LL SAY HE'S A **STINGER**!

I AM MY OWN ENGINEER, CARPENTER, PLUMBER AND GARDENER. IT'S A **GOOD** THING, YOU KNOW.

IT BRUSHES THE **NEWGATE** COBWEBS AWAY, AND PLEASES THE AGED.

YOU WOULDN'T MIND BEING **INTRODUCED** TO THE AGED, WOULD YOU?

WE WENT INTO THE CASTLE, AND FOUND SITTING BY A FIRE, A VERY OLD MAN – CHEERFUL, COMFORTABLE, AND WELL CARED FOR, BUT INTENSELY **DEAF.**

HERE'S MR. PIP, AGED PARENT, AND I WISH YOU COULD HEAR HIS NAME. NOD AWAY AT HIM, MR. PIP; THAT'S WHAT HE **LIKES.** NOD AWAY AT HIM, IF YOU PLEASE, LIKE **WINKING!**

ALL RIGHT, **JOHN,** ALL RIGHT.

WE **LEFT** HIM BESTIRRING HIMSELF TO FEED THE FOWLS, AND SAT DOWN TO OUR **PUNCH** IN THE ARBOUR.

IT'S TAKEN ME A GOOD MANY **YEARS** TO BRING THE PROPERTY UP TO ITS PRESENT PITCH OF PERFECTION.

I HOPE MR. JAGGERS ADMIRES IT?

NEVER **SEEN** IT. NEVER **HEARD** OF IT. NEVER SEEN THE AGED. NEVER HEARD OF HIM. NO; THE OFFICE IS **ONE** THING, AND PRIVATE LIFE IS **ANOTHER.**

WHEN I GO TO THE OFFICE, I LEAVE THE **CASTLE** BEHIND ME.

YOU'LL **OBLIGE** ME BY DOING THE **SAME.** I DON'T WISH IT PROFESSIONALLY SPOKEN ABOUT. IT'S GETTING NEAR GUN-FIRE. IT'S THE AGED'S **TREAT.**

INSIDE THE CASTLE, WE FOUND THE AGED HEATING THE **POKER** AS A PRELIMINARY TO THIS GREAT NIGHTLY CEREMONY.

WEMMICK STOOD WITH HIS WATCH IN HIS HAND UNTIL THE MOMENT WAS COME FOR HIM TO TAKE THE RED-HOT POKER AND REPAIR TO THE **BATTERY.**

HE TOOK IT AND WENT OUT, AND PRESENTLY THE STINGER WENT OFF WITH A **BANG** THAT SHOOK THE CRAZY LITTLE BOX OF A COTTAGE, AND MADE EVERY GLASS AND TEACUP RING.

BOOOOOM

I HEERD HIM!

SUPPER WAS **EXCELLENT,** AS WAS MY LITTLE TURRET BEDROOM.

WEMMICK WAS UP **EARLY** IN THE MORNING AND OUR BREAKFAST WAS AS **GOOD** AS THE SUPPER. AT HALF-PAST EIGHT WE STARTED FOR LITTLE BRITAIN.

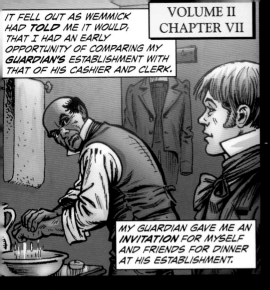

IT FELL OUT AS WEMMICK HAD **TOLD** ME IT WOULD, THAT I HAD AN EARLY OPPORTUNITY OF COMPARING MY **GUARDIAN'S** ESTABLISHMENT WITH THAT OF HIS CASHIER AND CLERK.

VOLUME II CHAPTER VII

MY GUARDIAN GAVE ME AN **INVITATION** FOR MYSELF AND FRIENDS FOR DINNER AT HIS ESTABLISHMENT.

THE **HOUSEKEEPER** APPEARED WITH THE FIRST DISH FOR THE TABLE.

OUR CONVERSATION TURNED UPON OUR **ROWING** FEATS. DRUMMLE WAS RALLIED FOR COMING UP BEHIND IN HIS SLOW AMPHIBIOUS WAY. UPON THIS, DRUMMLE INFORMED OUR HOST THAT AS TO STRENGTH, HE COULD SCATTER US LIKE **CHAFF**. THE **SPIDER**, AS MR. JAGGERS CALLED HIM, FELL BARING HIS ARM TO SHOW HOW **MUSCULAR** IT WAS, AND WE ALL FELL TO BARING OUR ARMS IN A RIDICULOUS MANNER.

THE HOUSEKEEPER WAS AT THAT TIME **CLEARING** THE TABLE. MY GUARDIAN SUDDENLY CLAPPED HIS LARGE HAND ON THE HOUSEKEEPER'S, LIKE A **TRAP**, AS SHE STRETCHED IT ACROSS THE TABLE.

IF YOU TALK OF STRENGTH, I'LL **SHOW** YOU A WRIST. MOLLY, LET THEM SEE YOUR **WRIST**.

Master, don't.

MOLLY, LET THEM SEE **BOTH** YOUR WRISTS. **SHOW** THEM. COME!

THERE'S **POWER** HERE. VERY FEW MEN HAVE THE POWER OF WRIST THAT THIS WOMAN HAS.

IT'S **REMARKABLE** WHAT FORCE OF **GRIP** THERE IS IN THESE HANDS.

THAT'LL DO, MOLLY. YOU HAVE BEEN **ADMIRED**, AND CAN GO.

AT HALF-PAST NINE, GENTLEMEN, WE MUST BREAK UP. PRAY MAKE THE BEST USE OF YOUR TIME.

AND AT HALF-PAST NINE WE DEPARTED.

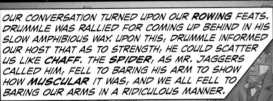

A MONTH OR SO LATER, I RECEIVED A LETTER BY THE POST.

My dear Mr. Pip:
I write this by request of Mr. Gargery, for to let you know that he is going to London, and would be glad if agreeable to be allowed to see you. He would call at Barnard's Hotel Tuesday morning 9 o'clock.
Your poor sister is much the same as when you left. We talk of you in the kitchen every night, and wonder what you are doing. No more, dear Mr. Pip, from your ever obliged and affectionate servant,
Biddy.
P.S. he wishes me most particular to write what larks.

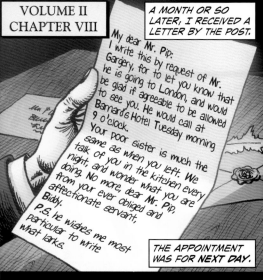

THE APPOINTMENT WAS FOR **NEXT DAY**.

LET ME CONFESS **EXACTLY** WITH WHAT FEELINGS I LOOKED FORWARD TO JOE'S COMING. NOT WITH PLEASURE, THOUGH I WAS BOUND TO HIM BY SO MANY TIES – NO, WITH CONSIDERABLE DISTURBANCE, **MORTIFICATION**, AND A KEEN SENSE OF **INCONGRUITY**.

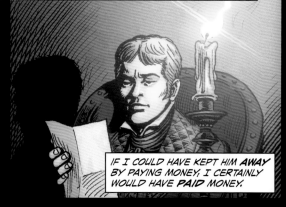

IF I COULD HAVE KEPT HIM **AWAY** BY PAYING MONEY, I CERTAINLY WOULD HAVE **PAID** MONEY.

I GOT UP **EARLY** IN THE MORNING, AND CAUSED OUR ROOMS IN BARNARD'S INN TO ASSUME THEIR MOST **SPLENDID** APPEARANCE. AS THE TIME APPROACHED I SHOULD HAVE LIKED TO **RUN AWAY**, BUT PRESENTLY I HEARD JOE ON THE STAIRCASE.

I **KNEW** IT WAS JOE BY HIS **CLUMSY** MANNER OF COMING UP STAIRS. AT LAST HE STOPPED OUTSIDE OUR DOOR, AND GAVE A FAINT SINGLE RAP.

≒tap≒

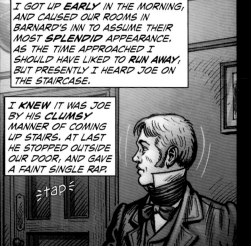

JOE, HOW ARE YOU, JOE?

PIP, HOW **AIR** YOU, PIP?

I AM GLAD TO **SEE** YOU, JOE.

WHICH YOU HAVE THAT GROWED, AND THAT SWELLED, AND THAT – GENTLE-FOLKED – AS TO BE SURE YOU ARE A **HONOUR** TO YOUR KING AND COUNTRY.

AND YOU, JOE, LOOK **WONDERFULLY** WELL.

US TWO BEING ALONE, SIR...

JOE, HOW CAN YOU CALL ME, SIR?

US TWO BEING ALONE, AND ME HAVING THE INTENTION TO STAY NOT MANY MINUTES MORE, I WILL NOW MENTION WHAT HAVE LED TO MY HAVING THE PRESENT HONOUR.

WELL, SIR, I WERE AT THE BARGEMEN T'OTHER NIGHT, WHEN THERE COME UP, PUMBLECHOOK, WHICH HIS MANNERS IS GIVEN TO BLUSTEROUS, PIP, AND HIS WORD WERE, "JOSEPH, MISS HAVISHAM SHE WISH TO SPEAK TO YOU."

NEXT DAY, SIR, HAVING CLEANED MYSELF, I GO AND I SEE MISS A.

MISS A., JOE? MISS HAVISHAM?

WHICH I SAY, SIR – MISS A., OR OTHERWAYS HAVISHAM. HER EXPRESSION AIR THEN AS FOLLERING: "MR. GARGERY. YOU AIR IN CORRESPONDENCE WITH MR. PIP? WOULD YOU TELL HIM, THAT ESTELLA HAS COME HOME AND WOULD BE GLAD TO SEE HIM."

I HAVE NOW CONCLUDED, SIR, AND, PIP, I WISH YOU EVER WELL AND EVER PROSPERING TO A GREATER AND A GREATER HEIGHT.

BUT YOU ARE NOT GOING NOW, JOE?

YES I AM.

PIP, DEAR OLD CHAP, LIFE IS MADE OF EVER SO MANY PARTINGS WELDED TOGETHER. IF THERE'S BEEN ANY FAULT AT ALL TODAY, IT'S MINE. YOU AND ME IS NOT TWO FIGURES TO BE TOGETHER IN LONDON; NOR YET ANYWHERES ELSE BUT WHAT IS PRIVATE.

IT AIN'T THAT I AM PROUD, BUT THAT I WANT TO BE RIGHT. I'M WRONG IN THESE CLOTHES. I'M WRONG OUT OF THE FORGE, THE KITCHEN, OR OFF TH' MESHES. AND SO GOD BLESS YOU, DEAR OLD PIP, OLD CHAP, GOD BLESS YOU!

HE TOUCHED ME GENTLY ON THE FOREHEAD AND WENT OUT.

IT WAS **CLEAR** THAT I MUST REPAIR TO OUR TOWN NEXT DAY; AND I SECURED MY BOX-PLACE BY TOMORROW'S AFTERNOON COACH.

IN THE FIRST FLOW OF MY **REPENTANCE**, IT WAS EQUALLY CLEAR THAT I MUST **STAY** AT **JOE'S**. BUT LATER, I BEGAN TO **INVENT** REASONS AND MAKE **EXCUSES** FOR PUTTING UP AT THE BLUE BOAR.

NEXT DAY, I ARRIVED ON THE GROUND WITH A QUARTER OF AN HOUR TO SPARE. AT THAT TIME, IT WAS CUSTOMARY TO CARRY **CONVICTS** DOWN TO THE DOCKYARDS BY STAGE-COACH.

AS I HAD OFTEN HEARD OF THEM IN THE CAPACITY OF **OUTSIDE** PASSENGERS, I WAS NOT SURPRISED WHEN I FOUND THERE WERE **TWO CONVICTS** GOING DOWN WITH ME.

YOU DON'T **MIND** THEM HANDEL?

OH NO! I DON'T MIND THEM.

SEE! THERE THEY ARE. WHAT A DEGRADED AND **VILE** SIGHT IT IS!

THE TWO CONVICTS WERE HANDCUFFED TOGETHER, AND HAD IRONS ON THEIR LEGS – IRONS OF A PATTERN I KNEW WELL. **ONE** WAS TALLER AND STOUTER THAN THE OTHER.

I **KNEW** HIS HALF-CLOSED EYE AT ONE GLANCE. **THERE** STOOD THE MAN WHO HAD SHOWED ME THE **FILE** AT **THE JOLLY BARGEMEN!**

E WEATHER WAS MISERABLY **RAW**. MADE US ALL **LETHARGIC** FORE WE HAD GONE FAR.

I **DOZED OFF**, MYSELF, IN CONSIDERING THE QUESTION WHETHER I SHOULD **RESTORE** A COUPLE OF **POUNDS** STERLING TO THIS CREATURE BEFORE LOSING SIGHT OF HIM, AND HOW IT COULD **BEST** BE DONE.

73

IN THE ACT OF DIPPING FORWARD, I WOKE IN A **FRIGHT**. THE VERY **FIRST** WORDS I HEARD THEM INTERCHANGE AS I BECAME CONSCIOUS WERE THE WORDS OF MY OWN **THOUGHT**...

...TWO ONE POUND NOTES.

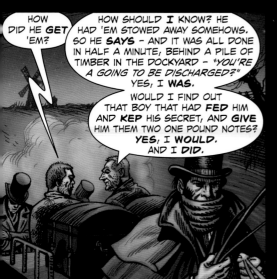

HOW DID HE **GET** 'EM?

HOW SHOULD **I** KNOW? HE HAD 'EM STOWED AWAY SOMEHOWS. SO HE **SAYS** – AND IT WAS ALL DONE IN HALF A MINUTE, BEHIND A PILE OF TIMBER IN THE DOCKYARD – "YOU'RE A GOING TO BE DISCHARGED?" YES, I **WAS**.

WOULD I FIND OUT THAT BOY THAT HAD **FED** HIM AND **KEP** HIS SECRET, AND **GIVE** HIM THEM TWO ONE POUND NOTES? **YES, I WOULD.** AND I **DID**.

MORE FOOL **YOU**. I'D HAVE SPENT 'EM ON A MAN, IN WITTLES AND DRINK. HE MUST HAVE BEEN A GREEN ONE. MEAN TO SAY HE KNOWED **NOTHING** OF YOU?

NOT A **HA'PORTH**. DIFFERENT GANGS AND DIFFERENT SHIPS. HE WAS TRIED **AGAIN** FOR PRISON BREAKING, AND GOT MADE A **LIFER.**

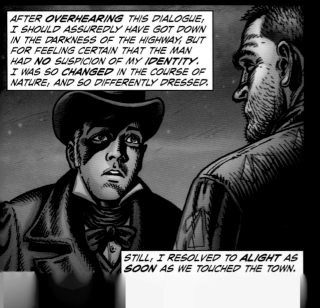

AFTER **OVERHEARING** THIS DIALOGUE, I SHOULD ASSUREDLY HAVE GOT DOWN IN THE DARKNESS OF THE HIGHWAY, BUT FOR FEELING CERTAIN THAT THE MAN HAD **NO** SUSPICION OF MY **IDENTITY**. I WAS SO **CHANGED** IN THE COURSE OF NATURE, AND SO DIFFERENTLY DRESSED.

STILL, I RESOLVED TO **ALIGHT** AS **SOON** AS WE TOUCHED THE TOWN.

THE CONVICTS WENT THEIR WAY WITH THE COACH. I COULD NOT HAVE SAID **WHAT** I WAS **AFRAID** OF, BUT THERE WAS **GREAT** FEAR UPON ME, AS I WALKED ON TO THE BLUE BOAR.

BETIMES IN THE MORNING I WAS UP AND OUT. IT WAS TOO **EARLY** YET TO GO TO MISS HAVISHAM'S, SO I LOITERED INTO THE COUNTRY, THINKING ABOUT MY PATRONESS, AND PAINTING **BRILLIANT** PICTURES OF HER **PLANS** FOR ME.

VOLUME II
CHAPTER X

I SO SHAPED OUT MY WALK AS TO **ARRIVE** AT THE GATE AT MY OLD TIME. WHEN I HAD RUNG AT THE BELL WITH AN **UNSTEADY** HAND, I TURNED MY BACK UPON THE GATE.

SHE HAD **ADOPTED** ESTELLA, SHE HAD AS **GOOD** AS ADOPTED **ME**, AND IT COULD NOT **FAIL** TO BE HER **INTENTION** TO BRING US **TOGETHER**.

ORLICK!

AH, YOUNG MASTER, THERE'S **MORE** CHANGES THAN **YOURS**. BUT COME IN. IT'S OPPOSED TO MY ORDERS TO HOLD THE GATE OPEN.

THEN YOU HAVE **LEFT** THE FORGE?

DO THIS **LOOK** LIKE THE **FORGE?**

ORLICK SOUNDED A BELL, AND **LEFT** ME TO ASCEND THE STAIRCASE IN THE **DARK**. I TAPPED IN MY OLD WAY AT THE DOOR OF MISS HAVISHAM'S ROOM.

tap-ta-tap

PIP'S RAP. **COME IN**, PIP

SITTING **NEAR** HER WAS AN ELEGANT LADY WHOM I HAD **NEVER** SEEN.

COME IN, PIP, HOW DO YOU **DO**, PIP?

SO YOU KISS MY HAND AS IF I WERE A **QUEEN**, EH? – WELL?

I HEARD, MISS HAVISHAM, THAT YOU WERE SO **KIND** AS TO WISH ME TO COME AND **SEE** YOU, AND I CAME **DIRECTLY**.

WELL?

THE LADY WHOM I HAD **NEVER** SEEN BEFORE, LIFTED UP HER **EYES** AND LOOKED AT ME...

...AND THEN I SAW THAT THE EYES WERE **ESTELLA'S** EYES.

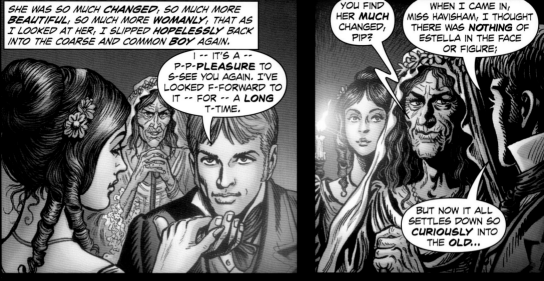

SHE WAS SO MUCH **CHANGED**, SO MUCH MORE **BEAUTIFUL**, SO MUCH MORE **WOMANLY**, THAT AS I LOOKED AT HER, I SLIPPED **HOPELESSLY** BACK INTO THE COARSE AND COMMON **BOY** AGAIN.

I -- IT'S A -- P-P-**PLEASURE** TO S-SEE YOU AGAIN. I'VE LOOKED F-FORWARD TO IT -- FOR -- A **LONG** T-TIME.

YOU FIND HER **MUCH** CHANGED, PIP?

WHEN I CAME IN, MISS HAVISHAM, I THOUGHT THERE WAS **NOTHING** OF ESTELLA IN THE FACE OR FIGURE;

BUT NOW IT ALL SETTLES DOWN SO **CURIOUSLY** INTO THE **OLD**...

WHAT? YOU ARE NOT GOING TO SAY INTO THE OLD ESTELLA? SHE WAS **PROUD** AND **INSULTING**. DON'T YOU **REMEMBER**?

THAT WAS **LONG** AGO, AND I KNEW NO **BETTER** THEN.

I HAVE NO DOUBT THAT YOU ARE QUITE **RIGHT**. I WAS VERY **DISAGREEABLE**.

WHEN WE HAD **CONVERSED** FOR A WHILE, MISS HAVISHAM SENT US TWO OUT TO WALK IN THE NEGLECTED GARDEN. I, **TREMBLING** IN SPIRIT AND WORSHIPPING THE VERY **HEM** OF HER DRESS; SHE, QUITE **COMPOSED** AND MOST DECIDEDLY **NOT** WORSHIPPING THE HEM OF **MINE**.

AS WE CAME **BACK** INTO THE YARD, I **SHOWED** HER WHERE SHE HAD GIVEN ME MY MEAT AND DRINK.

I DON'T **REMEMBER**.

NOT **REMEMBER** THAT YOU MADE ME **CRY**?

NO.

ESTELLA NOT REMEMBERING OR MINDING IN THE **LEAST**, MADE ME CRY **AGAIN**, INWARDLY.

YOU MUST KNOW, THAT I HAVE **NO HEART** – IF THAT HAS ANYTHING TO DO WITH MY MEMORY.

OH! I HAVE A **HEART** TO BE **STABBED** IN OR **SHOT** IN, I HAVE NO DOUBT. BUT YOU KNOW WHAT I **MEAN**.

I HAVE NO **SOFTNESS** THERE, NO – SYMPATHY; SENTIMENT – **NONSENSE**.

WHAT **WAS** IT THAT WAS BORNE IN UPON MY MIND WHEN SHE LOOKED ATTENTIVELY AT ME? ANYTHING THAT I HAD SEEN IN MISS HAVISHAM?

NO, IT WAS **NOT** MISS HAVISHAM. **WHO** THEN?

I LOOKED **AGAIN**, AND THE SUGGESTION WAS **GONE**.

AT LAST WE WENT BACK INTO THE HOUSE, AND THERE I HEARD, WITH SURPRISE, THAT MY **GUARDIAN** WAS THERE ON **BUSINESS** AND WOULD COME TO **DINNER.**

MISS HAVISHAM WAS IN HER CHAIR AND **WAITING** FOR ME. IT WAS LIKE PUSHING THE CHAIR ITSELF BACK INTO THE **PAST,** WHEN WE BEGAN THE OLD CIRCUIT ROUND ABOUT THE **ASHES** OF THE BRIDAL FEAST.

IS SHE BEAUTIFUL, GRACEFUL, WELL-GROWN?

DO YOU **ADMIRE** HER?

EVERYBODY **MUST** WHO **SEES** HER, MISS HAVISHAM.

LOVE HER, **LOVE HER,** LOVE HER!

IF SHE **FAVOURS** YOU, **LOVE** HER. IF SHE **WOUNDS** YOU, **LOVE** HER. IF SHE **TEARS** YOUR HEART TO **PIECES,** LOVE HER, **LOVE** HER!

HEAR ME, PIP! I ADOPTED HER, TO BE LOVED. I BRED HER AND EDUCATED HER, TO BE LOVED. **LOVE HER!**

AAAEEEEEEEK!

AS I DREW HER DOWN AGAIN, I WAS CONSCIOUS OF A SCENT THAT I **KNEW,** AND TURNING, SAW MY GUARDIAN.

MISS HAVISHAM MADE A STRONG ATTEMPT TO **COMPOSE** HERSELF, AND STAMMERED THAT HE WAS AS PUNCTUAL AS EVER.

MISS HAVISHAM SENT US DOWN TO OUR **DINNER.** AS MR. JAGGERS AND I GROPED OUR WAY DOWN-STAIRS, HE TOLD ME MISS HAVISHAM **NEVER** ALLOWED HERSELF TO BE **SEEN** EATING OR DRINKING, BUT WANDERED ABOUT AT **NIGHT** AND THEN LAID HANDS ON SUCH FOOD AS SHE TOOK.

PRAY, SIR, MAY I ASK YOU A QUESTION?

ESTELLA'S **NAME.** IS IT **HAVISHAM** OR...

IT **IS** HAVISHAM.

AFTER DINNER, WE WENT UP TO MISS HAVISHAM'S ROOM, AND WE FOUR PLAYED AT **WHIST.**

WE PLAYED UNTIL NINE O'CLOCK, AND THEN IT WAS ARRANGED THAT WHEN **ESTELLA** CAME TO **LONDON** I SHOULD MEET HER **COACH.**

THEN I TOOK **LEAVE** OF HER.

MY GUARDIAN LAY AT THE BOAR IN THE **NEXT** ROOM TO MINE. FAR INTO THE NIGHT, MISS HAVISHAM'S WORDS, "LOVE HER, LOVE HER, LOVE HER!" SOUNDED IN MY EARS. A BURST OF **GRATITUDE** CAME UPON ME, THAT SHE SHOULD BE **DESTINED** FOR **ME,** ONCE THE BLACKSMITH'S BOY.

I NO LONGER THOUGHT THERE WAS ANYTHING **LOW** IN MY KEEPING AWAY FROM **JOE,** BECAUSE I KNEW ESTELLA WAS **CONTEMPTUOUS** OF HIM.

AFTER **CONSIDERING** THE MATTER WHILE DRESSING AT THE BLUE BOAR IN THE MORNING, I RESOLVED TO TELL MY GUARDIAN THAT I DOUBTED **ORLICK'S** BEING THE **RIGHT SORT** OF MAN TO FILL A POST OF **TRUST** AT MISS HAVISHAM'S.

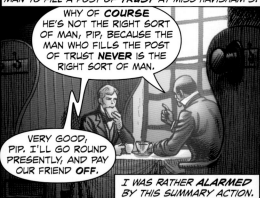

WHY OF **COURSE** HE'S NOT THE RIGHT SORT OF MAN, PIP; BECAUSE THE MAN WHO FILLS THE POST OF TRUST **NEVER** IS THE RIGHT SORT OF MAN.

VERY GOOD, PIP. I'LL GO ROUND PRESENTLY; AND PAY OUR FRIEND **OFF**.

I WAS RATHER **ALARMED** BY THIS SUMMARY ACTION.

JAGGERS AND I TOOK THE MID-DAY COACH BACK TO LONDON. AS **SOON** AS I ARRIVED, I WENT ON TO BARNARD'S INN.

MY DEAR HERBERT, I HAVE SOMETHING VERY **PARTICULAR** TO TELL YOU.

HERBERT, I **LOVE** – I **ADORE** – ESTELLA.

WELL? OF **COURSE** I KNOW **THAT**.

HOW DO YOU KNOW IT? I NEVER **TOLD** YOU.

TOLD ME! WHY, WHEN YOU TOLD ME YOUR OWN STORY, YOU TOLD ME **PLAINLY** THAT YOU BEGAN ADORING HER THE FIRST TIME YOU **SAW** HER.

I SAW HER **YESTERDAY**. AND IF I ADORED HER BEFORE, I NOW **DOUBLY** ADORE HER.

LUCKY FOR **YOU** THEN, IF YOU ARE PICKED OUT AND **ALLOTTED** TO HER.

AND NOW, HANDEL, I WANT TO **REPAY** CONFIDENCE WITH **CONFIDENCE**. I WANT TO SAY A WORD OR TWO CONCERNING MY FATHER'S SON.

I AM **ENGAGED**.

BUT IT'S A **SECRET**. NAME OF **CLARA**.

PERHAPS I OUGHT TO MENTION THAT SHE IS RATHER **BELOW** MY MOTHER'S **NONSENSICAL** FAMILY NOTIONS. I THINK HER FATHER WAS A SPECIES OF PURSER. HE'S AN INVALID NOW.

I HAVE NEVER **SEEN** HIM, FOR HE HAS ALWAYS KEPT TO HIS ROOM OVERHEAD. BUT I HAVE **HEARD** HIM CONSTANTLY. HE MAKES TREMENDOUS **ROWS** --

-- ROARS, AND PEGS AT THE FLOOR WITH SOME **FRIGHTFUL** INSTRUMENT!

HA, HA, HA!

THE **MOMENT** I BEGIN TO REALISE CAPITAL, IT IS MY INTENTION TO **MARRY** HER!

WE WARMLY SHOOK HANDS UPON OUR MUTUAL **CONFIDENCE**...

...AND WENT TO THE **THEATRE** TO SEE MR. WOPSLE IN DENMARK.

HAMLET
PRINCE OF DENMARK

HAYMARKET THEATRE

LEAVING THE THEATRE, IT OCCURRED TO ME – WAS I TO PLAY **HAMLET** TO MISS HAVISHAM'S **GHOST**?

I am to come to London the day after tomorrow by the midday coach. I believe it was settled you should meet me?

Miss Havisham has that impression, and I write in obedience to it. She sends you her regard.

Yours, Estella.

I BEGAN HAUNTING THE COACH-OFFICE IN CHEAPSIDE **BEFORE** THE COACH HAD **LEFT** THE BLUE BOAR IN OUR **TOWN**. I HAD PERFORMED THE FIRST HALF-HOUR OF A WATCH OF FOUR OR FIVE HOURS, WHEN **WEMMICK** RAN AGAINST ME.

HALLOA, MR. PIP. I SHOULD HARDLY HAVE THOUGHT THIS WAS **YOUR** BEAT. I AM GOING TO **NEWGATE**.

WOULD YOU LIKE TO **SEE** THE PLACE? HAVE YOU **TIME** TO SPARE?

I HAD SO **MUCH** TIME TO SPARE THAT THE PROPOSAL CAME AS A **RELIEF**. WEMMICK WALKED AMONG THE PRISONERS AND EXCHANGED WORDS WITH MANY. AS MR. JAGGERS'S SUBORDINATE, HE WAS HIGHLY **POPULAR**.

HOW ARE YOU, COLONEL?

ALL RIGHT, MR. WEMMICK.

EVERYTHING WAS DONE THAT **COULD** BE DONE, BUT THE EVIDENCE WAS TOO **STRONG** FOR US.

YES, IT WAS TOO STRONG, SIR, BUT I DON'T **CARE**.

I THINK I SHALL BE **OUT** OF THIS ON MONDAY; AND AM **GLAD** TO HAVE THE CHANCE OF BIDDING YOU **GOODBYE**.

*The recorder's report is made to-day, and he is **sure** to be **executed** on Monday.*

79

I RETURNED TO THE COACH-OFFICE WITH SOME THREE HOURS ON HAND. I CONSUMED THE TIME THINKING OF *ESTELLA* COMING TOWARDS ME, AND THOUGHT WITH ABSOLUTE *ABHORRENCE* OF THE *CONTRAST* BETWEEN THE JAIL AND HER.

I WAS STILL SHAKING THE *PRISON DUST* OFF MY CLOTHES, AND EXHALING ITS AIR FROM MY LUNGS, WHEN I SAW HER *FACE* AT THE COACH WINDOW.

I AM GOING TO *RICHMOND.* I AM TO HAVE A *CARRIAGE,* AND *YOU* ARE TO TAKE ME. YOU ARE TO PAY MY *CHARGES* OUT OF MY PURSE.

VOLUME II
CHAPTER XIV

OH, YOU *MUST* TAKE IT! WE HAVE NO CHOICE, YOU AND I, BUT TO *OBEY* OUR INSTRUCTIONS.

WILL YOU *REST* HERE A LITTLE?

YES, I AM TO REST A LITTLE, AND DRINK SOME TEA, AND *YOU* ARE TO *TAKE CARE* OF ME THE WHILE.

HER TONE, AS IF OUR ASSOCIATION WERE *FORCED* UPON US, AND WE MERE *PUPPETS*, GAVE ME PAIN.

WHERE ARE YOU *GOING* TO, AT RICHMOND?

I AM GOING TO LIVE, AT A *GREAT* EXPENSE, WITH A LADY THERE, WHO HAS THE POWER OF TAKING ME ABOUT, AND *INTRODUCING* ME TO PEOPLE.

AND HOW DO YOU *THRIVE* WITH MR. POCKET?

I LIVE QUITE PLEASANTLY THERE – AT LEAST, AS PLEASANTLY AS I *COULD* ANYWHERE, AWAY FROM *YOU.*

YOU SILLY BOY, HOW CAN YOU TALK SUCH **NONSENSE?** YOUR FRIEND MR. MATTHEW, I BELIEVE, IS **SUPERIOR** TO THE **REST** OF HIS FAMILY?

AS FOR THE REST, THEY BESET MISS HAVISHAM WITH REPORTS TO YOUR **DISADVANTAGE.** THEY **WATCH** YOU AND WRITE **LETTERS** ABOUT YOU.

YOU CAN SCARCELY **REALISE** THE **HATRED** THEY FEEL FOR YOU.

OH, THOSE **PEOPLE** WITH MISS HAVISHAM, AND THE **TORTURES** THEY UNDERGO!

IT IS NOT EASY FOR EVEN YOU TO KNOW WHAT **SATISFACTION** IT GIVES ME TO SEE THOSE PEOPLE **THWARTED.**

AFTER TEA, WE GOT INTO OUR POST-COACH AND DROVE AWAY.

WHAT PLACE IS **THAT?**

ERRM... NEWGATE PRISON.

WRETCHES!

WE CAME TO RICHMOND ALL TOO **SOON.**

GOOD NIGHT.

I STOOD LOOKING AT THE HOUSE, THINKING HOW **HAPPY** I SHOULD BE IF I LIVED THERE WITH HER, AND KNOWING THAT I NEVER WAS HAPPY WITH HER, BUT ALWAYS **MISERABLE.**

81

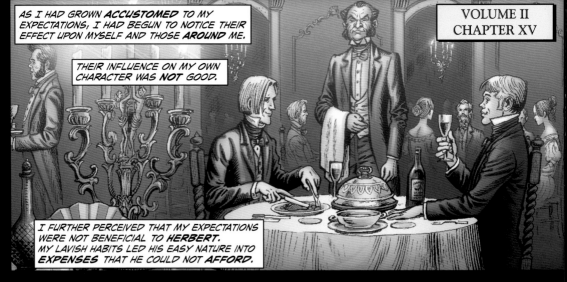

AS I HAD GROWN **ACCUSTOMED** TO MY EXPECTATIONS, I HAD BEGUN TO NOTICE THEIR EFFECT UPON MYSELF AND THOSE **AROUND** ME.

THEIR INFLUENCE ON MY OWN CHARACTER WAS **NOT** GOOD.

I FURTHER PERCEIVED THAT MY EXPECTATIONS WERE NOT BENEFICIAL TO **HERBERT.** MY LAVISH HABITS LED HIS EASY NATURE INTO **EXPENSES** THAT HE COULD NOT **AFFORD.**

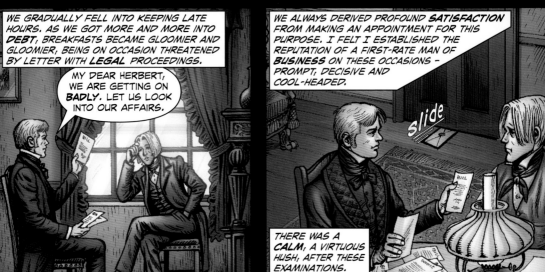

WE GRADUALLY FELL INTO KEEPING LATE HOURS. AS WE GOT MORE AND MORE INTO **DEBT,** BREAKFASTS BECAME GLOOMIER AND GLOOMIER, BEING ON OCCASION THREATENED BY LETTER WITH **LEGAL** PROCEEDINGS.

MY DEAR HERBERT, WE ARE GETTING ON **BADLY.** LET US LOOK INTO OUR AFFAIRS.

WE ALWAYS DERIVED PROFOUND **SATISFACTION** FROM MAKING AN APPOINTMENT FOR THIS PURPOSE. I FELT I ESTABLISHED THE REPUTATION OF A FIRST-RATE MAN OF **BUSINESS** ON THESE OCCASIONS – PROMPT, DECISIVE AND COOL-HEADED.

slide

THERE WAS A **CALM,** A VIRTUOUS HUSH, AFTER THESE EXAMINATIONS.

IT'S FOR **YOU,** HANDEL. I HOPE THERE IS NOTHING THE MATTER.

THE LETTER WAS SIGNED TRABB & Cº, AND BEGGED TO INFORM ME THAT MRS. J. GARGERY HAD **DEPARTED** THIS **LIFE** ON MONDAY LAST...

...AND THAT MY ATTENDANCE WAS REQUESTED AT THE **INTERMENT** ON MONDAY NEXT AT THREE O'CLOCK.

THE FIGURE OF MY SISTER IN HER CHAIR BY THE FIRE **HAUNTED** ME NIGHT AND DAY.

I WROTE TO JOE TO OFFER CONSOLATION AND TO **ASSURE** HIM THAT I WOULD COME TO THE FUNERAL.

VOLUME II
CHAPTER XVI

DEAR JOE, HOW **ARE** YOU?

PIP, OLD CHAP, YOU KNOWED HER WHEN SHE WERE A **FINE FIGURE** OF A WOMAN.

Here they come!

Here they are!

WE WENT INTO THE CHURCHYARD, CLOSE TO THE GRAVES OF MY UNKNOWN **PARENTS**. THERE, MY SISTER WAS LAID **QUIETLY** IN THE **EARTH**.

AFTERWARDS, BIDDY, JOE, AND I HAD A COLD DINNER TOGETHER IN THE **BEST PARLOUR.** JOE WAS SO EXCEEDINGLY **PARTICULAR** WHAT HE DID WITH HIS KNIFE AND FORK, THAT THERE WAS GREAT **RESTRAINT** UPON US.

BUT HE WAS VERY MUCH **PLEASED** BY MY ASKING IF I MIGHT SLEEP IN MY **OWN** LITTLE ROOM, AND I FELT THAT I HAD DONE RATHER A **GREAT** THING IN MAKING THE REQUEST.

AS EVENING CLOSED IN, I TOOK **BIDDY** FOR A LITTLE **TALK.**

I SUPPOSE IT WILL BE **DIFFICULT** FOR YOU TO REMAIN HERE NOW, BIDDY DEAR?

OH! I CAN'T DO SO, MR. PIP.

HOW ARE YOU GOING TO **LIVE?** IF YOU WANT ANY MO--

HOW AM I GOING TO LIVE? I'LL **TELL** YOU, MR. PIP. I AM GOING TO TRY TO GET THE PLACE OF MISTRESS IN THE **NEW SCHOOL** NEARLY FINISHED HERE.

I HAVE NOT HEARD THE **PARTICULARS** OF MY SISTER'S DEATH, BIDDY.

THEY ARE VERY SLIGHT, **POOR** THING. SHE HAD BEEN IN ONE OF HER **BAD STATES** FOR FOUR DAYS, WHEN SHE SAID QUITE PLAINLY, *"JOE."*

I **RAN** AND FETCHED MR. GARGERY, AND SHE LAID HER HEAD ON HIS SHOULDER. SHE PRESENTLY SAID *"JOE"* AGAIN, AND ONCE *"PARDON,"* AND ONCE *"PIP."* AN HOUR LATER, SHE WAS **GONE.**

DO YOU KNOW WHAT IS BECOME OF ORLICK? HAVE YOU **SEEN** HIM?

WHY ARE YOU **LOOKING** AT THAT DARK TREE?

I SAW HIM **THERE** ON THE NIGHT SHE **DIED.** AND I HAVE SEEN HIM THERE, SINCE WE HAVE BEEN WALKING **HERE.** HE WAS NOT THERE A MINUTE, AND HE IS **GONE.**

I SHOULD THINK FROM THE **COLOUR** OF HIS CLOTHES THAT HE IS WORKING IN THE **QUARRIES.**

IT REVIVED MY UTMOST INDIGNATION TO FIND THAT SHE WAS STILL **PURSUED** BY THIS FELLOW.

I WILL TAKE **ANY** PAINS TO **DRIVE** HIM OUT OF THE **COUNTRY.**

BY DEGREES SHE LED ME INTO MORE **TEMPERATE** TALK.

YOU MUST KNOW THAT JOE **LOVES** YOU AND NEVER COMPLAINS ABOUT **ANYTHING.** HE DOES HIS DUTY WITH A **GENTLE** HEART.

BIDDY, WE MUST **OFTEN** SPEAK OF THESE THINGS, FOR I SHALL BE OFTEN DOWN HERE NOW. I AM NOT GOING TO LEAVE POOR JOE **ALONE.**

ARE YOU QUITE **SURE**, THEN, THAT YOU **WILL** COME TO SEE HIM **OFTEN?**

OH DEAR ME! THIS REALLY IS A VERY **BAD** SIDE OF HUMAN NATURE!

DON'T SAY ANY **MORE**, IF YOU PLEASE, BIDDY. THIS **SHOCKS** ME VERY MUCH!

I KEPT BIDDY AT A **DISTANCE** FOR THE REMAINDER OF THE EVENING.

AS OFTEN AS I WAS **RESTLESS** IN THE NIGHT, I REFLECTED WHAT AN INJURY, WHAT AN **INJUSTICE**, BIDDY HAD DONE ME. EARLY IN THE MORNING, I WAS TO GO.

GOOD-BY, DEAR JOE! – I SHALL BE DOWN **SOON**, AND **OFTEN.**

NEVER TOO SOON, SIR, AND **NEVER** TOO OFTEN, PIP.

BIDDY, I AM NOT ANGRY; BUT I AM **HURT.**

DON'T BE HURT – LET ONLY **ME** BE HURT, IF I HAVE BEEN **UNGENEROUS.**

ONCE MORE, THE MISTS WERE RISING AS I WALKED AWAY. IF THEY DISCLOSED TO ME THAT I SHOULD **NOT** COME BACK, AND THAT BIDDY WAS QUITE **RIGHT**, ALL I CAN SAY IS...

...THEY WERE QUITE **RIGHT** TOO.

VOLUME II
CHAPTER XVII

HERBERT AND I WENT ON FROM BAD TO **WORSE**, IN THE WAY OF INCREASING OUR **DEBTS**.

TIME WENT ON, AND I CAME OF **AGE**. WE HAD LOOKED FORWARD TO MY ONE-AND-TWENTIETH **BIRTHDAY** WITH A CROWD OF **SPECULATIONS**, FOR WE BOTH CONSIDERED THAT MY GUARDIAN COULD HARDLY HELP SAYING SOMETHING **DEFINITE** ON THAT OCCASION.

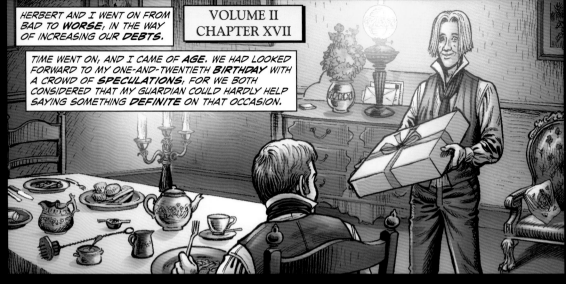

I RECEIVED AN OFFICIAL NOTE FROM WEMMICK, INFORMING ME THAT MR. JAGGERS WOULD BE GLAD IF I WOULD CALL UPON HIM AT FIVE IN THE AFTERNOON OF THE AUSPICIOUS DAY. THIS CONVINCED US THAT SOMETHING **GREAT** WAS TO HAPPEN.

WELL, PIP – I MUST CALL YOU **MR. PIP** TODAY.

CONGRATULATIONS, MR. PIP.

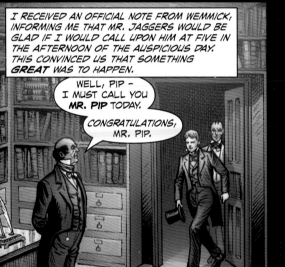

NOW MY YOUNG **FRIEND**, I AM GOING TO HAVE A **WORD** WITH YOU.

WHAT DO YOU SUPPOSE YOU ARE LIVING AT THE **RATE** OF?

I AM UNABLE TO **ANSWER** THAT QUESTION.

I **THOUGHT** SO!

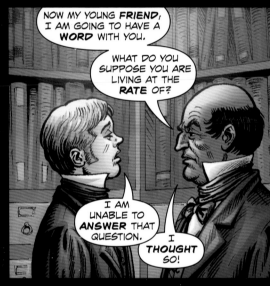

NOW, HAVE YOU **ANYTHING** TO ASK **ME?**

OF COURSE IT WOULD BE A GREAT RELIEF TO ME TO ASK YOU SEVERAL QUESTIONS, SIR, BUT I REMEMBER YOUR **PROHIBITION**.

IS MY **BENEFACTOR** TO BE MADE **KNOWN** TO ME TODAY?

NO. ASK ANOTHER.

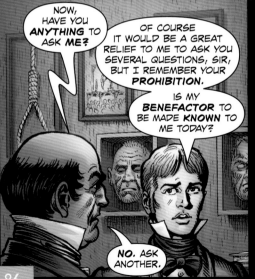

HAVE -- I -- ANYTHING TO **RECEIVE**, SIR?

I THOUGHT WE SHOULD COME TO IT! YOU HAVE BEEN DRAWING PRETTY **FREELY** HERE; YOUR NAME OCCURS PRETTY **OFTEN** IN WEMMICK'S CASH-BOOK; BUT YOU ARE IN **DEBT**, OF COURSE?

I AM **AFRAID** I MUST SAY YES, SIR.

THAT IS A BANK-NOTE FOR **FIVE HUNDRED** POUNDS.

NOW, THAT HANDSOME SUM OF MONEY, PIP, IS YOUR **OWN** -- A PRESENT TO YOU ON THIS DAY; IN EARNEST OF YOUR **EXPECTATIONS.**

AND AT THE **RATE** OF THAT SUM OF MONEY PER ANNUM, AND NO **HIGHER**, YOU ARE TO LIVE UNTIL THE DONOR OF THE **WHOLE** APPEARS.

THAT IS TO SAY; YOU WILL NOW TAKE YOUR MONEY AFFAIRS **ENTIRELY** INTO YOUR OWN HANDS.

MR JAGGERS, I HAVE **ANOTHER** QUESTION.

IS IT LIKELY THAT MY **PATRON** WILL SOON -- -- WILL SOON **COME** TO LONDON, OR **SUMMON** ME ANYWHERE **ELSE?**

COME! THAT'S A QUESTION I MUST **NOT** BE **ASKED** -- A QUESTION THAT MIGHT **COMPROMISE** ME. THAT'S ALL I HAVE TO SAY.

FROM THIS LAST SPEECH I DERIVED THE NOTION THAT MISS HAVISHAM HAD **NOT** TAKEN HIM INTO HER **CONFIDENCE** AS TO HER DESIGNING **ME** FOR **ESTELLA**, AND THAT HE **RESENTED** THIS AND WOULD HAVE NOTHING TO DO WITH IT.

IF THAT IS **ALL** YOU HAVE TO SAY; SIR, THERE CAN BE **NOTHING** LEFT FOR **ME** TO SAY.

I WENT INTO THE OUTER OFFICE TO TALK TO WEMMICK.

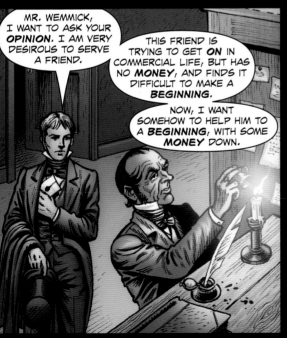

MR. WEMMICK, I WANT TO ASK YOUR **OPINION.** I AM VERY DESIROUS TO SERVE A FRIEND.

THIS FRIEND IS TRYING TO GET **ON** IN COMMERCIAL LIFE, BUT HAS NO **MONEY**, AND FINDS IT DIFFICULT TO MAKE A **BEGINNING.**

NOW, I WANT SOMEHOW TO HELP HIM TO A **BEGINNING**, WITH SOME **MONEY** DOWN.

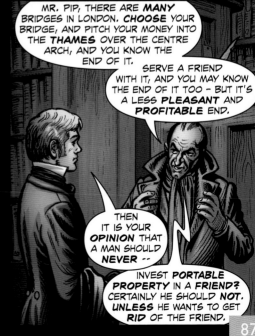

MR. PIP, THERE ARE **MANY** BRIDGES IN LONDON. **CHOOSE** YOUR BRIDGE, AND PITCH YOUR MONEY INTO THE **THAMES** OVER THE CENTRE ARCH, AND YOU KNOW THE END OF IT.

SERVE A FRIEND WITH IT, AND YOU MAY KNOW THE END OF IT TOO -- BUT IT'S A LESS **PLEASANT** AND **PROFITABLE** END.

THEN IT IS YOUR **OPINION** THAT A MAN SHOULD **NEVER** --

INVEST **PORTABLE PROPERTY** IN A **FRIEND?** CERTAINLY HE SHOULD **NOT. UNLESS** HE WANTS TO GET **RID** OF THE FRIEND.

VOLUME II CHAPTER XVIII

I DEVOTED THE NEXT SUNDAY AFTERNOON TO A *PILGRIMAGE* TO THE CASTLE.

I WAS ADMITTED BY THE *AGED*, WHO TOLD ME HIS SON WOULD *SOON* BE HOME FROM HIS AFTERNOON WALK. WE WENT IN AND SAT DOWN BY THE FIRESIDE.

THE OLD GENTLEMAN CHATTED IN HIS CHIRPING WAY; AND I *NODDED* AT HIM VIGOROUSLY. AFTER A GREAT DEAL OF NODDING, I WAS STARTLED BY A SUDDEN *CLICK* BY THE CHIMNEY...

Click

MY SON'S COME HOME!

John

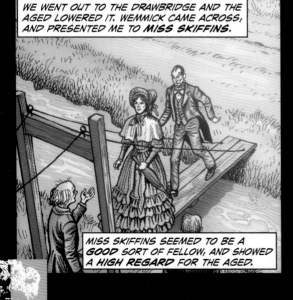

WE WENT OUT TO THE DRAWBRIDGE AND THE AGED LOWERED IT. WEMMICK CAME ACROSS, AND PRESENTED ME TO *MISS SKIFFINS*.

MISS SKIFFINS SEEMED TO BE A *GOOD* SORT OF FELLOW, AND SHOWED A *HIGH REGARD* FOR THE AGED.

SHE WAS A *FREQUENT* VISITOR AT THE CASTLE; FOR WEMMICK SHOWED ME THAT THE INGENIOUS CONTRIVANCE BY THE CHIMNEY HAD A *SECOND* FLAP WITH *"MISS SKIFFINS"* ON IT.

Miss Skiffins   John

WEMMICK INVITED ME TO TAKE A WALK ROUND THE PROPERTY; AND I **SEIZED** THE OPPORTUNITY. I INFORMED HIM THAT I WAS **ANXIOUS** ON BEHALF OF HERBERT POCKET. I TOLD HIM HOW HERBERT AND I HAD FIRST MET, AND GLANCED AT HIS HOME, CHARACTER, AND LACK OF MEANS.

I FEAR THAT HE MIGHT HAVE DONE **BETTER** WITHOUT ME AND MY EXPECTATIONS.

I HAVE GREAT **AFFECTION** FOR HERBERT. HOW CAN I BEST TRY TO HELP HIM TO SOME PRESENT INCOME AND GRADUALLY BUY HIM ON TO SOME SMALL PARTNERSHIP WITHOUT HIS **KNOWLEDGE**?

WELL YOU KNOW, MR. PIP, I MUST TELL YOU ONE THING. THIS IS DEVILISH **GOOD** OF YOU.

I'LL PUT ON MY CONSIDERING-CAP, AND I THINK ALL YOU WANT TO DO MAY BE DONE BY DEGREES. SKIFFINS (THAT'S HER BROTHER) IS AN **ACCOUNTANT** AND **AGENT**. I'LL LOOK HIM UP AND GO TO **WORK** FOR YOU.

I THANK YOU TEN THOUSAND TIMES.

BEFORE A **WEEK** WAS OUT, I RECEIVED A NOTE FROM WEMMICK, DATED WALWORTH, STATING THAT HE HAD MADE SOME **ADVANCE** IN THE MATTER.

THE UPSHOT WAS, THAT WE FOUND A WORTHY YOUNG SHIPPING-BROKER, ONE **CLARRIKER**, NOT LONG ESTABLISHED IN BUSINESS, WHO WANTED **CAPITAL**, AND, IN DUE COURSE OF TIME, A **PARTNER**.

BETWEEN HIM AND ME, **SECRET ARTICLES** WERE SIGNED OF WHICH HERBERT WAS THE SUBJECT. I PAID HIM **HALF** OF MY FIVE HUNDRED POUNDS DOWN, AND ENGAGED FOR SUNDRY OTHER PAYMENTS.

MISS SKIFFINS'S BROTHER **CONDUCTED** THE NEGOTIATION. WEMMICK PERVADED IT, BUT **NEVER APPEARED** IN IT. THE WHOLE BUSINESS WAS SO **CLEVERLY** MANAGED, THAT HERBERT HAD NOT THE **LEAST SUSPICION** OF IT.

I NEVER SHALL **FORGET** THE RADIANT FACE WITH WHICH HERBERT CAME HOME AND TOLD ME OF HIS HAVING FALLEN IN WITH ONE CLARRIKER, AND HIS BELIEF THAT THE **OPENING** HAD COME AT **LAST**.

DAY BY DAY, HIS HOPES GREW **STRONGER** AND HIS FACE **BRIGHTER**.

I HAD THE **GREATEST** DIFFICULTY IN RESTRAINING MY TEARS OF TRIUMPH WHEN I SAW HIM SO **HAPPY**.

BOTH IN AND OUT OF MRS. BRANDLEY'S HOUSE, I SUFFERED *EVERY* KIND OF *TORTURE* THAT ESTELLA COULD *CAUSE* ME.

IF THAT *STAID* OLD HOUSE IN RICHMOND SHOULD EVER COME TO BE *HAUNTED* WHEN I AM DEAD, IT WILL BE HAUNTED, SURELY, BY *MY* GHOST. *O*, THE MANY, MANY NIGHTS AND DAYS THROUGH WHICH MY UNQUIET SPIRIT *HAUNTED* THAT HOUSE WHEN ESTELLA LIVED THERE!

THE LADY WITH WHOM SHE LIVED, MRS. BRANDLEY BY NAME, WAS A WIDOW, WHO HAD BEEN A *FRIEND* OF MISS HAVISHAM'S BEFORE HER *SECLUSION*.

SHE HAD ADMIRERS WITHOUT *END*, AND MADE USE OF ME TO *TEASE* THEM. SHE USED OUR VERY FAMILIARITY TO PUT A CONSTANT SLIGHT ON MY *DEVOTION*.

I SAW HER *OFTEN* AT RICHMOND...

PIP, PIP, WILL YOU *NEVER* TAKE *WARNING*?

OF *WHAT*? WARNING NOT TO BE ATTRACTED BY *YOU*, DO YOU MEAN, ESTELLA?

IF YOU DON'T *KNOW* WHAT I MEAN, YOU ARE *BLIND*.

PIP, MISS HAVISHAM *WISHES* TO HAVE ME FOR A DAY AT SATIS HOUSE. *YOU* ARE TO TAKE ME *THERE*, AND BRING ME *BACK*, IF YOU WILL.

CAN YOU TAKE ME? THE DAY AFTER TOMORROW, IF YOU PLEASE.

WE WENT DOWN ON THE NEXT DAY BUT ONE.

MISS HAVISHAM HUNG UPON HER *BEAUTY*, HER WORDS AND GESTURES, AS THOUGH SHE WERE *DEVOURING* HER.

HOW DOES SHE *USE* YOU, PIP; HOW *DOES* SHE USE YOU?

SHE EXTORTED FROM ESTELLA THE NAMES OF ALL THE MEN WHOM SHE HAD FASCINATED, AND DWELT UPON THE ROLL WITH WITCH-LIKE *EAGERNESS*.

I SAW IN THIS THAT ESTELLA WAS SET TO WREAK MISS HAVISHAM'S *REVENGE* ON MEN, AND THAT SHE WAS *NOT* TO BE GIVEN TO ME UNTIL SHE HAD *GRATIFIED* IT FOR A TERM.

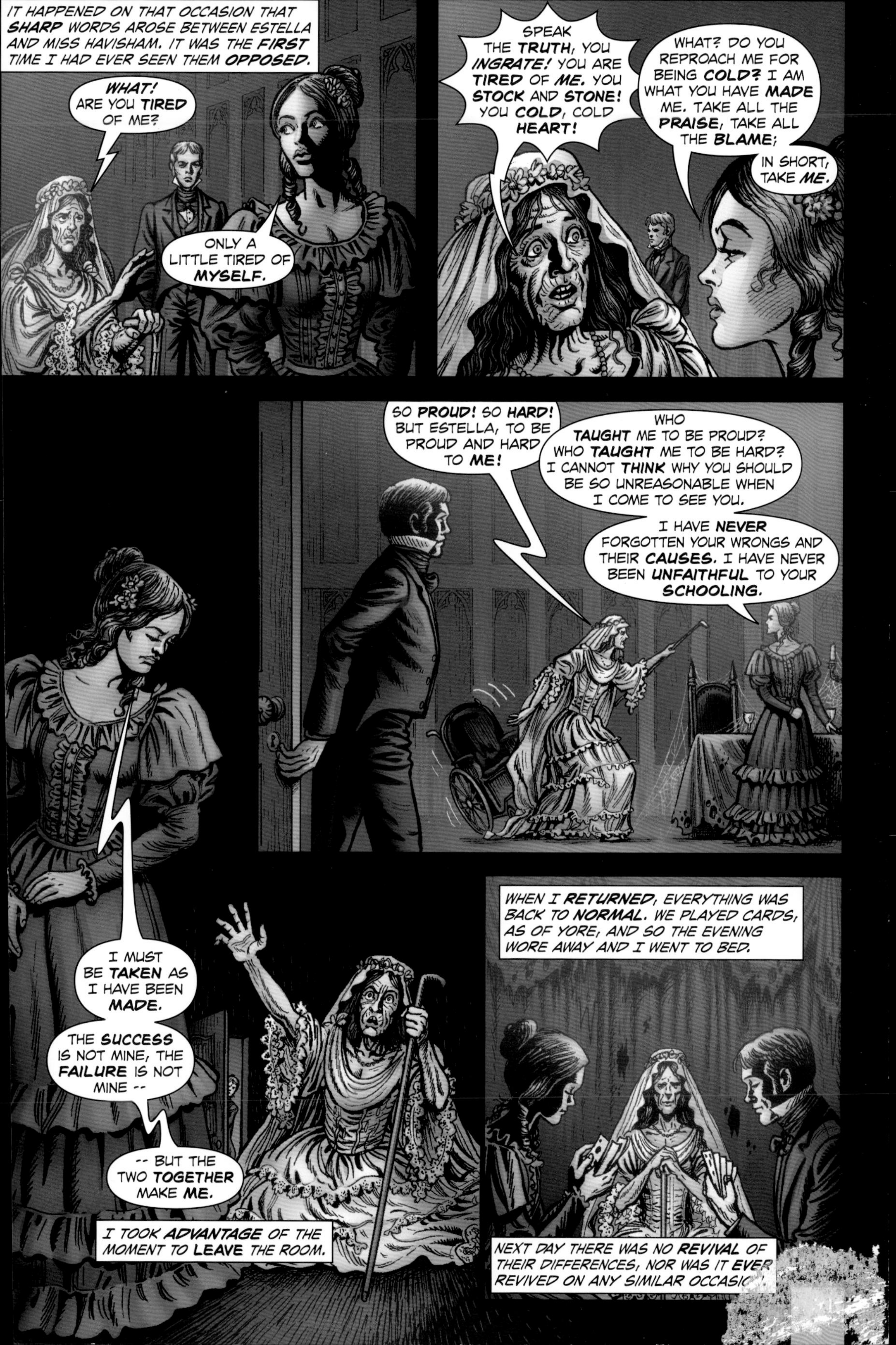

IT HAPPENED ON THAT OCCASION THAT SHARP WORDS AROSE BETWEEN ESTELLA AND MISS HAVISHAM. IT WAS THE FIRST TIME I HAD EVER SEEN THEM OPPOSED.
WHAT! ARE YOU TIRED OF ME?
ONLY A LITTLE TIRED OF MYSELF.
SPEAK THE TRUTH, YOU INGRATE! YOU ARE TIRED OF ME. YOU STOCK AND STONE! YOU COLD, COLD HEART!
WHAT? DO YOU REPROACH ME FOR BEING COLD? I AM WHAT YOU HAVE MADE ME. TAKE ALL THE PRAISE, TAKE ALL THE BLAME;
IN SHORT, TAKE ME.
SO PROUD! SO HARD! BUT ESTELLA, TO BE PROUD AND HARD TO ME!
WHO TAUGHT ME TO BE PROUD? WHO TAUGHT ME TO BE HARD? I CANNOT THINK WHY YOU SHOULD BE SO UNREASONABLE WHEN I COME TO SEE YOU.
I HAVE NEVER FORGOTTEN YOUR WRONGS AND THEIR CAUSES. I HAVE NEVER BEEN UNFAITHFUL TO YOUR SCHOOLING.
I MUST BE TAKEN AS I HAVE BEEN MADE.
THE SUCCESS IS NOT MINE, THE FAILURE IS NOT MINE --
-- BUT THE TWO TOGETHER MAKE ME.
I TOOK ADVANTAGE OF THE MOMENT TO LEAVE THE ROOM.
WHEN I RETURNED, EVERYTHING WAS BACK TO NORMAL. WE PLAYED CARDS, AS OF YORE; AND SO THE EVENING WORE AWAY AND I WENT TO BED.
NEXT DAY THERE WAS NO REVIVAL OF THEIR DIFFERENCES, NOR WAS IT EVER REVIVED ON ANY SIMILAR OCCASIO

HERBERT AND I WERE ELECTED INTO A **CLUB** CALLED THE FINCHES OF THE GROVE, AND THE **FIRST** FINCH I SAW WAS **BENTLEY DRUMMLE.**

THE PRESIDING FINCH CALLED UPON MR. DRUMMLE TO TOAST A LADY. WHAT WAS MY INDIGNANT **SURPRISE** WHEN HE CALLED UPON THE COMPANY TO PLEDGE HIM TO...

ESTELLA OF RICHMOND, GENTLEMEN, AND A **PEERLESS** BEAUTY!

I **KNOW** THAT LADY.

AND SO DO **I.**

I BECAME HIGHLY **INCENSED** BY THIS, BUT SOON LEARNED HOW THEY HAD DANCED TOGETHER **SEVERAL** TIMES.

I CANNOT EXPRESS WHAT **PAIN** IT GAVE ME TO THINK THAT ESTELLA SHOULD SHOW **ANY** FAVOUR TO THIS CONTEMPTIBLE BOOBY. I SOON FOUND OUT THAT DRUMMLE HAD BEGUN TO FOLLOW HER **CLOSELY,** AND THAT SHE **ALLOWED** HIM TO DO IT.

SOON HE WAS **ALWAYS** IN PURSUIT OF HER, AND HE AND I CROSSED ONE ANOTHER EVERY DAY.

AT AN ASSEMBLY BALL AT RICHMOND, THE BLUNDERING DRUMMLE SO HUNG ABOUT ESTELLA AND WITH SO MUCH **TOLERATION** ON HER PART, THAT I RESOLVED TO **SPEAK** TO HER WHILE SHE WAITED FOR MRS. BRANDLEY TO TAKE HER HOME.

ESTELLA, **DO** LOOK AT THAT FELLOW IN THE CORNER **YONDER,** LOOKING OVER AT US.

WHY **SHOULD** I LOOK AT HIM? WHAT IS HE TO **ME?**

ESTELLA, DO **HEAR** ME SPEAK.

IT MAKES ME **WRETCHED** THAT YOU SHOULD ENCOURAGE A MAN SO GENERALLY **DESPISED** AS DRUMMLE.

PIP, DON'T BE **FOOLISH** ABOUT ITS **EFFECT** ON YOU. IT MAY HAVE ITS EFFECT ON **OTHERS,** AND MAY BE **MEANT** TO HAVE. IT'S NOT **WORTH** DISCUSSING.

DO YOU **DECEIVE** AND **ENTRAP** HIM, ESTELLA?

YES, AND **MANY** OTHERS – **ALL** OF THEM BUT **YOU.**

HERE IS MRS. BRANDLEY. I'LL SAY NO **MORE.**

GREAT EVENT, THE **TURNING POINT** OF MY LIFE, NOW APPEARS IN VIEW. I WAS THREE-AND-TWENTY YEARS OF AGE, AND NOT ANOTHER **WORD** HAD I HEARD CONCERNING MY **EXPECTATIONS**.

VOLUME II
CHAPTER XX

IT WAS WRETCHED WEATHER, STORMY AND WET. I LOOKED THROUGH THE BLACK WINDOWS TO SEE THE LAMPS IN THE COURT WERE ALL **BLOWN OUT**.

HERBERT'S BUSINESS WAS STILL PROGRESSING, AND HAD TAKEN HIM ON A JOURNEY TO **MARSEILLES**, SO I WAS **ALONE**. MR. POCKET AND I HAD LONG PARTED COMPANY AS TO OUR ORIGINAL RELATIONS, THOUGH WE CONTINUED ON THE **BEST** TERMS.

NOTWITHSTANDING MY **INABILITY** TO SETTLE TO **ANYTHING**, I READ REGULARLY SO MANY HOURS A DAY. AT ELEVEN O'CLOCK, I HEARD A **FOOTSTEP** ON THE **STAIR**.

CLUMP

REMEMBERING THAT THE STAIRCASE LIGHTS WERE BLOWN **OUT**, I TOOK UP MY READING-LAMP AND WENT OUT. WHOEVER WAS BELOW HAD **STOPPED** ON SEEING MY LAMP, FOR ALL WAS **QUIET**.

THERE IS SOMEONE **DOWN** THERE, IS THERE NOT? WHAT FLOOR DO YOU **WANT?**

THE **TOP**.

MR. PIP.

THAT IS **MY** NAME. THERE IS NOTHING THE **MATTER?**

NOTHING THE MATTER.

I SAW A **FACE** THAT WAS **STRANGE** TO ME, LOOKING UP WITH AN INCOMPREHENSIBLE AIR OF BEING **PLEASED** BY THE **SIGHT** OF ME.

PRAY WHAT IS YOUR **BUSINESS?** DO YOU WISH TO COME **IN?**

YES, I WISH TO COME IN. I WILL **EXPLAIN** MY BUSINESS, MASTER.

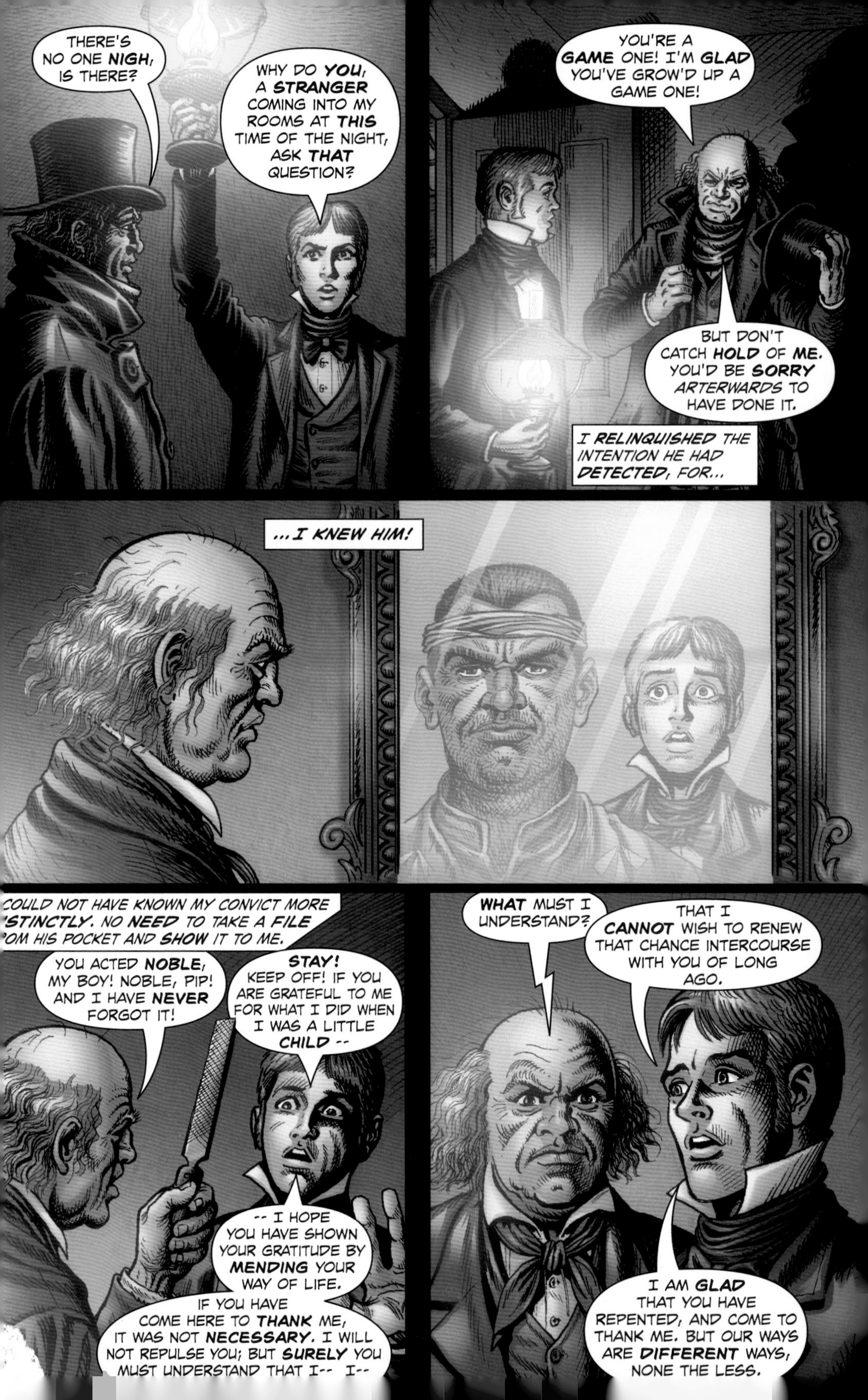
THERE'S NO ONE NIGH, IS THERE?
WHY DO YOU, A STRANGER COMING INTO MY ROOMS AT THIS TIME OF THE NIGHT, ASK THAT QUESTION?
YOU'RE A GAME ONE! I'M GLAD YOU'VE GROW'D UP A GAME ONE!
BUT DON'T CATCH HOLD OF ME. YOU'D BE SORRY ARTERWARDS TO HAVE DONE IT.
I RELINQUISHED THE INTENTION HE HAD DETECTED, FOR...
...I KNEW HIM!
COULD NOT HAVE KNOWN MY CONVICT MORE 'STINCTLY. NO NEED TO TAKE A FILE OM HIS POCKET AND SHOW IT TO ME.
YOU ACTED NOBLE, MY BOY! NOBLE, PIP! AND I HAVE NEVER FORGOT IT!
STAY! KEEP OFF! IF YOU ARE GRATEFUL TO ME FOR WHAT I DID WHEN I WAS A LITTLE CHILD --
-- I HOPE YOU HAVE SHOWN YOUR GRATITUDE BY MENDING YOUR WAY OF LIFE.
IF YOU HAVE COME HERE TO THANK ME, IT WAS NOT NECESSARY. I WILL NOT REPULSE YOU; BUT SURELY YOU MUST UNDERSTAND THAT I-- I--
WHAT MUST I UNDERSTAND?
THAT I CANNOT WISH TO RENEW THAT CHANCE INTERCOURSE WITH YOU OF LONG AGO.
I AM GLAD THAT YOU HAVE REPENTED, AND COME TO THANK ME. BUT OUR WAYS ARE DIFFERENT WAYS, NONE THE LESS.

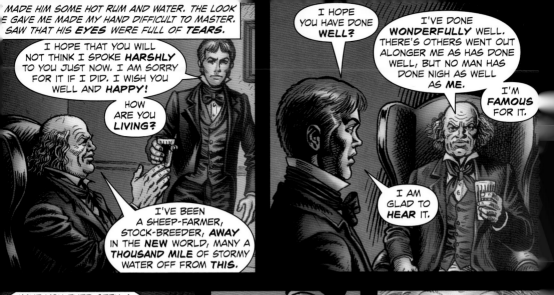

MADE HIM SOME HOT RUM AND WATER. THE LOOK E GAVE ME MADE MY HAND DIFFICULT TO MASTER. SAW THAT HIS **EYES** WERE FULL OF **TEARS.**

I HOPE THAT YOU WILL NOT THINK I SPOKE **HARSHLY** TO YOU JUST NOW. I AM SORRY FOR IT IF I DID. I WISH YOU WELL AND **HAPPY!**

HOW ARE YOU **LIVING?**

I'VE BEEN A SHEEP-FARMER, STOCK-BREEDER, **AWAY** IN THE **NEW** WORLD; MANY A **THOUSAND MILE** OF STORMY WATER OFF FROM **THIS.**

I HOPE YOU HAVE DONE **WELL?**

I'VE DONE **WONDERFULLY** WELL. THERE'S OTHERS WENT OUT ALONGER ME AS HAS DONE WELL, BUT NO MAN HAS DONE NIGH AS WELL AS **ME.**

I'M **FAMOUS** FOR IT.

I AM GLAD TO **HEAR** IT.

HAVE YOU EVER SEEN A **MESSENGER** YOU ONCE SENT TO ME, SINCE HE UNDERTOOK THAT **TRUST?** HE CAME **FAITHFULLY,** AND BROUGHT ME THE TWO **ONE-POUND** NOTES.

TO A POOR BOY THEY WERE A LITTLE **FORTUNE.** BUT, LIKE YOU, I HAVE DONE WELL SINCE, AND YOU **MUST** LET ME PAY THEM **BACK.**

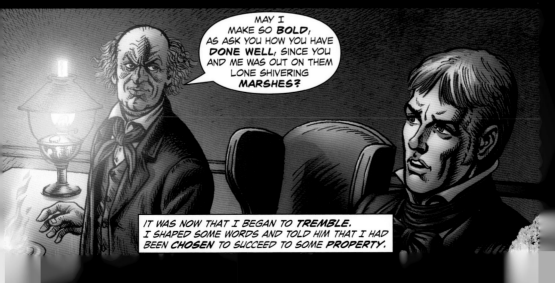

MAY I MAKE SO **BOLD,** AS ASK YOU HOW YOU HAVE **DONE WELL,** SINCE YOU AND ME WAS OUT ON THEM LONE SHIVERING **MARSHES?**

IT WAS NOW THAT I BEGAN TO **TREMBLE.** I SHAPED SOME WORDS AND TOLD HIM THAT I HAD BEEN **CHOSEN** TO SUCCEED TO SOME **PROPERTY.**

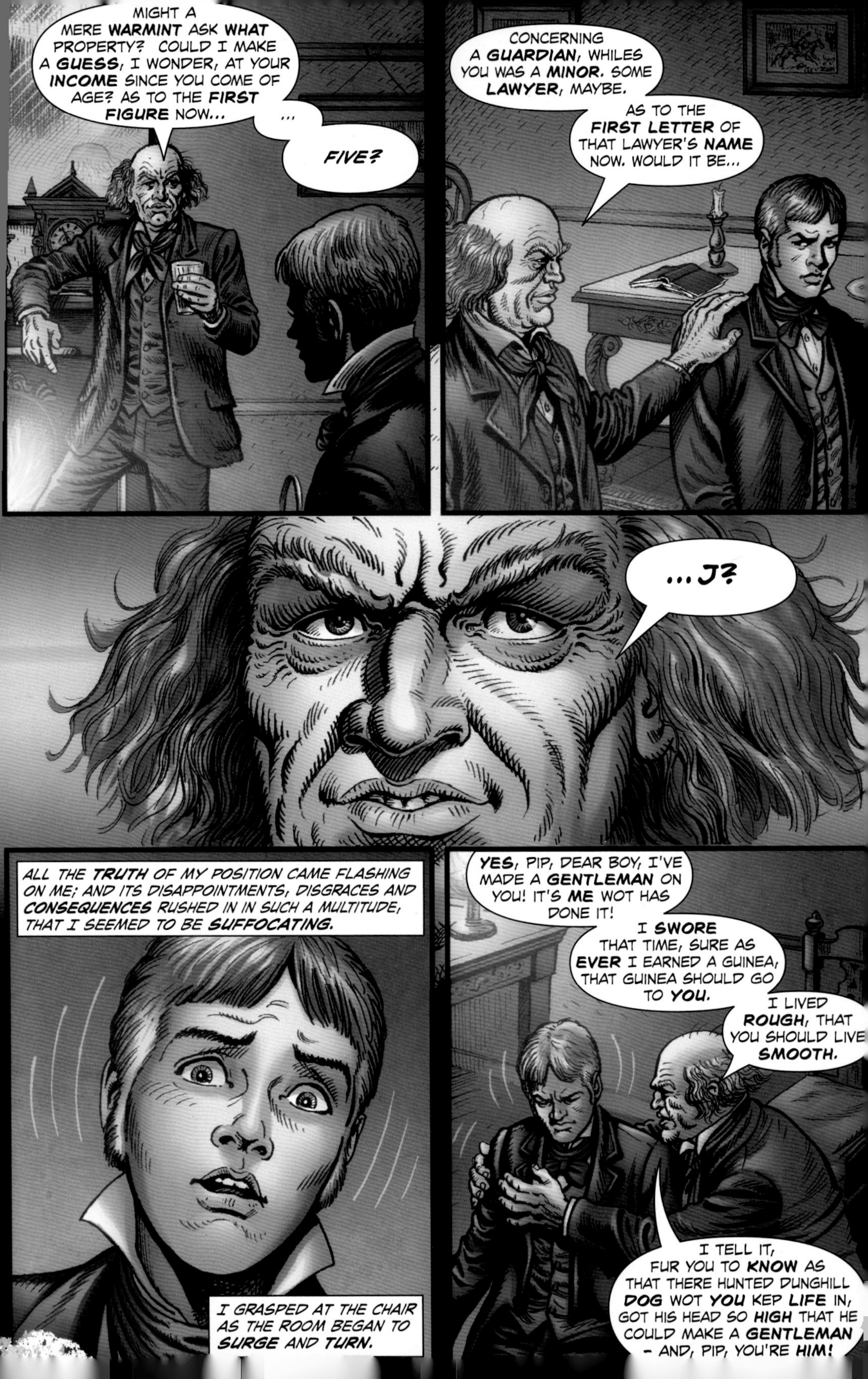
MIGHT A MERE WARMINT ASK WHAT PROPERTY? COULD I MAKE A GUESS, I WONDER, AT YOUR INCOME SINCE YOU COME OF AGE? AS TO THE FIRST FIGURE NOW...
...
FIVE?
CONCERNING A GUARDIAN, WHILES YOU WAS A MINOR. SOME LAWYER, MAYBE.
AS TO THE FIRST LETTER OF THAT LAWYER'S NAME NOW. WOULD IT BE...
...J?
ALL THE TRUTH OF MY POSITION CAME FLASHING ON ME; AND ITS DISAPPOINTMENTS, DISGRACES AND CONSEQUENCES RUSHED IN IN SUCH A MULTITUDE, THAT I SEEMED TO BE SUFFOCATING.
I GRASPED AT THE CHAIR AS THE ROOM BEGAN TO SURGE AND TURN.
YES, PIP, DEAR BOY, I'VE MADE A GENTLEMAN ON YOU! IT'S ME WOT HAS DONE IT!
I SWORE THAT TIME, SURE AS EVER I EARNED A GUINEA, THAT GUINEA SHOULD GO TO YOU.
I LIVED ROUGH, THAT YOU SHOULD LIVE SMOOTH.
I TELL IT, FUR YOU TO KNOW AS THAT THERE HUNTED DUNGHILL DOG WOT YOU KEP LIFE IN, GOT HIS HEAD SO HIGH THAT HE COULD MAKE A GENTLEMAN - AND, PIP, YOU'RE HIM!

THE **ABHORRENCE** IN WHICH I HELD THE MAN, THE **DREAD** I FELT, COULD NOT HAVE BEEN EXCEEDED IF HE HAD BEEN SOME TERRIBLE **BEAST.**

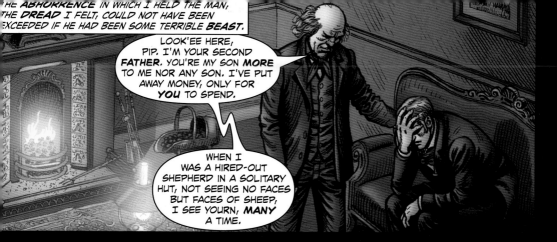

LOOK'EE HERE, PIP. I'M YOUR SECOND **FATHER.** YOU'RE MY SON **MORE** TO ME NOR ANY SON. I'VE PUT AWAY MONEY, ONLY FOR **YOU** TO SPEND.

WHEN I WAS A HIRED-OUT SHEPHERD IN A SOLITARY HUT, NOT SEEING NO FACES BUT FACES OF SHEEP, I SEE YOURN, **MANY** A TIME.

AND I SAYS, "LORD STRIKE ME DEAD! BUT WOT, IF I GETS LIBERTY AND MONEY, I'LL MAKE THAT BOY A **GENTLEMAN!"** AND I **DONE** IT.

WHY, **LOOK** AT YOU, DEAR BOY! LOOK AT THESE HERE LODGINGS O'YOURN, FIT FOR A **LORD!** LOOK AT YOUR CLOTHES; BETTER AIN'T TO BE GOT! AND YOUR BOOKS TOO, MOUNTING UP BY **HUNDREDS!**

DON'T YOU MIND **TALKING,** DEAR BOY. YOU AIN'T LOOKED FORWARD TO THIS AS I HAVE; YOU WOSN'T PREPARED FOR THIS AS I WOS.

BUT DIDN'T YOU **NEVER** THINK IT MIGHT BE **ME?**

OH NO, **NO.** NEVER, **NEVER!**

WAS THERE NO ONE **ELSE?**

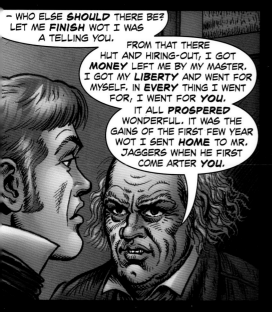

– WHO ELSE **SHOULD** THERE BE? LET ME **FINISH** WOT I WAS A TELLING YOU.

FROM THAT THERE HUT AND HIRING-OUT, I GOT **MONEY** LEFT ME BY MY MASTER. I GOT MY **LIBERTY** AND WENT FOR MYSELF. IN **EVERY** THING I WENT FOR, I WENT FOR **YOU.**

IT ALL **PROSPERED** WONDERFUL. IT WAS THE GAINS OF THE FIRST FEW YEAR WOT I SENT **HOME** TO MR. JAGGERS WHEN HE FIRST COME ARTER **YOU.**

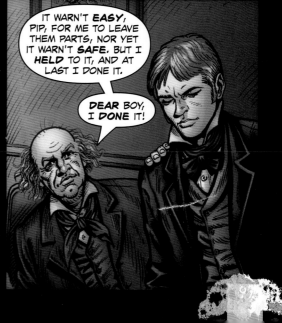

IT WARN'T **EASY,** PIP, FOR ME TO LEAVE THEM PARTS, NOR YET IT WARN'T **SAFE.** BUT I **HELD** TO IT, AND AT LAST I DONE IT.

DEAR BOY, I **DONE** IT!

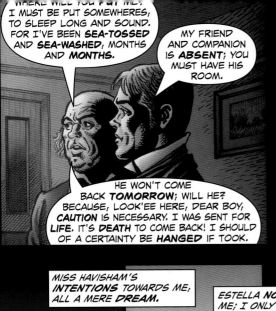

WHERE WILL YOU PUT ME? I MUST BE PUT SOMEWHERES, TO SLEEP LONG AND SOUND. FOR I'VE BEEN **SEA-TOSSED** AND **SEA-WASHED**, MONTHS AND **MONTHS**.

MY FRIEND AND COMPANION IS **ABSENT**; YOU MUST HAVE HIS ROOM.

HE WON'T COME BACK **TOMORROW**; WILL HE? BECAUSE, LOOK'EE HERE, DEAR BOY, **CAUTION** IS NECESSARY. I WAS SENT FOR **LIFE**. IT'S **DEATH** TO COME BACK! I SHOULD OF A CERTAINTY BE **HANGED** IF TOOK.

AFTER HIS RUM AND BISCUIT SUPPER HE BADE ME **GOOD NIGHT** IN HERBERT'S ROOM. I SAT DOWN BY THE FIRE, AFRAID TO GO TO BED. I THEN BEGAN **FULLY** TO KNOW HOW **WRECKED** I WAS.

MISS HAVISHAM'S **INTENTIONS** TOWARDS ME, ALL A MERE **DREAM**.

ESTELLA **NOT** DESIGNED FOR ME; I ONLY SUFFERED IN SATIS HOUSE AS A **STING** FOR GREEDY **RELATIONS**.

SHARPEST AND DEEPEST PAIN OF ALL, IT WAS FOR THIS **CONVICT** THAT I HAD **DESERTED** JOE.

I SLEPT, WITHOUT PARTING FROM THE PERCEPTION OF MY **WRETCHEDNESS**.

WHEN I AWOKE, THE FIRE WAS **DEAD**, THE CANDLES **OUT**, AND THE **WIND** AND **RAIN** INTENSIFIED THE THICK BLACK **DARKNESS**.

I HAD TO TAKE **PRECAUTIONS** TO ENSURE THE **SAFETY** OF MY DREADED VISITOR. I RESOLVED TO ANNOUNCE THAT MY **UNCLE** HAD **UNEXPECTEDLY** COME FROM THE **COUNTRY**.

I HEARD A NOISE **OUTSIDE**...

WHAT ARE YOU **DOING** THERE?

!?!

VOLUME III
CHAPTER I

IT TROUBLED ME THAT THERE SHOULD HAVE BEEN A **LURKER** ON THE STAIRS, ON THAT NIGHT OF **ALL** NIGHTS. I ASKED THE WATCHMAN WHETHER HE HAD ADMITTED **ANY** UNFAMILIAR FIGURE AT HIS GATE.

THE NIGHT BEING SO **BAD**, SIR, UNCOMMON **FEW** HAVE COME IN AT MY GATE. ABOUT ELEVEN O'CLOCK, A **STRANGER** ASKED FOR YOU.

ERM... MY **UNCLE**. YES.

YOU **SAW** HIM, SIR? LIKEWISE THE PERSON **WITH** HIM?

PERSON **WITH HIM?**

I **JUDGED** THE PERSON TO BE WITH HIM.

THE PERSON **STOPPED** WHEN YOUR UNCLE STOPPED TO MAKE INQUIRY OF ME, AND TOOK THIS WAY WHEN YOUR **UNCLE** TOOK THIS WAY.

AT BREAKFAST...

I DO NOT EVEN KNOW BY WHAT **NAME** TO CALL YOU. I HAVE GIVEN OUT THAT YOU ARE MY **UNCLE**.

THAT'S **IT**, DEAR BOY! CALL ME **UNCLE**.

YOU ASSUMED **SOME** NAME, I SUPPOSE, ON BOARD **SHIP?**

YES, DEAR BOY. I TOOK THE NAME OF **PROVIS**.

WHAT IS YOUR **REAL** NAME?

MAGWITCH, CHRISEN'D **ABEL.**

WERE YOU **KNOWN** IN LONDON, ONCE? WERE YOU -- **TRIED** -- IN LONDON?

WHICH **TIME** – THE **LAST** TIME? YES, I FIRST KNOWED MR. **JAGGERS** THAT WAY. JAGGERS WAS **FOR** ME.

WHEN YOU CAME HERE LAST NIGHT, AND ASKED THE WATCHMAN THE WAY, HAD YOU ANYONE **WITH** YOU? WAS ANYONE **ELSE** THERE?

WITH **ME?** NO, DEAR BOY. I DIDN'T TAKE PARTICULAR NOTICE, NOT KNOWING THE **WAYS** OF THE PLACE. BUT I THINK THERE **WAS** A PERSON, TOO, COME IN ALONGER ME.

AND THIS IS THE **GENTLEMAN** WHAT I **MADE!** IT DOES ME GOOD FUR TO LOOK AT YOU, DEAR BOY!

I MUSTN'T SEE MY GENTLEMAN A **FOOTING** IT IN THE **MIRE** OF THE STREETS; THERE MUSTN'T BE NO **MUD** ON HIS BOOTS. MY GENTLEMAN MUST HAVE **HORSES**, PIP!

HORSES TO RIDE, AND HORSES TO DRIVE, AND HORSES FOR HIS SERVANT TO RIDE AND DRIVE AS **WELL!**

THERE'S SOMETHING WORTH **SPENDING** IN THAT THERE BOOK, DEAR BOY. IT'S YOURN. DON'T YOU BE **AFEERD** ON IT.

THERE'S **MORE** WHERE THAT COME FROM.

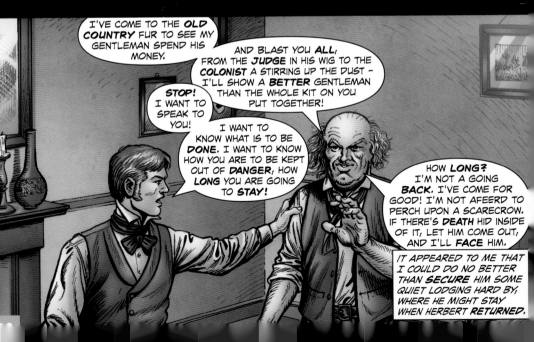

I'VE COME TO THE **OLD COUNTRY** FUR TO SEE MY GENTLEMAN SPEND HIS MONEY.

AND BLAST YOU **ALL,** FROM THE **JUDGE** IN HIS WIG TO THE **COLONIST** A STIRRING UP THE DUST – I'LL SHOW A **BETTER** GENTLEMAN THAN THE WHOLE KIT ON YOU PUT TOGETHER!

STOP! I WANT TO SPEAK TO YOU!

I WANT TO KNOW WHAT IS TO BE **DONE.** I WANT TO KNOW HOW YOU ARE TO BE KEPT OUT OF **DANGER,** HOW **LONG** YOU ARE GOING TO **STAY!**

HOW **LONG?** I'M NOT A GOING **BACK.** I'VE COME FOR GOOD! I'M NOT AFEERD TO PERCH UPON A SCARECROW. IF THERE'S **DEATH** HID INSIDE OF IT, LET HIM COME OUT, AND I'LL **FACE** HIM.

IT APPEARED TO ME THAT I COULD DO NO BETTER THAN SECURE HIM SOME QUIET LODGING HARD BY, WHERE HE MIGHT STAY WHEN HERBERT RETURNED.

I WAS **FORTUNATE** TO SECURE THE SECOND FLOOR OF A NEARBY LODGING-HOUSE FOR MY **UNCLE**, MR. PROVIS. THIS BUSINESS TRANSACTED, I TURNED MY FACE, ON MY OWN ACCOUNT, TO **LITTLE BRITAIN**.

NOW, PIP, BE **CAREFUL**. DON'T COMMIT **YOURSELF**, AND DON'T COMMIT **ANY** ONE. DON'T TELL ME ANYTHING; I DON'T WANT TO **KNOW** – I AM NOT **CURIOUS**.

HE **KNOWS** THE MAN HAS COME!

MR. JAGGERS, I MERELY WANT TO **ASSURE** MYSELF THAT WHAT I HAVE BEEN TOLD IS **TRUE**. I HAVE NO HOPE OF ITS BEING **UNTRUE**, BUT AT LEAST I MAY **VERIFY** IT.

BUT DID YOU SAY "**TOLD**" OR "**INFORMED**"?

TOLD WOULD SEEM TO IMPLY VERBAL COMMUNICATION. YOU CAN'T HAVE **VERBAL** COMMUNICATION WITH A MAN IN **NEW SOUTH WALES**, YOU KNOW.

I WILL SAY, **INFORMED**, MR. JAGGERS. I HAVE BEEN INFORMED BY A PERSON NAMED **ABEL MAGWITCH**, THAT HE IS THE **BENEFACTOR** SO LONG UNKNOWN TO ME.

THAT IS THE MAN. IN **NEW SOUTH WALES**.

AND **ONLY** HE?

AND ONLY **HE**.

I AM NOT SO UNREASONABLE, SIR, AS TO THINK YOU AT ALL RESPONSIBLE FOR MY **MISTAKES** AND **WRONG CONCLUSIONS**; BUT I ALWAYS SUPPOSED IT WAS MISS **HAVISHAM**.

AS YOU SAY, PIP, I AM NOT AT **ALL** RESPONSIBLE FOR **THAT**.

WHEN MAGWITCH FIRST WROTE TO ME – FROM NEW SOUTH WALES – HE APPEARED TO HINT IN HIS LETTER AT SOME DISTANT IDEA OF **SEEING** YOU IN **ENGLAND**.

I CAUTIONED HIM THAT I MUST HEAR NO **MORE** OF THAT; THAT HIS PRESENTING HIMSELF HERE WOULD RENDER HIM LIABLE TO THE **EXTREME** PENALTY OF THE **LAW**. I GAVE MAGWITCH THAT CAUTION. HE GUIDED HIMSELF BY IT, NO DOUBT.

WE **WISHED** EACH OTHER A "GOOD DAY" AND SHOOK HANDS.

I RECOILED FROM PROVIS WITH A **STRONGER** REPULSION, THE **FONDER** HE BECAME OF ME.

WHEN HE WAS NOT ASLEEP, OR PLAYING PATIENCE WITH A RAGGED PACK OF CARDS, HE WOULD ASK ME TO **READ** TO HIM – "FOREIGN LANGUAGE, DEAR BOY!"

EXPECTING **HERBERT** ALL THE TIME, I DARED NOT GO **OUT**, EXCEPT WHEN I TOOK HIM FOR AN AIRING AFTER **DARK**.

THIS LASTED FOR ABOUT **FIVE DAYS**.

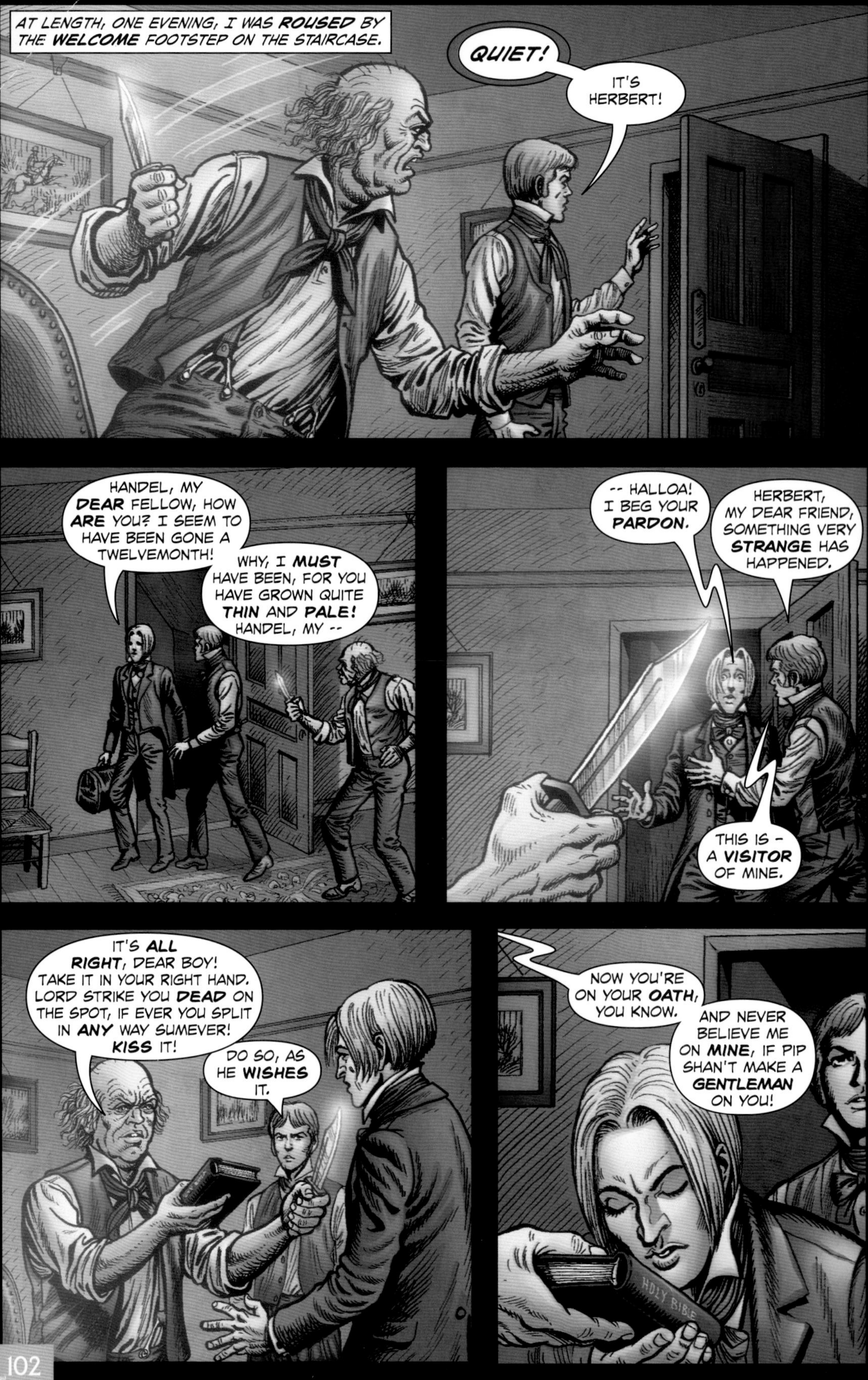
AT LENGTH, ONE EVENING, I WAS ROUSED BY THE WELCOME FOOTSTEP ON THE STAIRCASE.
QUIET!
IT'S HERBERT!
HANDEL, MY DEAR FELLOW, HOW ARE YOU? I SEEM TO HAVE BEEN GONE A TWELVEMONTH!
WHY, I MUST HAVE BEEN, FOR YOU HAVE GROWN QUITE THIN AND PALE! HANDEL, MY --
-- HALLOA! I BEG YOUR PARDON.
HERBERT, MY DEAR FRIEND, SOMETHING VERY STRANGE HAS HAPPENED.
THIS IS - A VISITOR OF MINE.
IT'S ALL RIGHT, DEAR BOY! TAKE IT IN YOUR RIGHT HAND. LORD STRIKE YOU DEAD ON THE SPOT, IF EVER YOU SPLIT IN ANY WAY SUMEVER! KISS IT!
DO SO, AS HE WISHES IT.
NOW YOU'RE ON YOUR OATH, YOU KNOW.
AND NEVER BELIEVE ME ON MINE, IF PIP SHAN'T MAKE A GENTLEMAN ON YOU!
HOLY BIBLE

IN VAIN SHOULD I ATTEMPT TO DESCRIBE THE **ASTONISHMENT** OF HERBERT, WHEN HE AND I AND PROVIS SAT DOWN BEFORE THE FIRE, AND I RECOUNTED THE **SECRET**.

I SAW MY **OWN** FEELINGS REFLECTED IN HERBERT'S FACE, AND NOT LEAST AMONG THEM, **REPUGNANCE**.

HERBERT AND I WERE ANXIOUS FOR THE TIME WHEN PROVIS WOULD GO TO HIS **LODGING**, BUT HE SAT **LATE**. IT WAS **MIDNIGHT** BEFORE I TOOK HIM ROUND TO ESSEX STREET.

WHEN HIS DOOR CLOSED, I EXPERIENCED THE FIRST **RELIEF** I HAD KNOWN SINCE THE NIGHT OF HIS **ARRIVAL**.

STILL, SOMETHING MUST BE **DONE**. HE IS INTENT UPON VARIOUS NEW **EXPENSES** – HORSES, CARRIAGES, LAVISH APPEARANCES OF ALL KINDS. HE MUST BE **STOPPED** SOMEHOW.

YOU MEAN THAT YOU **CAN'T** ACCEPT --

-- HOW **CAN** I? THINK OF HIM! **LOOK** AT HIM! YET I AM AFRAID THE DREADFUL TRUTH IS THAT HE IS STRONGLY ATTACHED TO ME. WAS THERE **EVER** SUCH A **FATE**!

AFTER ALL, NEVER TAKING ANOTHER **PENNY** FROM HIM, THINK WHAT I **OWE** HIM ALREADY! THEN AGAIN: I AM HEAVILY IN **DEBT**, WHO HAVE NOW **NO** EXPECTATIONS.

I HAVE BEEN BRED TO **NO** CALLING --

-- AND AM FIT FOR **NOTHING**!

THE MAIN THING TO BE DONE, IS TO GET HIM **OUT** OF **ENGLAND**. YOU WILL HAVE TO GO **WITH** HIM, AND THEN HE MAY BE **INDUCED** TO GO.

THAT DONE, **EXTRICATE** YOURSELF, IN HEAVEN'S NAME, AND WE'LL SEE IT OUT **TOGETHER**, DEAR OLD BOY.

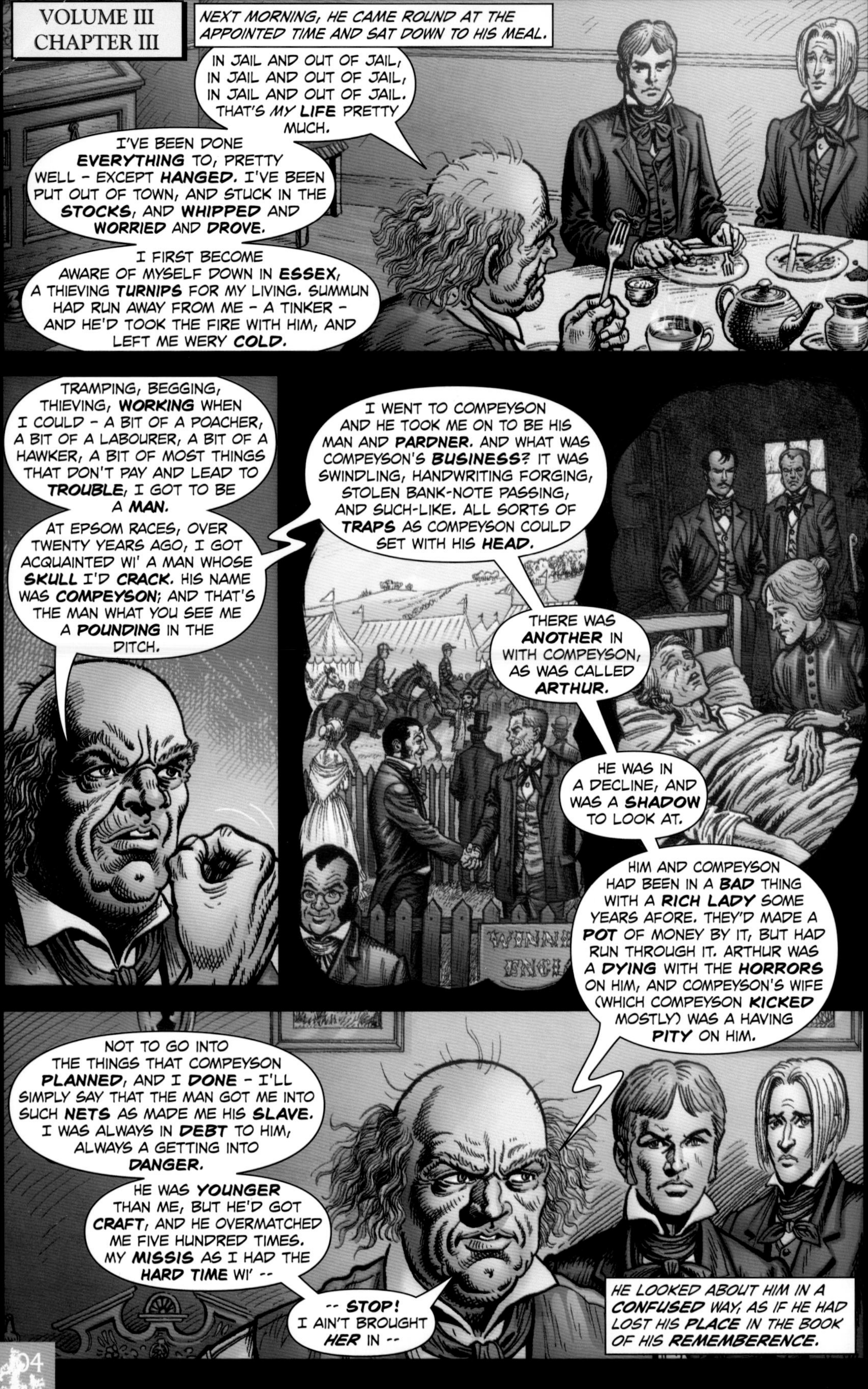
VOLUME III
CHAPTER III
NEXT MORNING, HE CAME ROUND AT THE APPOINTED TIME AND SAT DOWN TO HIS MEAL.
IN JAIL AND OUT OF JAIL, IN JAIL AND OUT OF JAIL, IN JAIL AND OUT OF JAIL. THAT'S MY LIFE PRETTY MUCH.
I'VE BEEN DONE EVERYTHING TO, PRETTY WELL - EXCEPT HANGED. I'VE BEEN PUT OUT OF TOWN, AND STUCK IN THE STOCKS, AND WHIPPED AND WORRIED AND DROVE.
I FIRST BECOME AWARE OF MYSELF DOWN IN ESSEX, A THIEVING TURNIPS FOR MY LIVING. SUMMUN HAD RUN AWAY FROM ME - A TINKER - AND HE'D TOOK THE FIRE WITH HIM, AND LEFT ME WERY COLD.
TRAMPING, BEGGING, THIEVING, WORKING WHEN I COULD - A BIT OF A POACHER, A BIT OF A LABOURER, A BIT OF A HAWKER, A BIT OF MOST THINGS THAT DON'T PAY AND LEAD TO TROUBLE, I GOT TO BE A MAN.
AT EPSOM RACES, OVER TWENTY YEARS AGO, I GOT ACQUAINTED WI' A MAN WHOSE SKULL I'D CRACK. HIS NAME WAS COMPEYSON; AND THAT'S THE MAN WHAT YOU SEE ME A POUNDING IN THE DITCH.
I WENT TO COMPEYSON AND HE TOOK ME ON TO BE HIS MAN AND PARDNER. AND WHAT WAS COMPEYSON'S BUSINESS? IT WAS SWINDLING, HANDWRITING FORGING, STOLEN BANK-NOTE PASSING, AND SUCH-LIKE. ALL SORTS OF TRAPS AS COMPEYSON COULD SET WITH HIS HEAD.
THERE WAS ANOTHER IN WITH COMPEYSON, AS WAS CALLED ARTHUR.
HE WAS IN A DECLINE, AND WAS A SHADOW TO LOOK AT.
HIM AND COMPEYSON HAD BEEN IN A BAD THING WITH A RICH LADY SOME YEARS AFORE. THEY'D MADE A POT OF MONEY BY IT, BUT HAD RUN THROUGH IT. ARTHUR WAS A DYING WITH THE HORRORS ON HIM, AND COMPEYSON'S WIFE (WHICH COMPEYSON KICKED MOSTLY) WAS A HAVING PITY ON HIM.
NOT TO GO INTO THE THINGS THAT COMPEYSON PLANNED, AND I DONE - I'LL SIMPLY SAY THAT THE MAN GOT ME INTO SUCH NETS AS MADE ME HIS SLAVE. I WAS ALWAYS IN DEBT TO HIM, ALWAYS A GETTING INTO DANGER.
HE WAS YOUNGER THAN ME, BUT HE'D GOT CRAFT, AND HE OVERMATCHED ME FIVE HUNDRED TIMES. MY MISSIS AS I HAD THE HARD TIME WI' --
-- STOP! I AIN'T BROUGHT HER IN --
HE LOOKED ABOUT HIM IN A CONFUSED WAY, AS IF HE HAD LOST HIS PLACE IN THE BOOK OF HIS REMEMBERENCE.

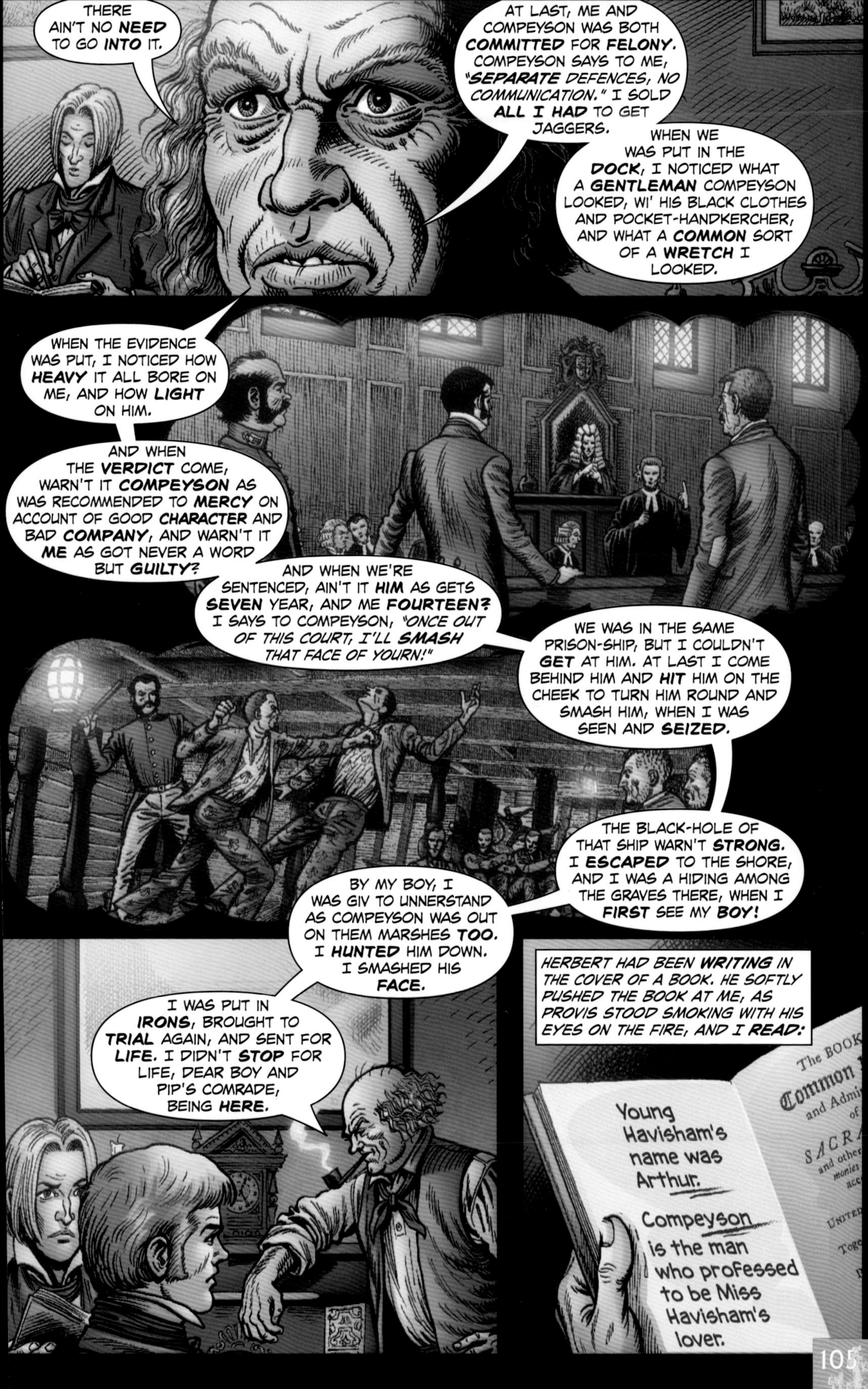

THERE AIN'T NO NEED TO GO INTO IT.
AT LAST, ME AND COMPEYSON WAS BOTH COMMITTED FOR FELONY. COMPEYSON SAYS TO ME, "SEPARATE DEFENCES, NO COMMUNICATION." I SOLD ALL I HAD TO GET JAGGERS.
WHEN WE WAS PUT IN THE DOCK, I NOTICED WHAT A GENTLEMAN COMPEYSON LOOKED, WI' HIS BLACK CLOTHES AND POCKET-HANDKERCHER, AND WHAT A COMMON SORT OF A WRETCH I LOOKED.
WHEN THE EVIDENCE WAS PUT, I NOTICED HOW HEAVY IT ALL BORE ON ME, AND HOW LIGHT ON HIM.
AND WHEN THE VERDICT COME, WARN'T IT COMPEYSON AS WAS RECOMMENDED TO MERCY ON ACCOUNT OF GOOD CHARACTER AND BAD COMPANY, AND WARN'T IT ME AS GOT NEVER A WORD BUT GUILTY?
AND WHEN WE'RE SENTENCED, AIN'T IT HIM AS GETS SEVEN YEAR, AND ME FOURTEEN? I SAYS TO COMPEYSON, "ONCE OUT OF THIS COURT, I'LL SMASH THAT FACE OF YOURN!"
WE WAS IN THE SAME PRISON-SHIP, BUT I COULDN'T GET AT HIM. AT LAST I COME BEHIND HIM AND HIT HIM ON THE CHEEK TO TURN HIM ROUND AND SMASH HIM, WHEN I WAS SEEN AND SEIZED.
THE BLACK-HOLE OF THAT SHIP WARN'T STRONG. I ESCAPED TO THE SHORE, AND I WAS A HIDING AMONG THE GRAVES THERE, WHEN I FIRST SEE MY BOY!
BY MY BOY, I WAS GIV TO UNNERSTAND AS COMPEYSON WAS OUT ON THEM MARSHES TOO. I HUNTED HIM DOWN. I SMASHED HIS FACE.
I WAS PUT IN IRONS, BROUGHT TO TRIAL AGAIN, AND SENT FOR LIFE. I DIDN'T STOP FOR LIFE, DEAR BOY AND PIP'S COMRADE, BEING HERE.
HERBERT HAD BEEN WRITING IN THE COVER OF A BOOK. HE SOFTLY PUSHED THE BOOK AT ME, AS PROVIS STOOD SMOKING WITH HIS EYES ON THE FIRE, AND I READ:
Young Havisham's name was Arthur.
Compeyson is the man who professed to be Miss Havisham's lover.

I RESOLVED NEVER TO BREATHE A **WORD** OF ESTELLA TO **PROVIS**. BUT BEFORE I COULD GO ABROAD, I FELT THAT I MUST **SEE** BOTH ESTELLA AND MISS HAVISHAM.

TO RICHMOND I WENT, BUT ESTELLA'S MAID TOLD ME THAT SHE HAD GONE TO **SATIS HOUSE**. SHE HAD NEVER YET GONE **WITHOUT ME** BEFORE.

NEXT DAY, I SET OFF FOR MISS HAVISHAM'S BY THE EARLY MORNING COACH. WHEN WE DROVE UP TO THE BLUE BOAR, WHOM SHOULD I SEE, BUT **BENTLEY DRUMMLE**!

YOU HAVE JUST COME **DOWN?**

BEASTLY PLACE – **YOUR** PART OF THE COUNTRY, I THINK?

YES, I AM TOLD IT IS VERY LIKE **YOUR** SHROPSHIRE.

NOT IN THE **LEAST** LIKE IT. LARGE TRACT OF **MARSHES**, I BELIEVE?

I AM GOING OUT FOR A RIDE, AND MEAN TO **EXPLORE**. CURIOUS LITTLE PUBLIC-HOUSES – AND SMITHIES – AND THAT.

HE CALLED TO THE WAITER, THEN **GLANCED** AT ME, WITH AN INSOLENT **TRIUMPH** ON HIS GREAT-JOWLED FACE.

IS THAT HORSE OF MINE **READY?**

LOOK HERE, YOU SIR. THE **LADY** WON'T RIDE TO-DAY; THE WEATHER WON'T **DO**. AND I DON'T **DINE**, BECAUSE I'M GOING TO DINE AT THE **LADY'S**.

MR. DRUMMLE, I DID NOT **SEEK** THIS CONVERSATION, AND I DON'T THINK IT AN **AGREEABLE** ONE.

WITH YOUR LEAVE, I WILL SUGGEST THAT WE HOLD **NO** KIND OF COMMUNICATION IN **FUTURE**.

QUITE **MY** OPINION. BUT DON'T LOSE YOUR **TEMPER**. HAVEN'T YOU LOST **ENOUGH** WITHOUT THAT?

YOU QUITE **UNDERSTAND** THAT THE YOUNG LADY DON'T RIDE TO-DAY; AND THAT **I** DINE AT THE **YOUNG LADY'S**.

WE SAT IN **SILENCE** UNTIL I WATCHED HIM LEAVE.

HEAVILY OUT OF SORTS, I WENT TO THE MEMORABLE OLD HOUSE.

VOLUME III CHAPTER V

WHAT WIND BLOWS YOU **HERE**, PIP?

MISS HAVISHAM, I WENT TO **RICHMOND** YESTERDAY TO **SPEAK** TO ESTELLA;

AND FINDING THAT SOME WIND HAD BLOWN HER **HERE**, I **FOLLOWED**.

WHAT I HAD TO SAY TO **ESTELLA**, MISS HAVISHAM, I WILL SAY BEFORE **YOU**, PRESENTLY. IT WILL **NOT** DISPLEASE YOU.

I AM AS **UNHAPPY** AS YOU CAN EVER HAVE MEANT ME TO BE.

I HAVE FOUND OUT WHO MY PATRON IS. IT IS NOT A **FORTUNATE** DISCOVERY, AND IS NOT LIKELY EVER TO ENRICH ME IN REPUTATION, STATION, FORTUNE, **ANYTHING**.

THERE ARE REASONS WHY I MUST SAY **NO MORE** OF THAT. IT IS NOT **MY** SECRET, BUT **ANOTHER'S**.

WHEN YOU FIRST CAUSED ME TO BE **BROUGHT** HERE, MISS HAVISHAM, I SUPPOSE I DID REALLY COME HERE, AS ANY CHANCE BOY MIGHT HAVE COME, LIKE A **SERVANT**, TO GRATIFY A **WHIM**, AND BE **PAID** FOR IT? AND MR. **JAGGERS** --

MR. JAGGERS HAD **NOTHING** TO DO WITH IT. HIS BEING **MY** LAWYER, AND HIS BEING THE LAWYER OF YOUR **PATRON**, IS A **COINCIDENCE**.

BUT WHEN I FELL INTO THE **MISTAKE** I HAVE SO LONG REMAINED IN, YOU LET ME GO **ON**. IN **HUMOURING** MY MISTAKE, YOU **PUNISHED** YOUR SELF-SEEKING RELATIONS.

I **DID**. WHY, THEY WOULD HAVE IT SO!

AND **YOU** MADE YOUR **OWN** SNARES. I NEVER MADE THEM.

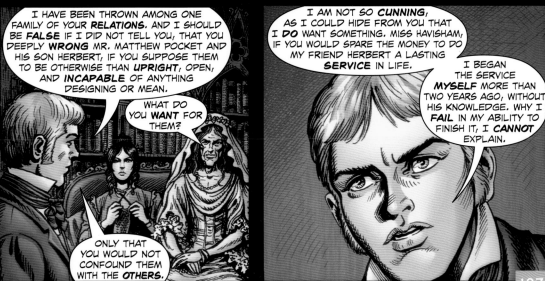

I HAVE BEEN THROWN AMONG ONE FAMILY OF YOUR **RELATIONS**. AND I SHOULD BE **FALSE** IF I DID NOT TELL YOU, THAT YOU DEEPLY **WRONG** MR. MATTHEW POCKET AND HIS SON HERBERT, IF YOU SUPPOSE THEM TO BE OTHERWISE THAN **UPRIGHT**, OPEN, AND **INCAPABLE** OF ANYTHING DESIGNING OR MEAN.

WHAT DO YOU **WANT** FOR THEM?

ONLY THAT YOU WOULD NOT CONFOUND THEM WITH THE **OTHERS**.

I AM NOT SO **CUNNING**, AS I COULD HIDE FROM YOU THAT I **DO** WANT SOMETHING. MISS HAVISHAM, IF YOU WOULD SPARE THE MONEY TO DO MY FRIEND HERBERT A LASTING **SERVICE** IN LIFE.

I BEGAN THE SERVICE **MYSELF** MORE THAN TWO YEARS AGO, WITHOUT HIS KNOWLEDGE. WHY I **FAIL** IN MY ABILITY TO FINISH IT, I **CANNOT** EXPLAIN.

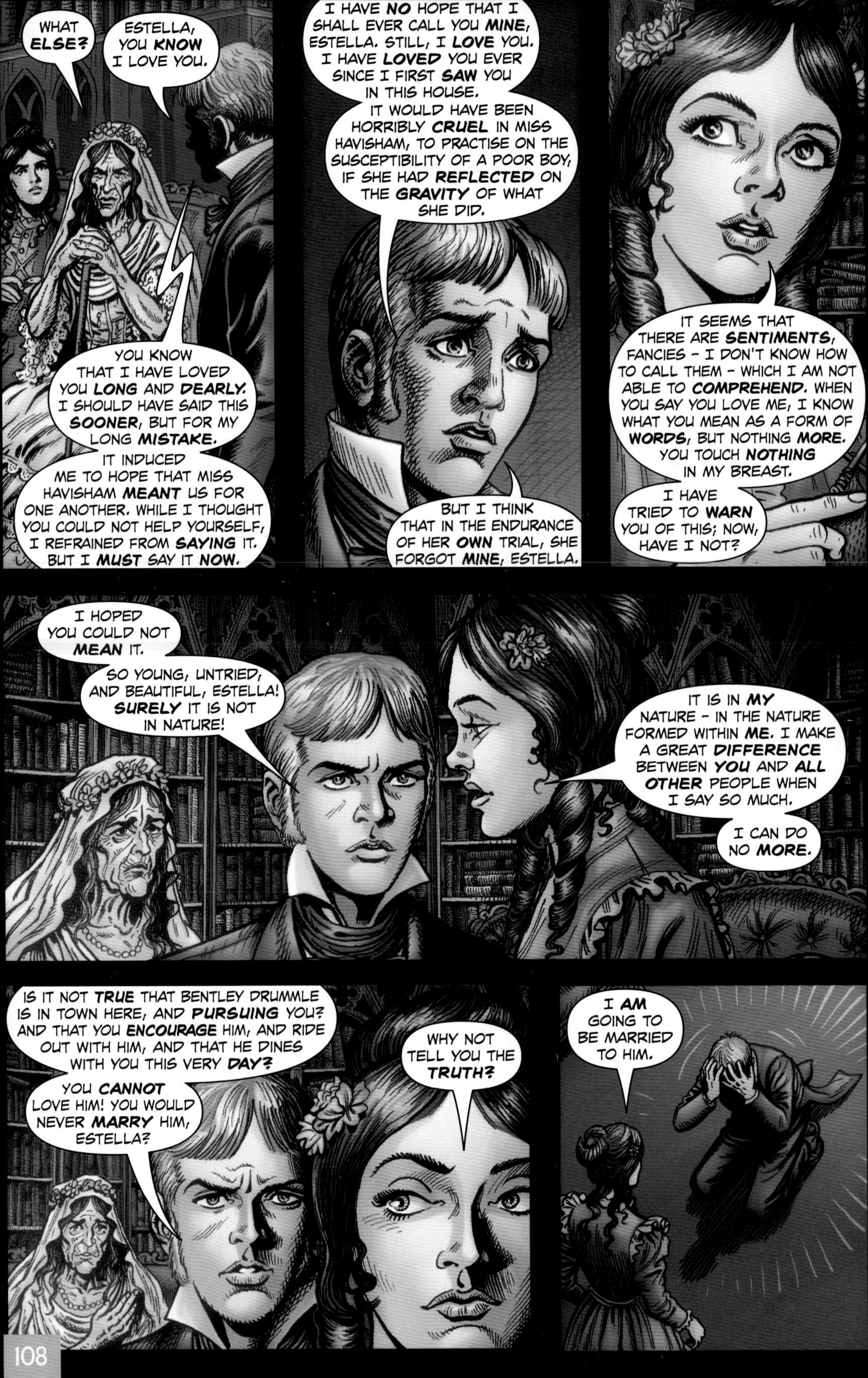
WHAT ELSE?
ESTELLA, YOU KNOW I LOVE YOU.
YOU KNOW THAT I HAVE LOVED YOU LONG AND DEARLY. I SHOULD HAVE SAID THIS SOONER, BUT FOR MY LONG MISTAKE.
IT INDUCED ME TO HOPE THAT MISS HAVISHAM MEANT US FOR ONE ANOTHER. WHILE I THOUGHT YOU COULD NOT HELP YOURSELF, I REFRAINED FROM SAYING IT. BUT I MUST SAY IT NOW.
I HAVE NO HOPE THAT I SHALL EVER CALL YOU MINE, ESTELLA. STILL, I LOVE YOU. I HAVE LOVED YOU EVER SINCE I FIRST SAW YOU IN THIS HOUSE.
IT WOULD HAVE BEEN HORRIBLY CRUEL IN MISS HAVISHAM, TO PRACTISE ON THE SUSCEPTIBILITY OF A POOR BOY, IF SHE HAD REFLECTED ON THE GRAVITY OF WHAT SHE DID.
BUT I THINK THAT IN THE ENDURANCE OF HER OWN TRIAL, SHE FORGOT MINE, ESTELLA.
IT SEEMS THAT THERE ARE SENTIMENTS, FANCIES - I DON'T KNOW HOW TO CALL THEM - WHICH I AM NOT ABLE TO COMPREHEND. WHEN YOU SAY YOU LOVE ME, I KNOW WHAT YOU MEAN AS A FORM OF WORDS, BUT NOTHING MORE. YOU TOUCH NOTHING IN MY BREAST.
I HAVE TRIED TO WARN YOU OF THIS; NOW, HAVE I NOT?
I HOPED YOU COULD NOT MEAN IT.
SO YOUNG, UNTRIED, AND BEAUTIFUL, ESTELLA! SURELY IT IS NOT IN NATURE!
IT IS IN MY NATURE - IN THE NATURE FORMED WITHIN ME. I MAKE A GREAT DIFFERENCE BETWEEN YOU AND ALL OTHER PEOPLE WHEN I SAY SO MUCH.
I CAN DO NO MORE.
IS IT NOT TRUE THAT BENTLEY DRUMMLE IS IN TOWN HERE, AND PURSUING YOU? AND THAT YOU ENCOURAGE HIM, AND RIDE OUT WITH HIM, AND THAT HE DINES WITH YOU THIS VERY DAY?
YOU CANNOT LOVE HIM! YOU WOULD NEVER MARRY HIM, ESTELLA?
WHY NOT TELL YOU THE TRUTH?
I AM GOING TO BE MARRIED TO HIM.

DEAREST ESTELLA, DO **NOT** LET MISS HAVISHAM LEAD YOU INTO THIS **FATAL** STEP. PUT ME ASIDE FOR **EVER**, BUT BESTOW YOURSELF ON SOME **WORTHIER** PERSON THAN DRUMMLE!

MISS HAVISHAM GIVES YOU TO **HIM**, AS THE GREATEST **SLIGHT** AND **INJURY** THAT COULD BE DONE TO THE MANY FAR BETTER MEN WHO **ADMIRE** YOU, AND TO THE FEW WHO TRULY **LOVE** YOU.

WHY DO YOU INTRODUCE THE NAME OF MY MOTHER BY ADOPTION? IT IS MY **OWN** ACT. **THERE!** I SHALL DO WELL **ENOUGH**, AND SO WILL MY **HUSBAND**.

MISS HAVISHAM WOULD HAVE HAD ME **WAIT**, AND NOT MARRY YET, BUT I AM **TIRED** OF THE LIFE I HAVE LED, WHICH HAS VERY **FEW** CHARMS FOR ME.

O ESTELLA! EVEN IF I REMAINED IN ENGLAND AND COULD HOLD MY HEAD UP WITH THE **REST**, HOW COULD I SEE YOU DRUMMLE'S **WIFE!**

NONSENSE, **NONSENSE**. THIS WILL **PASS** IN NO TIME. AND YOU WILL GET ME OUT OF YOUR THOUGHTS IN A **WEEK**.

OUT OF MY **THOUGHTS!**

YOU ARE PART OF MY **EXISTENCE**, PART OF **MYSELF**.

YOU HAVE BEEN IN EVERY PROSPECT I HAVE EVER **SEEN** SINCE I **FIRST** CAME HERE A ROUGH COMMON BOY, WHOSE POOR HEART YOU WOUNDED EVEN **THEN**.

TO THE LAST **HOUR** OF MY LIFE, YOU CANNOT CHOOSE BUT REMAIN PART OF MY CHARACTER, PART OF THE LITTLE **GOOD** IN ME, PART OF THE **EVIL**. OH, GOD **BLESS** YOU, GOD **FORGIVE** YOU!

ALL **DONE**, ALL **GONE!** I WENT OUT AT THE GATE. FOR A WHILE, I HID MYSELF AMONG SOME LANES, AND THEN STRUCK OFF TO **WALK** ALL THE WAY TO **LONDON**.

FOR I COULD NOT BEAR TO GO BACK TO THE INN AND SEE **DRUMMLE**, OR SIT UPON THE COACH AND BE SPOKEN TO. I COULD DO **NOTHING** HALF SO GOOD AS **TIRE** MYSELF OUT.

IT WAS PAST **MIDNIGHT** WHEN I CROSSED LONDON BRIDGE. I CAME IN AT THE WHITEFRIARS GATE, MUDDY AND **WEARY** – THE NIGHT-PORTER EXAMINED ME **CLOSELY**.

I **THOUGHT** IT WAS YOU, SIR. HERE'S A **NOTE**. THE MESSENGER THAT BROUGHT IT SAID WOULD YOU BE SO GOOD AS **READ** IT BY MY **LANTERN?**

MUCH **SURPRISED** BY THE REQUEST, I TOOK THE NOTE. IT WAS DIRECTED TO **PHILIP PIP, ESQUIRE**, AND ON THE TOP WERE THE WORDS, **"PLEASE READ THIS, HERE."**

I OPENED IT AND READ INSIDE, IN **WEMMICK'S** WRITING...

Don't go home. W.

VOLUME III
CHAPTER VI

TURNING FROM THE GATE, I GOT A LATE HACKNEY CHARIOT TO THE HUMMUMS IN COVENT GARDEN, WHERE A BED COULD BE GOT AT **ANY** HOUR OF NIGHT. THE CHAMBERLAIN SHOWED ME INTO A BEDROOM.

I HAD LEFT DIRECTIONS THAT I WAS TO BE CALLED AT SEVEN, FOR IT WAS PLAIN THAT I MUST SEE WEMMICK **IMMEDIATELY**.

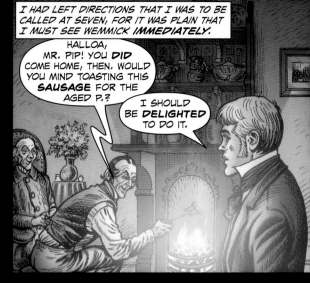

HALLOA, MR. PIP! YOU **DID** COME HOME, THEN. WOULD YOU MIND TOASTING THIS **SAUSAGE** FOR THE AGED P.?

I SHOULD BE **DELIGHTED** TO DO IT.

I GOT INTO BED AND LAY THERE WEARY AND **WRETCHED**, MY MIND MUCH OCCUPIED WITH THE QUESTION OF **WHY** I COULD NOT GO HOME, AND ALSO WITH THOUGHTS OF **ESTELLA**.

AT LAST I **DOZED** IN SHEER EXHAUSTION.

NOW, MR. PIP. YOU UNDERSTAND WE ARE IN OUR **PRIVATE** AND PERSONAL CAPACITIES.

I ACCIDENTALLY HEARD, YESTERDAY MORNING, BEING IN A **CERTAIN** PLACE WHERE I ONCE TOOK YOU – IT'S AS WELL NOT TO MENTION NAMES –

THAT A CERTAIN PERSON OF **COLONIAL** PURSUITS HAD MADE SOME LITTLE STIR IN PART OF THE WORLD WHERE MANY PEOPLE GO, NOT ALWAYS IN GRATIFICATION OF THEIR OWN INCLINATIONS – BY DISAPPEARING, AND BEING NO MORE **HEARD** OF THEREABOUTS.

FROM WHICH, CONJECTURES HAD BEEN RAISED, AND **THEORIES** FORMED.

I ALSO HEARD THAT YOU HAD BEEN **WATCHED** AT YOUR CHAMBERS. BY WHOM, I WON'T GO INTO, AS IT MIGHT **CLASH** WITH **OFFICIAL** RESPONSIBILITIES.

AFTER A LITTLE MEDITATION, I TOLD HIM THAT I WOULD LIKE TO ASK A **QUESTION**, SUBJECT TO HIS ANSWERING OR NOT ANSWERING, AS HE DEEMED RIGHT. HE NODDED.

YOU HAVE HEARD OF A MAN OF BAD CHARACTER, WHOSE TRUE NAME IS **COMPEYSON**? IS HE **LIVING**? IS HE IN **LONDON**?

TO THESE QUESTIONS WEMMICK **NODDED**, AND WENT ON WITH HIS BREAKFAST.

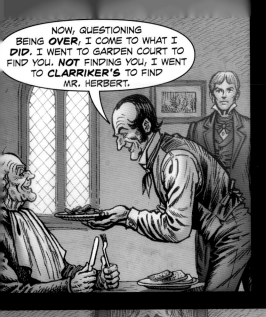

NOW, QUESTIONING BEING **OVER**, I COME TO WHAT I **DID**. I WENT TO GARDEN COURT TO FIND YOU. **NOT** FINDING YOU, I WENT TO **CLARRIKER'S** TO FIND MR. HERBERT.

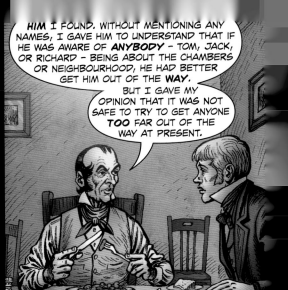

HIM I FOUND. WITHOUT MENTIONING ANY NAMES, I GAVE HIM TO UNDERSTAND THAT IF HE WAS AWARE OF **ANYBODY** – TOM, JACK, OR RICHARD – BEING ABOUT THE CHAMBERS OR NEIGHBOURHOOD, HE HAD BETTER GET HIM OUT OF THE **WAY**.

BUT I GAVE MY OPINION THAT IT WAS NOT SAFE TO TRY TO GET ANYONE **TOO** FAR OUT OF THE WAY AT PRESENT.

MR. HERBERT STRUCK OUT A **PLAN**. HE MENTIONED TO ME THAT HE IS COURTING A YOUNG LADY WHO HAS A BEDRIDDEN PA. WHICH PA LIES A-BED IN A BOW-WINDOW WHERE HE CAN SEE THE **SHIPS** ON THE RIVER.

THE HOUSE IS KEPT, IT SEEMS, BY A RESPECTABLE WIDOW WHO HAS A FURNISHED UPPER FLOOR TO LET. MR. HERBERT PUT IT TO ME, WHAT DID I THINK OF THAT AS A **TEMPORARY** TENEMENT FOR TOM, JACK, OR RICHARD?

I THOUGHT VERY **WELL** OF IT.

AFTER A WHILE AND WHEN **PRUDENT**, IF YOU **SHOULD** WANT TO SLIP ANYONE ON BOARD A FOREIGN **PACKET-BOAT**, THERE HE IS – READY.

WELL, SIR! MR. HERBERT **THREW** HIMSELF INTO THE BUSINESS, AND BY NINE O'CLOCK LAST NIGHT HE HOUSED TOM, JACK, OR RICHARD QUITE **SUCCESSFULLY**. AND NOW, MR. PIP, I HAVE PROBABLY DONE THE MOST I **CAN** DO.

THANK YOU FOR **ALL** YOUR HELP.

YOU ARE VERY WELCOME. I MUST BE OFF.

IF YOU HAD NOTHING MORE **PRESSING** TO DO THAN TO KEEP HERE TILL DARK, THAT'S WHAT I SHOULD ADVISE. IT WOULD DO YOU **GOOD** TO HAVE A PERFECTLY QUIET DAY WITH THE AGED.

I SOON FELL **ASLEEP** BEFORE WEMMICK'S FIRE, AND WHEN IT WAS QUITE **DARK**, I LEFT THE AGED.

I FOUND THE HOUSE UPON *MILL POND BANK.*

MRS. WHIMPLE RESPONDED...

KNOCK

KNOCK

ALL IS **WELL**, HANDEL. HE IS QUITE **SATISFIED**, THOUGH EAGER TO **SEE** YOU. MY DEAR GIRL IS WITH HER FATHER.

IF YOU'LL **WAIT** TILL SHE COMES DOWN, I'LL MAKE YOU KNOWN TO HER, AND THEN WE'LL GO UP-STAIRS.

BANG BANG

BANG BANG

AARGH!

THAT'S HER **FATHER**. I AM AFRAID HE IS A SAD OLD RASCAL, BUT I HAVE **NEVER** SEEN HIM. MRS. WHIMPLE IS THE **BEST** OF HOUSEWIVES, AND I REALLY DON'T KNOW WHAT MY CLARA WOULD DO WITHOUT HER MOTHERLY HELP. FOR, CLARA HAS NO MOTHER OF HER **OWN**, HANDEL, AND NO RELATION IN THE WORLD BUT OLD **GRUFFANDGRIM**.

THUMP

SURELY THAT'S NOT HIS **NAME**, HERBERT?

NO, NO, THAT'S **MY** NAME FOR HIM. HIS NAME IS MR. BARLEY.

AS WE WERE CONVERSING IN A **LOW** TONE WHILE OLD BARLEY'S GROWL **VIBRATED** OVERHEAD, THE DOOR OPENED, AND A VERY PRETTY DARK-EYED GIRL CAME IN. HERBERT, **BLUSHING**, PRESENTED HER AS **CLARA**.

THERE WAS SOMETHING SO **NATURAL** AND WINNING, SO CONFIDING, **LOVING** AND INNOCENT, AND SOMETHING SO **GENTLE** IN HER THAT I WOULD NOT HAVE **UNDONE** THE ENGAGEMENT BETWEEN HER AND HERBERT FOR ALL THE **MONEY** IN THE POCKET-BOOK I HAD **NEVER** OPENED.

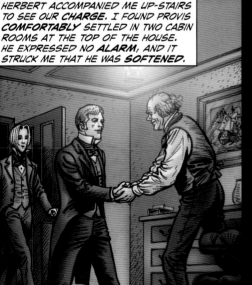

HERBERT ACCOMPANIED ME UP-STAIRS TO SEE OUR **CHARGE**. I FOUND PROVIS **COMFORTABLY** SETTLED IN TWO CABIN ROOMS AT THE TOP OF THE HOUSE. HE EXPRESSED NO **ALARM**, AND IT STRUCK ME THAT HE WAS **SOFTENED**.

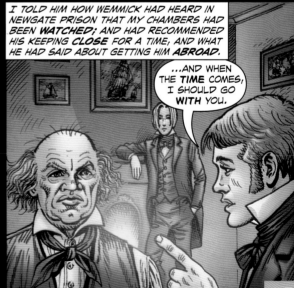

I TOLD HIM HOW WEMMICK HAD HEARD IN NEWGATE PRISON THAT MY CHAMBERS HAD BEEN **WATCHED**; AND HAD RECOMMENDED HIS KEEPING **CLOSE** FOR A TIME, AND WHAT HE HAD SAID ABOUT GETTING HIM **ABROAD**.

...AND WHEN THE **TIME** COMES, I SHOULD GO **WITH** YOU.

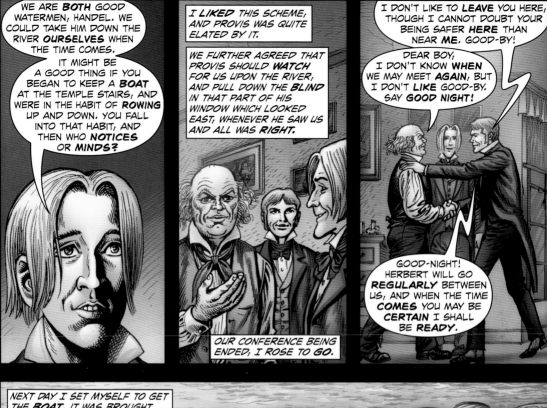

WE ARE **BOTH** GOOD WATERMEN, HANDEL. WE COULD TAKE HIM DOWN THE RIVER **OURSELVES** WHEN THE TIME COMES.

IT MIGHT BE A GOOD THING IF YOU BEGAN TO KEEP A **BOAT** AT THE TEMPLE STAIRS, AND WERE IN THE HABIT OF **ROWING** UP AND DOWN. YOU FALL INTO THAT HABIT, AND THEN WHO **NOTICES** OR **MINDS?**

I **LIKED** THIS SCHEME, AND PROVIS WAS QUITE ELATED BY IT.

WE FURTHER AGREED THAT PROVIS SHOULD **WATCH** FOR US UPON THE RIVER, AND PULL DOWN THE **BLIND** IN THAT PART OF HIS WINDOW WHICH LOOKED EAST, WHENEVER HE SAW US AND ALL WAS **RIGHT**.

OUR CONFERENCE BEING ENDED, I ROSE TO **GO**.

I DON'T LIKE TO **LEAVE** YOU HERE, THOUGH I CANNOT DOUBT YOUR BEING SAFER **HERE** THAN NEAR **ME**. GOOD-BY!

DEAR BOY, I DON'T KNOW **WHEN** WE MAY MEET **AGAIN**, BUT I DON'T **LIKE** GOOD-BY. SAY **GOOD NIGHT!**

GOOD-NIGHT! HERBERT WILL GO **REGULARLY** BETWEEN US, AND WHEN THE TIME **COMES** YOU MAY BE **CERTAIN** I SHALL BE **READY**.

NEXT DAY I SET MYSELF TO GET THE **BOAT**. IT WAS BROUGHT ROUND TO THE TEMPLE-STAIRS, AND LAY WHERE I COULD **REACH** HER WITHIN A **MINUTE** OR TWO.

I BEGAN TO GO OUT AS FOR TRAINING AND PRACTICE: SOMETIMES **ALONE**, SOMETIMES WITH **HERBERT**.

THE FIRST TIME I PASSED MILL POND BANK, HERBERT AND I WERE PULLING A PAIR OF OARS. BOTH IN GOING AND RETURNING, WE SAW THE **BLIND** TOWARDS THE EAST COME **DOWN**.

STILL, I COULD NOT GET RID OF THE NOTION OF BEING **WATCHED**.

114

SOME WEEKS PASSED WITHOUT **CHANGE**. WE WAITED FOR WEMMICK, AND HE MADE NO **SIGN**. MY WORLDLY AFFAIRS BEGAN TO WEAR A **GLOOMY** APPEARANCE, AND I WAS PRESSED FOR **MONEY** BY **SEVERAL** CREDITORS.

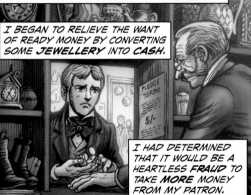

I BEGAN TO RELIEVE THE WANT OF READY MONEY BY CONVERTING SOME **JEWELLERY** INTO **CASH**.

I HAD DETERMINED THAT IT WOULD BE A HEARTLESS **FRAUD** TO TAKE **MORE** MONEY FROM MY PATRON.

AS TIME WORE ON, AN IMPRESSION SETTLED UPON ME THAT ESTELLA WAS **MARRIED**. **FEARFUL** OF HAVING IT **CONFIRMED**, I AVOIDED THE NEWSPAPERS AND BEGGED HERBERT **NEVER** TO SPEAK OF HER.

IT WAS AN **UNHAPPY** LIFE, WITH ONE DOMINANT **ANXIETY**.

CONDEMNED TO SUSPENSE, I ROWED ABOUT IN MY BOAT...

...AND **WAITED**, WAITED, AS I BEST **COULD**.

LATE IN THE MONTH OF FEBRUARY, IT WAS A RAW EVENING – AND I THOUGHT I WOULD GO TO THE **PLAY** AND SEE **MR. WOPSLE**.

IT IS THE **STRANGEST** THING! YOU'LL HARDLY **BELIEVE** WHAT I AM GOING TO TELL YOU. YOU REMEMBER IN **OLD** TIMES A CERTAIN CHRISTMAS DAY, WHEN YOU WERE QUITE A CHILD AND THERE WAS A **CHASE** AFTER TWO **CONVICTS?**

YES, I REMEMBER **ALL** THAT.

THEN MR. PIP, ONE OF THOSE TWO PRISONERS SAT **BEHIND** YOU **TONIGHT**. THE ONE WHO HAD BEEN **MAULED** – I'LL SWEAR I **SAW** HIM!

I CANNOT **EXAGGERATE** THE ENHANCED DISQUIET INTO WHICH THIS CONVERSATION THREW ME, OR THE SPECIAL AND PECULIAR **TERROR** I FELT AT COMPEYSON'S HAVING BEEN BEHIND ME, "LIKE A **GHOST**".

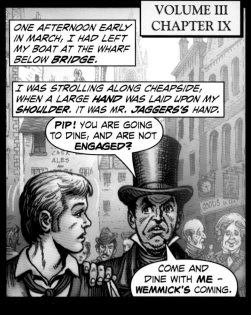

ONE AFTERNOON EARLY IN MARCH, I HAD LEFT MY BOAT AT THE WHARF BELOW **BRIDGE**.

I WAS STROLLING ALONG CHEAPSIDE, WHEN A LARGE **HAND** WAS LAID UPON MY **SHOULDER**. IT WAS MR. **JAGGERS'S** HAND.

PIP! YOU ARE GOING TO DINE, AND ARE NOT **ENGAGED**?

COME AND DINE WITH **ME** – **WEMMICK'S** COMING.

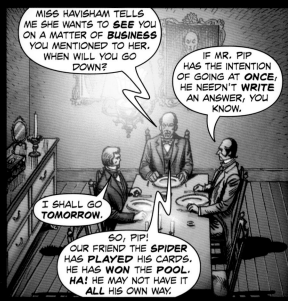

MISS HAVISHAM TELLS ME SHE WANTS TO **SEE** YOU ON A MATTER OF **BUSINESS** YOU MENTIONED TO HER. WHEN WILL YOU GO DOWN?

IF MR. PIP HAS THE INTENTION OF GOING AT **ONCE**, HE NEEDN'T **WRITE** AN ANSWER, YOU KNOW.

I SHALL GO **TOMORROW**.

SO, PIP! OUR FRIEND THE **SPIDER** HAS **PLAYED** HIS CARDS. HE HAS **WON** THE **POOL**. HA! HE MAY NOT HAVE IT **ALL** HIS OWN WAY.

IF HE SHOULD **BEAT** HER, HE MAY GET THE **STRENGTH** ON HIS SIDE; IF IT SHOULD BE A QUESTION OF **INTELLECT**, HE CERTAINLY WILL **NOT**.

SO, HERE'S TO MRS. BENTLEY DRUMMLE! MAY THE QUESTION OF **SUPREMACY** BE SETTLED TO THE LADY'S **SATISFACTION**!

NOW, **MOLLY**, MOLLY, MOLLY, **MOLLY**, HOW **SLOW** YOU ARE TODAY!

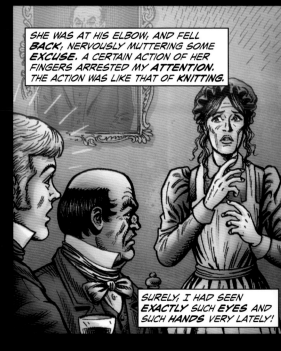

SHE WAS AT HIS ELBOW, AND FELL **BACK**, NERVOUSLY MUTTERING SOME **EXCUSE**. A CERTAIN ACTION OF HER FINGERS ARRESTED MY **ATTENTION**. THE ACTION WAS LIKE THAT OF **KNITTING**.

SURELY, I HAD SEEN **EXACTLY** SUCH **EYES** AND SUCH **HANDS** VERY LATELY!

I LOOKED AT THOSE **HANDS**, AT THOSE **EYES**, AT THAT FLOWING **HAIR**; AND I COMPARED THEM WITH OTHER HANDS, EYES, AND HAIR – AND WITH WHAT THOSE MIGHT BE AFTER TWENTY YEARS OF A **STORMY** LIFE.

I THOUGHT OF THE INEXPLICABLE **FEELING** THAT HAD COME OVER ME WHEN I SAW A FACE AT A STAGE-COACH WINDOW; AND LATER IN A CARRIAGE PASSING **NEWGATE**.

AND I FELT ABSOLUTELY **CERTAIN** THAT THIS WOMAN WAS ESTELLA'S **MOTHER**.

WEMMICK AND I TOOK OUR LEAVE *EARLY*, AND LEFT TOGETHER.

WEMMICK, DO YOU REMEMBER TELLING ME, BEFORE I FIRST WENT TO MR. JAGGERS'S PRIVATE HOUSE, TO NOTICE THAT *HOUSEKEEPER?*

A WILD BEAST *TAMED*, YOU CALLED HER. HOW DID MR. JAGGERS TAME HER?

THAT'S HIS *SECRET*. SHE HAS BEEN WITH HIM *MANY* A LONG YEAR.

I WISH YOU *WOULD* TELL ME HER STORY – I FEEL A *PARTICULAR* INTEREST IN IT.

I DON'T KNOW *ALL* OF HER STORY, BUT WHAT I *DO* KNOW, I'LL *TELL* YOU.

A SCORE OR SO OF YEARS AGO, THAT WOMAN WAS *TRIED* AT THE OLD BAILEY FOR *MURDER*, AND WAS *ACQUITTED*.

SHE WAS A VERY HANDSOME YOUNG WOMAN. MR. JAGGERS WAS FOR HER, AND WORKED THE CASE IN A WAY QUITE *ASTONISHING*.

SHE LED A TRAMPING LIFE AND HAD MARRIED *YOUNG* "OVER THE BROOMSTICK".

IT WAS A CASE OF *JEALOUSY*. THE MURDERED PERSON WAS A WOMAN A GOOD TEN YEARS *OLDER*, AND MUCH LARGER AND *STRONGER*.

SHE WAS FOUND *DEAD* IN A BARN – THERE HAD BEEN A *VIOLENT* STRUGGLE. SHE WAS BRUISED AND SCRATCHED, AND HAD BEEN *CHOKED*.

THERE WAS *NO* REASONABLE EVIDENCE TO IMPLICATE *ANY* PERSON BUT *THIS* WOMAN.

THE PROSECUTION ATTEMPTED TO SET UP, IN PROOF OF HER JEALOUSY, THAT SHE WAS UNDER STRONG SUSPICION OF HAVING *DESTROYED* HER THREE-YEAR-OLD *CHILD* BY HER HUSBAND TO *REVENGE* HERSELF UPON HIM.

WELL, SIR! IT HAPPENED THAT THIS WOMAN WAS SO VERY *ARTFULLY* DRESSED FROM THE TIME OF HER APPREHENSION, THAT SHE LOOKED *SLIGHTER* THAN SHE REALLY *WAS*.

AND, ON THE *IMPROBABILITIES* OF HER BEING ABLE TO DO IT, MR. JAGGERS RESTED HIS CASE.

TO SUM UP, SIR, MR. JAGGERS WAS ALTOGETHER TOO MANY FOR THE *JURY*, AND THEY GAVE IN. IN FACT, THE CASE COULD ALMOST BE SAID TO HAVE *MADE* HIM.

SHE WENT INTO HIS SERVICE IMMEDIATELY AFTER HER ACQUITTAL, *TAMED* AS SHE IS NOW.

DO YOU REMEMBER THE *SEX* OF THE *CHILD?*

SAID TO HAVE BEEN A *GIRL*.

WE EXCHANGED A CORDIAL GOODNIGHT, AND I WENT HOME WITH *NEW* MATTER FOR MY THOUGHTS, THOUGH WITH NO *RELIEF* FROM THE OLD.

THE BEST LIGHT OF THE DAY WAS **GONE** WHEN I REACHED SATIS HOUSE. AN ELDERLY WOMAN, A **SERVANT**, OPENED THE GATE. I FOUND MISS HAVISHAM IN THE ROOM WITH THE GREAT TABLE, SITTING BY AN ASHY FIRE, **LOST** IN **CONTEMPLATION**.

THERE WAS AN AIR OF UTTER **LONELINESS** UPON HER, THAT MOVED ME TO **PITY**.

IT IS I, **PIP**. MR. JAGGERS GAVE ME YOUR NOTE **YESTERDAY**, AND I HAVE LOST **NO** TIME.

THANK YOU. I WANT TO **PURSUE** THAT SUBJECT YOU MENTIONED TO ME WHEN YOU WERE LAST HERE, AND TO SHOW YOU THAT I AM NOT **ALL** STONE.

YOU SAID, SPEAKING FOR YOUR **FRIEND**, THAT YOU COULD TELL ME HOW TO DO SOMETHING **USEFUL** AND **GOOD**.

I EXPLAINED TO HER THE SECRET HISTORY OF THE **PARTNERSHIP**. I TOLD HER HOW I HAD HOPED TO COMPLETE THE TRANSACTION OUT OF MY MEANS, BUT HOW I WAS **DISAPPOINTED**.

SO. AND HOW **MUCH** MONEY IS WANTING TO **COMPLETE** THE PURCHASE?

NINE HUNDRED POUNDS.

IF I GIVE YOU MONEY FOR THIS PURPOSE, YOU WILL KEEP **MY** SECRET AS YOU HAVE KEPT YOUR **OWN**?

QUITE AS FAITHFULLY.

YOU ARE STILL ON **FRIENDLY** TERMS WITH MR. JAGGERS?

QUITE. I **DINED** WITH HIM YESTERDAY.

THIS IS AN AUTHORITY TO HIM TO PAY YOU THE **MONEY** FOR YOUR FRIEND. BUT IS THERE **NOTHING** I CAN DO FOR YOU YOURSELF?

THANK YOU, MISS HAVISHAM. AND THANK YOU FOR THE **QUESTION**, BUT THERE IS NOTHING.

MY **NAME** IS ON THE FIRST LEAF. IF YOU CAN EVER WRITE UNDER MY NAME, *"I FORGIVE HER"*, THOUGH EVER SO LONG AFTER MY BROKEN HEART IS **DUST** – PRAY DO IT!

O MISS HAVISHAM, I CAN DO IT **NOW**.

THERE HAVE BEEN SORE **MISTAKES**; AND MY LIFE HAS BEEN A **BLIND** AND **THANKLESS** ONE; BUT I WANT FORGIVENESS AND DIRECTION FAR TOO MUCH, TO BE **BITTER** WITH **YOU**.

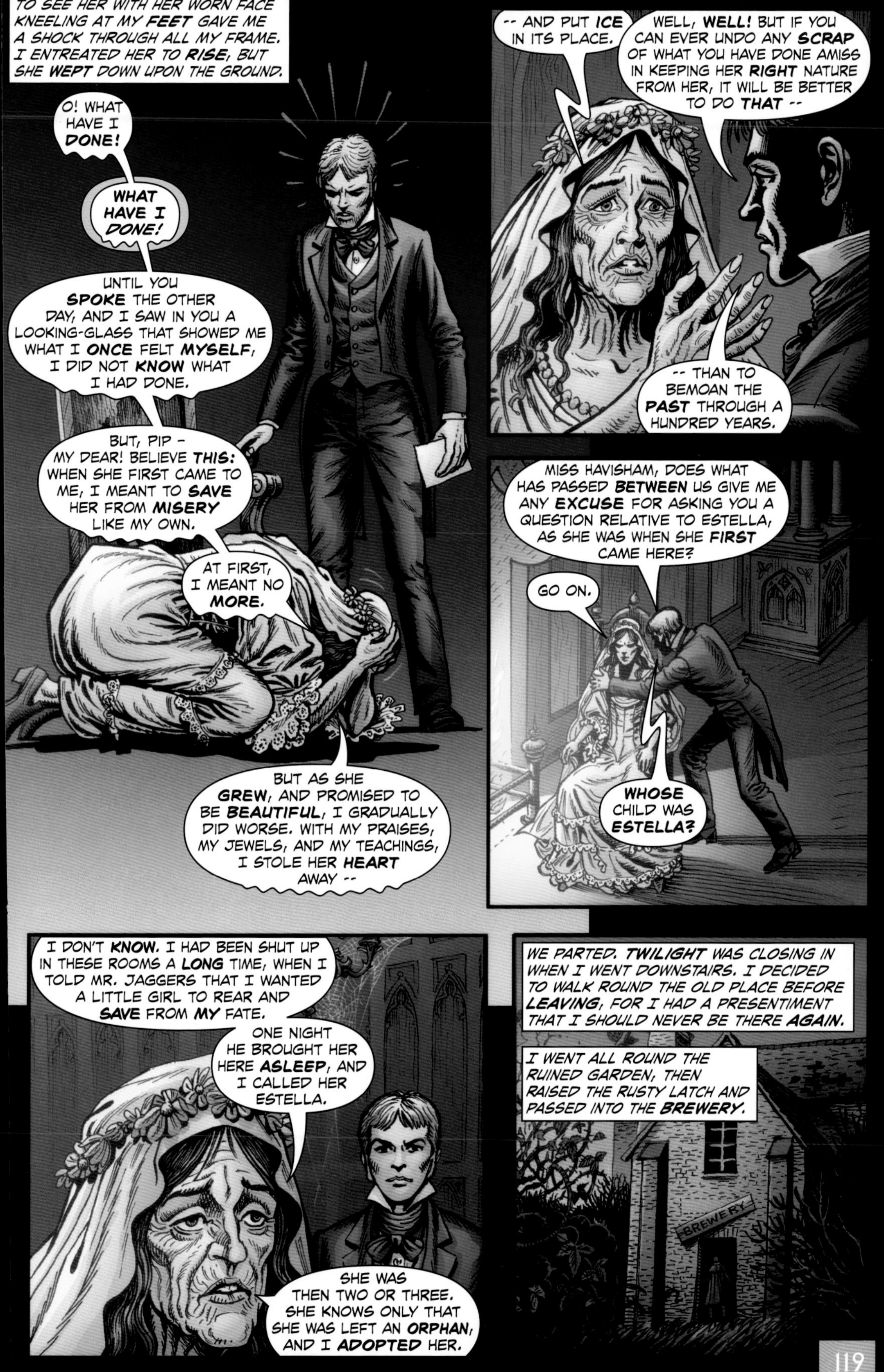
TO SEE HER WITH HER WORN FACE KNEELING AT MY FEET GAVE ME A SHOCK THROUGH ALL MY FRAME. I ENTREATED HER TO RISE; BUT SHE WEPT DOWN UPON THE GROUND.
O! WHAT HAVE I DONE!
WHAT HAVE I DONE!
UNTIL YOU SPOKE THE OTHER DAY, AND I SAW IN YOU A LOOKING-GLASS THAT SHOWED ME WHAT I ONCE FELT MYSELF, I DID NOT KNOW WHAT I HAD DONE.
BUT, PIP – MY DEAR! BELIEVE THIS: WHEN SHE FIRST CAME TO ME, I MEANT TO SAVE HER FROM MISERY LIKE MY OWN.
AT FIRST, I MEANT NO MORE.
BUT AS SHE GREW, AND PROMISED TO BE BEAUTIFUL, I GRADUALLY DID WORSE. WITH MY PRAISES, MY JEWELS, AND MY TEACHINGS, I STOLE HER HEART AWAY --
-- AND PUT ICE IN ITS PLACE.
WELL, WELL! BUT IF YOU CAN EVER UNDO ANY SCRAP OF WHAT YOU HAVE DONE AMISS IN KEEPING HER RIGHT NATURE FROM HER, IT WILL BE BETTER TO DO THAT --
-- THAN TO BEMOAN THE PAST THROUGH A HUNDRED YEARS.
MISS HAVISHAM, DOES WHAT HAS PASSED BETWEEN US GIVE ME ANY EXCUSE FOR ASKING YOU A QUESTION RELATIVE TO ESTELLA, AS SHE WAS WHEN SHE FIRST CAME HERE?
GO ON.
WHOSE CHILD WAS ESTELLA?
I DON'T KNOW. I HAD BEEN SHUT UP IN THESE ROOMS A LONG TIME, WHEN I TOLD MR. JAGGERS THAT I WANTED A LITTLE GIRL TO REAR AND SAVE FROM MY FATE.
ONE NIGHT HE BROUGHT HER HERE ASLEEP, AND I CALLED HER ESTELLA.
SHE WAS THEN TWO OR THREE. SHE KNOWS ONLY THAT SHE WAS LEFT AN ORPHAN, AND I ADOPTED HER.
WE PARTED. TWILIGHT WAS CLOSING IN WHEN I WENT DOWNSTAIRS. I DECIDED TO WALK ROUND THE OLD PLACE BEFORE LEAVING, FOR I HAD A PRESENTIMENT THAT I SHOULD NEVER BE THERE AGAIN.
I WENT ALL ROUND THE RUINED GARDEN, THEN RAISED THE RUSTY LATCH AND PASSED INTO THE BREWERY.
BREWERY

I WAS GOING OUT AT THE OPPOSITE DOOR, WHEN I FANCIED THAT I SAW MISS HAVISHAM **HANGING** TO THE BEAM.

SO **STRONG** WAS THE IMPRESSION, THAT I STOOD UNDER THE BEAM **SHUDDERING** FROM HEAD TO FOOT BEFORE I KNEW IT WAS A **FANCY**.

IN GREAT TERROR OF THIS ILLUSION, I CAME OUT, AND PASSED INTO THE COURT-YARD. I RESOLVED TO GO UP-STAIRS AND **ASSURE** MYSELF THAT MISS HAVISHAM WAS **SAFE**.

I FOUND HER IN THE ROOM WHERE I HAD LEFT HER, SEATED **CLOSE** TO THE **FIRE**.

AAAARRRRRRRGGGGGHHHHH!!!!

I CLOSED WITH HER, *THREW HER DOWN*, AND GOT MY *GREAT-COAT* OVER HER.

I DRAGGED THE CLOTH FROM THE *TABLE*, AND WITH IT THE HEAP OF ROTTENNESS.

CLANK!

CHINK!

THEN WE WERE ON THE GROUND *STRUGGLING* LIKE DESPERATE ENEMIES.

SHE WAS **INSENSIBLE**, AND I WAS AFRAID TO HAVE HER MOVED OR TOUCHED. ASSISTANCE WAS SENT FOR, AND I **HELD** HER UNTIL IT **CAME**.

ON THE SURGEON'S COMING, I GOT UP, AND WAS ASTONISHED TO SEE THAT BOTH MY **HANDS** WERE **BURNT**, FOR I HAD NO **KNOWLEDGE** OF IT THROUGH FEELING.

THE SURGEON PRONOUNCED THAT SHE HAD RECEIVED **SERIOUS** HURTS, BUT THE MAIN DANGER LAY IN THE **NERVOUS SHOCK**.

AS I COULD DO NO **SERVICE** THERE, I DECIDED IN THE COURSE OF THE NIGHT, THAT I WOULD **RETURN** BY THE EARLY MORNING COACH.

AT ABOUT SIX O'CLOCK OF THE MORNING, THEREFORE, I LEANED OVER HER AND **TOUCHED** HER LIPS WITH **MINE**, JUST AS SHE SAID...

Take the pencil and write under my name, "I forgive her."

BACK AT OUR CHAMBERS, HERBERT DEVOTED THE DAY TO **ATTENDING** ON ME. HE WAS THE **KINDEST** OF NURSES, TAKING OFF THE BANDAGES, STEEPING THEM IN **COOLING** LIQUID AND REPLACING THEM WITH PATIENT TENDERNESS.

IS ALL **WELL** DOWN THE RIVER?

YES – I SAT WITH PROVIS LAST NIGHT, HANDEL, TWO GOOD HOURS. HE WAS VERY **COMMUNICATIVE**, AND TOLD ME MORE OF HIS LIFE. YOU REMEMBER HIS BREAKING OFF HERE ABOUT SOME **WOMAN** THAT HE HAD HAD GREAT **TROUBLE** WITH?

WELL! IT SEEMS THAT THE WOMAN WAS A YOUNG WOMAN, **JEALOUS** AND **REVENGEFUL** – REVENGEFUL TO THE **LAST** DEGREE.

TO **WHAT** LAST DEGREE?

MURDER.

VOLUME III
CHAPTER XI

SHE WAS **TRIED** FOR IT, AND MR. JAGGERS **DEFENDED** HER. THAT DEFENCE FIRST MADE HIS NAME KNOWN TO PROVIS. IT WAS ANOTHER, STRONGER, WOMAN WHO WAS THE VICTIM, AND THERE HAD BEEN A STRUGGLE – IN A BARN. THE VICTIM WAS FOUND **THROTTLED**. BUT THE WOMAN WAS **ACQUITTED**.

THIS YOUNG WOMAN AND PROVIS HAD A **CHILD**, OF WHOM PROVIS WAS EXCEEDINGLY **FOND.**

ON THE NIGHT IN QUESTION, THE YOUNG WOMAN PRESENTED HERSELF BEFORE PROVIS FOR ONE **MOMENT**, SWORE THAT SHE WOULD **DESTROY** THE CHILD, AND HE SHOULD NEVER SEE IT AGAIN; THEN, SHE **VANISHED**.

DID THE WOMAN **KEEP** HER **OATH?**

HE SAYS THAT SHE **DID**.

FEARING THAT HE SHOULD BE CALLED UPON TO DEPOSE ABOUT THE CHILD, AND SO BE THE **CAUSE** OF HER DEATH, HE HID HIMSELF OUT OF THE WAY; AND WAS ONLY VAGUELY TALKED OF AS A MAN CALLED **ABEL**, OUT OF WHOM THE **JEALOUSY** AROSE.

AFTER THE ACQUITTAL SHE **DISAPPEARED**.

HERBERT, DID HE TELL YOU **WHEN** THIS HAPPENED?

PARTICULARLY? HIS EXPRESSION WAS, "A ROUND **SCORE** O' YEAR AGO."

HE SAID THAT IT HAD HAPPENED SOME THREE OR FOUR YEARS BEFORE HE CAME UPON **YOU** IN THE **CHURCHYARD**, AND YOU BROUGHT INTO HIS MIND THE LITTLE GIRL SO TRAGICALLY **LOST**, WHO WOULD HAVE BEEN ABOUT **YOUR** AGE.

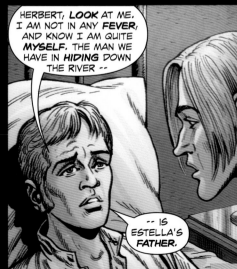

HERBERT, **LOOK** AT ME. I AM NOT IN ANY **FEVER**, AND KNOW I AM QUITE **MYSELF**. THE MAN WE HAVE IN **HIDING** DOWN THE RIVER --

-- IS **ESTELLA'S FATHER.**

WHAT *PURPOSE* I HAD IN VIEW IN *TRACING* ESTELLA'S PARENTAGE, I CANNOT SAY. BUT I WAS *SEIZED* WITH A FEVERISH CONVICTION THAT I *OUGHT* TO HUNT THE MATTER DOWN, AND SEE MR. JAGGERS AND COME AT THE BARE *TRUTH.*

EARLY NEXT MORNING, I TOOK MY WAY TO LITTLE BRITAIN, AND FOUND MR. JAGGERS AND WEMMICK *TOGETHER,* GOING OVER THE OFFICE ACCOUNTS.

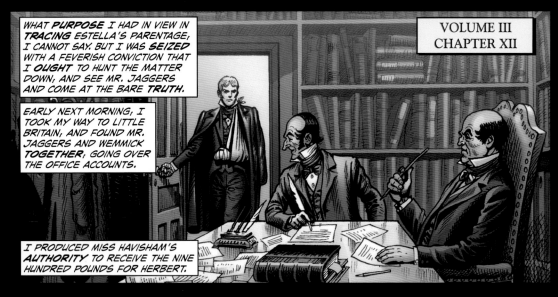

I PRODUCED MISS HAVISHAM'S *AUTHORITY* TO RECEIVE THE NINE HUNDRED POUNDS FOR HERBERT.

MR. JAGGERS'S EYES RETIRED *DEEPER* INTO HIS HEAD WHEN I HANDED HIM THE TABLETS, BUT HE GAVE THEM TO WEMMICK TO DRAW THE CHEQUE.

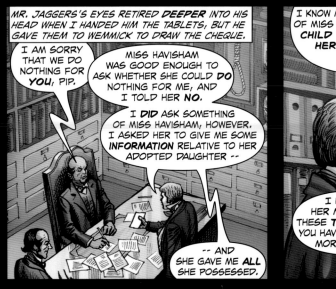

I AM SORRY THAT WE DO NOTHING FOR *YOU,* PIP.

MISS HAVISHAM WAS GOOD ENOUGH TO ASK WHETHER SHE COULD *DO* NOTHING FOR ME, AND I TOLD HER *NO.*

I *DID* ASK SOMETHING OF MISS HAVISHAM, HOWEVER. I ASKED HER TO GIVE ME SOME *INFORMATION* RELATIVE TO HER ADOPTED DAUGHTER --

-- AND SHE GAVE ME *ALL* SHE POSSESSED.

I KNOW MORE OF THE *HISTORY* OF MISS HAVISHAM'S ADOPTED *CHILD* THAN MISS HAVISHAM *HERSELF* DOES, SIR. I KNOW HER *MOTHER.*

MOTHER?

I HAVE *SEEN* HER MOTHER WITHIN THESE *THREE* DAYS. AND YOU HAVE SEEN HER STILL MORE *RECENTLY.*

PERHAPS I KNOW *MORE* OF ESTELLA'S HISTORY THAN EVEN *YOU* DO. I KNOW HER *FATHER* TOO.

A CERTAIN STOP THAT MR. JAGGERS CAME TO IN HIS MANNER *ASSURED* ME THAT HE DID *NOT* KNOW WHO HER FATHER WAS. THIS I HAD SUSPECTED FROM PROVIS'S ACCOUNT, HAVING PIECED TOGETHER THAT HE WAS NOT MR. JAGGERS'S CLIENT UNTIL SOME FOUR YEARS *LATER.*

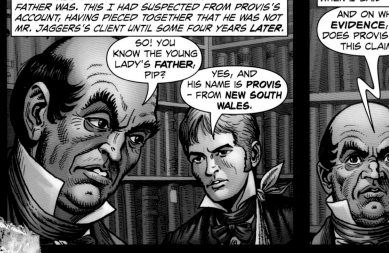

SO! YOU KNOW THE YOUNG LADY'S *FATHER,* PIP?

YES, AND HIS NAME IS *PROVIS* – FROM *NEW SOUTH WALES.*

EVEN MR. JAGGERS *STARTED* WHEN I SAID THOSE WORDS.

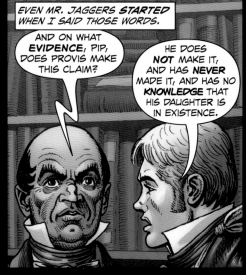

AND ON WHAT *EVIDENCE,* PIP, DOES PROVIS MAKE THIS CLAIM?

HE DOES *NOT* MAKE IT, AND HAS *NEVER* MADE IT, AND HAS NO *KNOWLEDGE* THAT HIS DAUGHTER IS IN EXISTENCE.

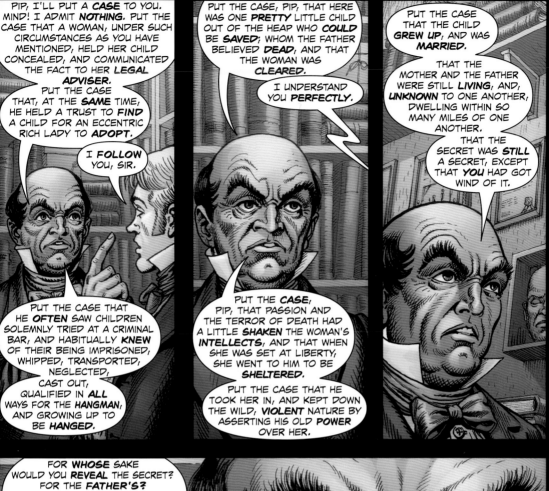

PIP, I'LL PUT A **CASE** TO YOU. MIND! I ADMIT **NOTHING**. PUT THE CASE THAT A WOMAN, UNDER SUCH CIRCUMSTANCES AS YOU HAVE MENTIONED, HELD HER CHILD CONCEALED, AND COMMUNICATED THE FACT TO HER **LEGAL ADVISER**.

PUT THE CASE THAT, AT THE **SAME** TIME, HE HELD A TRUST TO **FIND** A CHILD FOR AN ECCENTRIC RICH LADY TO **ADOPT**.

I **FOLLOW** YOU, SIR.

PUT THE CASE THAT HE **OFTEN** SAW CHILDREN SOLEMNLY TRIED AT A CRIMINAL BAR, AND HABITUALLY **KNEW** OF THEIR BEING IMPRISONED, WHIPPED, TRANSPORTED, NEGLECTED, CAST OUT, QUALIFIED IN **ALL** WAYS FOR THE **HANGMAN**, AND GROWING UP TO BE **HANGED**.

PUT THE CASE, PIP, THAT HERE WAS ONE **PRETTY** LITTLE CHILD OUT OF THE HEAP WHO **COULD** BE **SAVED**; WHOM THE FATHER BELIEVED **DEAD**, AND THAT THE WOMAN WAS **CLEARED**.

I UNDERSTAND YOU **PERFECTLY**.

PUT THE **CASE**, PIP, THAT PASSION AND THE TERROR OF DEATH HAD A LITTLE **SHAKEN** THE WOMAN'S **INTELLECTS**, AND THAT WHEN SHE WAS SET AT LIBERTY, SHE WENT TO HIM TO BE **SHELTERED**.

PUT THE CASE THAT HE TOOK HER IN, AND KEPT DOWN THE WILD, **VIOLENT** NATURE BY ASSERTING HIS OLD **POWER** OVER HER.

PUT THE CASE THAT THE CHILD **GREW UP**, AND WAS **MARRIED**.

THAT THE MOTHER AND THE FATHER WERE STILL **LIVING**, AND, **UNKNOWN** TO ONE ANOTHER, DWELLING WITHIN SO MANY MILES OF ONE ANOTHER.

THAT THE SECRET WAS **STILL** A SECRET, EXCEPT THAT **YOU** HAD GOT WIND OF IT.

FOR **WHOSE** SAKE WOULD YOU **REVEAL** THE SECRET? FOR THE **FATHER'S?** FOR THE **MOTHER'S?** I THINK **NOT**. FOR THE **DAUGHTER'S?** I THINK IT WOULD HARDLY **SERVE** HER TO DRAG HER BACK TO **DISGRACE**.

ADD THE CASE THAT YOU HAD **LOVED** HER, PIP, AND I TELL YOU THAT YOU HAD BETTER **CHOP OFF** BOTH THOSE BANDAGED **HANDS** OF YOURS.

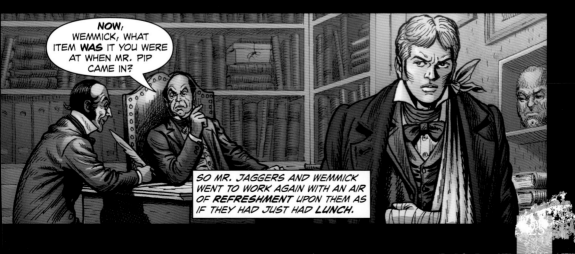

NOW, WEMMICK, WHAT ITEM **WAS** IT YOU WERE AT WHEN MR. PIP CAME IN?

SO MR. JAGGERS AND WEMMICK WENT TO WORK AGAIN WITH AN AIR OF **REFRESHMENT** UPON THEM AS IF THEY HAD JUST HAD **LUNCH**.

I WENT, WITH MY CHEQUE IN MY **POCKET**, TO MISS SKIFFINS'S BROTHER; AND WE WENT STRAIGHT TO **CLARRIKER**.

VOLUME III
CHAPTER XIII

CLARRIKER INFORMED THAT HIS AFFAIRS WERE **STEADILY PROGRESSING**, AND THAT HE WOULD **NOW** BE ABLE TO ESTABLISH A BRANCH-HOUSE IN THE **EAST**. HERBERT IN HIS **NEW CAPACITY** WOULD GO OUT AND TAKE **CHARGE** OF IT.

I FELT AS IF MY LAST **ANCHOR** WERE LOOSENING ITS HOLD, BUT THERE WAS RECOMPENSE IN THE **JOY** WITH WHICH HERBERT WOULD COME HOME AND TELL ME OF THESE **CHANGES**.

WE HAD NOW GOT WELL INTO **MARCH**. MY LEFT ARM WAS TAKING A LONG TIME TO HEAL, THOUGH MY RIGHT ARM WAS TOLERABLY **RESTORED**.

ON A MONDAY MORNING, WHEN HERBERT AND I WERE AT BREAKFAST, I RECEIVED THE FOLLOWING **LETTER** FROM WEMMICK BY THE POST...

Walworth.

Burn this as soon as read. Early in the week, or say Wednesday, you might do what you know of, if you felt disposed to try it.

Now Burn.

WHEN I HAD SHOWN THIS TO HERBERT, WE CONSIDERED WHAT TO **DO**. FOR OF COURSE, MY BEING **DISABLED** COULD NOW BE NO LONGER KEPT OUT OF VIEW.

I HAVE **THOUGHT** IT OVER AGAIN AND AGAIN, AND I THINK WE SHOULD TAKE **STARTOP**. A GOOD FELLOW, A SKILLED HAND, FOND OF US AND **HONOURABLE**. IT IS NECESSARY TO TELL HIM VERY **LITTLE**.

AS FOREIGN STEAMERS WOULD **LEAVE** LONDON AT ABOUT HIGH-WATER, OUR PLAN WAS TO GET DOWN THE RIVER BY A **PREVIOUS** EBB-TIDE, AND **LIE BY** IN SOME QUIET SPOT UNTIL WE COULD PULL OFF TO ONE.

WE WENT OUT AFTER BREAKFAST TO **PURSUE** OUR INVESTIGATIONS. WE FOUND THAT A STEAMER FOR **HAMBURG** WAS LIKELY TO SUIT OUR PURPOSE BEST, BUT NOTED DOWN WHAT **OTHER** STEAMERS WOULD LEAVE LONDON WITH THE SAME TIDE.

WE THEN SEPARATED FOR A FEW HOURS: I, TO GET SUCH PASSPORTS AS WERE **NECESSARY**; HERBERT, TO SEE **STARTOP** AT HIS LODGINGS.

WHEN WE MET AGAIN, HERBERT SAID THAT STARTOP WAS **MORE** THAN READY TO JOIN. WE ARRANGED THAT HERBERT SHOULD PREPARE PROVIS TO COME DOWN TO THE STAIRS HARD BY THE HOUSE, ON WEDNESDAY, WHEN HE SAW US **APPROACH**.

HAVING MADE OUR ARRANGEMENTS, I WENT HOME. THERE, I FOUND A **LETTER** DIRECTED TO **ME** – A **DIRTY** LETTER, THOUGH NOT ILL-WRITTEN. IT HAD BEEN DELIVERED BY **HAND**.

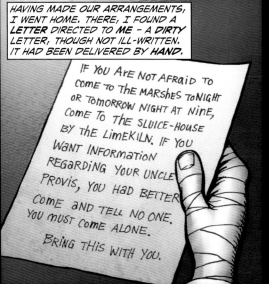

IF YOU ARE NOT AFRAID TO COME TO THE MARSHES TONIGHT OR TOMORROW NIGHT AT NINE, COME TO THE SLUICE-HOUSE BY THE LIMEKILN. IF YOU WANT INFORMATION REGARDING YOUR UNCLE PROVIS, YOU HAD BETTER COME AND TELL NO ONE. YOU MUST COME ALONE.

BRING THIS WITH YOU.

WHAT TO DO **NOW**, I COULD NOT TELL. AND THE WORST WAS, THAT I MUST DECIDE **QUICKLY**, OR MISS THE AFTERNOON COACH. THE REFERENCE TO PROVIS TURNED THE SCALE, AND I RESOLVED TO **GO**.

I LEFT A NOTE FOR **HERBERT**, TELLING HIM THAT AS I WAS GOING **AWAY**, I HAD DECIDED TO HURRY DOWN TO ASCERTAIN HOW MISS **HAVISHAM** WAS **FARING**.

I CAUGHT THE COACH JUST AS IT CAME OUT OF THE YARD. IT WAS **DARK** BEFORE WE GOT DOWN. I WENT TO SATIS HOUSE AND **INQUIRED** FOR MISS HAVISHAM; SHE WAS STILL VERY **ILL**.

I SOUGHT IN MY POCKETS FOR THE **LETTER**, BUT COULD NOT FIND IT.

I KNEW **VERY WELL**, HOWEVER, THE APPOINTED **PLACE** AND THE **HOUR**. TOWARDS THE MARSHES I NOW WENT STRAIGHT, HAVING NO TIME TO **SPARE**.

IT WAS A DARK NIGHT, AND THE MARSHES WERE VERY **DISMAL**. MY BACK WAS TURNED TOWARDS THE **LIGHTS** OF THE DISTANT HULKS AS I WALKED TOWARDS THE LIMEKILN.

FINALLY, I DREW NEAR TO THE KILN, WITH A SMALL STONE-QUARRY HARD BY. THE LIME WAS BURNING WITH A SLUGGISH **STIFLING** SMELL.

VOLUME III
CHAPTER XIV

I SAW A **LIGHT** IN THE OLD SLUICE-HOUSE.

THE LATCH ROSE UNDER MY HAND, AND THE **DOOR YIELDED...**

CREEEEEAK...

NOW I'VE **GOT** YOU!

WHAT **IS** THIS?

HELP, HELP!

UNBIND ME. LET ME **GO!**

WHY HAVE YOU **SET** UPON ME IN THE DARK?

BECAUSE I MEAN TO DO IT **ALL** MYSELF. **ONE** KEEPS A **SECRET** BETTER THAN **TWO**. OH YOU ENEMY, YOU **ENEMY!**

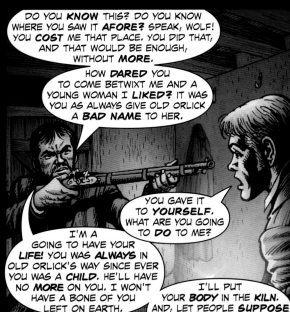

DO YOU **KNOW** THIS? DO YOU KNOW WHERE YOU SAW IT **AFORE?** SPEAK, WOLF! YOU **COST** ME THAT PLACE. YOU DID THAT, AND THAT WOULD BE ENOUGH, WITHOUT **MORE**.

HOW **DARED** YOU TO COME BETWIXT ME AND A YOUNG WOMAN I **LIKED?** IT WAS YOU AS ALWAYS GIVE OLD ORLICK A **BAD NAME** TO HER.

YOU GAVE IT TO **YOURSELF**. WHAT ARE YOU GOING TO **DO** TO ME?

I'M A GOING TO HAVE YOUR **LIFE!** YOU WAS **ALWAYS** IN OLD ORLICK'S WAY SINCE EVER YOU WAS A **CHILD**. HE'LL HAVE NO **MORE** ON YOU. I WON'T HAVE A BONE OF YOU LEFT ON EARTH.

I'LL PUT YOUR **BODY** IN THE **KILN**. AND, LET PEOPLE **SUPPOSE** WHAT THEY MAY, THEY SHALL NEVER **KNOW** NOTHING!

WOLF! OLD ORLICK'S A GOING TO **TELL** YOU SOMETHINK. IT WAS **YOU** AS DID FOR YOUR SHREW **SISTER**. I COME UPON HER FROM BEHIND. I GIV' IT HER! I LEFT HER FOR **DEAD**. BUT IT WARN'T OLD ORLICK AS DID IT; IT WAS **YOU**. YOU WAS **FAVOURED**, AND HE WAS BULLIED AND **BEAT**. NOW YOU **PAYS** FOR IT.

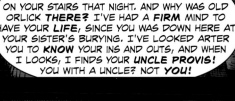

WOLF, I'LL TELL YOU SOMETHING **MORE**. IT WAS OLD ORLICK AS YOU TUMBLED OVER ON YOUR STAIRS THAT NIGHT. AND WHY WAS OLD ORLICK **THERE?** I'VE HAD A **FIRM** MIND TO HAVE YOUR **LIFE**, SINCE YOU WAS DOWN HERE AT YOUR SISTER'S BURYING. I'VE LOOKED ARTER YOU TO **KNOW** YOUR INS AND OUTS, AND WHEN I LOOKS, I FINDS YOUR **UNCLE PROVIS!** YOU WITH A UNCLE? NOT **YOU!**

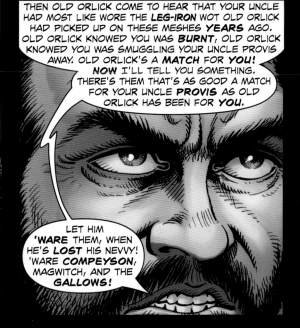

THEN OLD ORLICK COME TO HEAR THAT YOUR UNCLE HAD MOST LIKE WORE THE **LEG-IRON** WOT OLD ORLICK HAD PICKED UP ON THESE MESHES **YEARS** AGO. OLD ORLICK KNOWED YOU WAS **BURNT**, OLD ORLICK KNOWED YOU WAS SMUGGLING YOUR UNCLE PROVIS AWAY. OLD ORLICK'S A **MATCH** FOR **YOU!** **NOW** I'LL TELL YOU SOMETHING. THERE'S THEM THAT'S AS GOOD A MATCH FOR YOUR UNCLE **PROVIS** AS OLD ORLICK HAS BEEN FOR **YOU.**

LET HIM **'WARE** THEM, WHEN HE'S **LOST** HIS NEVVY! **'WARE COMPEYSON**, MAGWITCH, AND THE **GALLOWS!**

*HE DRAINED THE LAST FROM HIS BOTTLE, AND THREW IT AWAY WITH A SUDDEN **HURRY** OF **VIOLENCE**. HE STOOPED AND I SAW A **STONE-HAMMER** IN HIS HAND. I SHOUTED OUT AND STRUGGLED WITH ALL MY **MIGHT**.*

AARRGGHHH!!

GASP!

HA!

!

AARRRR!!

129

AFTER A **BLANK**, I FOUND THAT I WAS LYING UNBOUND ON THE FLOOR, WITH MY HEAD ON SOMEONE'S **KNEE**, AND LOOKING AT A **FACE** – THE FACE OF TRABB'S BOY!

I **THINK** HE'S ALL RIGHT, BUT AIN'T HE JUST **PALE** THOUGH!

HERBERT! GREAT HEAVEN!

AND OUR OLD COMRADE, **STARTOP!**

MY DEAR HANDEL, WHAT **HURT** HAVE YOU GOT? CAN YOU **STAND?**

YES, YES, I CAN **WALK.** I HAVE **NO** HURT BUT THIS THROBBING **ARM.**

THEY LAID IT BARE. IT WAS VIOLENTLY **SWOLLEN** AND **INFLAMED**, AND I COULD SCARCELY ENDURE TO HAVE IT **TOUCHED.**

ENTREATING HERBERT TO TELL ME **HOW** HE HAD COME TO MY **RESCUE**, I LEARNT THAT I HAD IN MY HURRY **DROPPED** THE LETTER, **OPEN**, IN OUR CHAMBERS.

COMING HOME WITH STARTOP, HE HAD **FOUND** IT.

TRABB'S BOY HAD SEEN ME PASSING MISS HAVISHAM'S, AND BECAME THEIR **GUIDE** TO THE SLUICE-HOUSE.

WE RELINQUISHED ALL THOUGHTS OF **PURSUING** ORLICK AT THAT TIME. BY DETAINING US THERE, SUCH A COURSE MIGHT BE **FATAL** TO **PROVIS**. ON GAINING THE TOWN, I PRESENTED TRABB'S BOY WITH TWO **GUINEAS** AND TOLD HIM THAT I WAS **SORRY** EVER TO HAVE HAD AN **ILL** OPINION OF HIM.

THIS MADE NO IMPRESSION ON HIM AT **ALL.** WE WENT BACK TO LONDON THAT NIGHT, THREE IN THE POST-CHAISE.

IT WAS **DAYLIGHT** WHEN WE REACHED HOME. I WENT AT ONCE TO **BED**, AND LAY IN BED ALL DAY.

MY BURNING **ARM** THROBBED, AND MY BURNING **HEAD** THROBBED.

HERBERT AND STARTOP KEPT ME VERY **QUIET**, AND KEPT MY ARM CONSTANTLY DRESSED.

AT **LAST** I SLEPT **SOUNDLY.**

WEDNESDAY MORNING WAS DAWNING WHEN I LOOKED OUT OF THE WINDOW. I FELT **STRONG** AND **WELL**. STARTOP LAY ASLEEP ON THE SOFA. I MADE UP THE FIRE, AND GOT SOME COFFEE READY.

OF ALL MY WORLDLY **POSSESSIONS** I TOOK NO MORE THAN THE FEW **NECESSARIES** THAT FILLED A **BAG**.

IN **GOOD** TIME, HERBERT AND STARTOP **STARTED UP** STRONG AND WELL.

OUR PLAN WAS **THIS**. THE TIDE, BEGINNING TO RUN **DOWN** AT NINE, AND BEING WITH US UNTIL THREE, WE INTENDED TO **CREEP** ON AFTER IT HAD TURNED, AND ROW **AGAINST** IT UNTIL **DARK**. WE SHOULD THEN BE WELL BELOW **GRAVESEND**, WHERE THE RIVER IS **BROAD** AND **SOLITARY**.

WE SHOULD LIE BY IN A LONELY **TAVERN** FOR THE **NIGHT**, AND AWAIT THE **STEAMERS** THAT WOULD START FROM LONDON ON **THURSDAY** MORNING.

FAITHFUL **DEAR** BOY, WELL **DONE**.

THANKYE, **THANKYE!**

I LOOKED **WARILY** FOR ANY TOKEN OF OUR BEING **SUSPECTED**. I SAW **NONE**. WE WERE CERTAINLY NOT FOLLOWED BY ANY BOAT. I FELT MORTIFIED TO BE OF SO LITTLE **USE** IN THE BOAT, BUT MY FRIENDS ROWED WITH A STEADY STROKE.

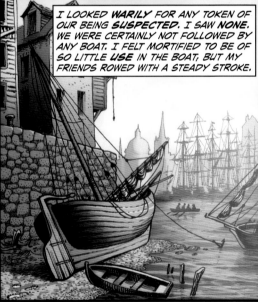

NIGHT **FELL**, AND STILL WE ROWED ON FOR FOUR OR FIVE DULL **MILES**. AT LENGTH WE DESCRIED THE LIGHT OF A LONELY **PUBLIC-HOUSE**, AND RAN ALONGSIDE A LITTLE CAUSEWAY. I STEPPED **ASHORE**.

IT WAS A **DIRTY** PLACE ENOUGH, BUT THERE WAS A **FIRE** IN THE **KITCHEN**, EGGS AND BACON TO **EAT**, AND TWO DOUBLE-BEDDED **ROOMS**.

WE WERE UP **EARLY**, AND ROWED OUT INTO THE TRACK OF THE STEAMER. IT WAS HALF-PAST ONE BEFORE WE SAW HER **SMOKE**, AND BEHIND IT THE SMOKE OF **ANOTHER** STEAMER.

AS THEY WERE COMING ON AT FULL **SPEED**, WE GOT THE BAGS **READY**. WE HAD ALL SHAKEN HANDS CORDIALLY...

...WHEN I SAW A FOUR-OARED **GALLEY** SHOOT OUT FROM UNDER THE **BANK** A LITTLE WAY AHEAD, AND ROW OUT INTO THE **SAME** TRACK.

THE GALLEY **CROSSED** US AND FELL **ALONGSIDE**. THE HAMBURG STEAMER WAS ALMOST **UPON** US, WHEN THE GALLEY **HAILED**:

YOU HAVE A RETURNED **TRANSPORT** THERE.

THAT'S THE MAN, WRAPPED IN THE **CLOAK**. HIS NAME IS **ABEL MAGWITCH**, OTHERWISE **PROVIS**.

I APPREHEND THAT MAN, AND CALL UPON HIM TO **SURRENDER**, AND YOU TO **ASSIST**.

THUD

STOP THE PADDLES!!

IT WAS THE FACE OF THE *OTHER* CONVICT OF *LONG AGO!*

KRASH

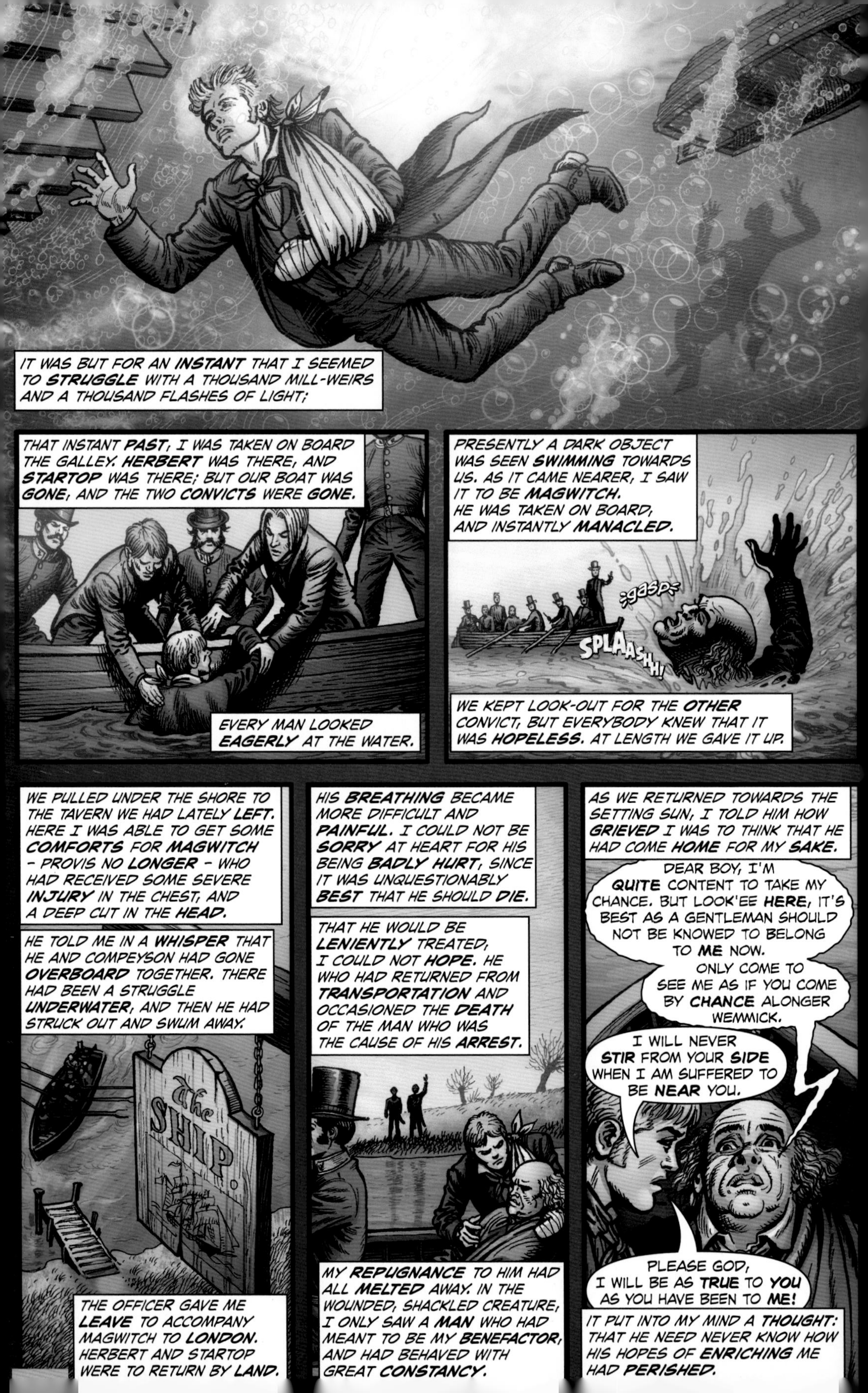
IT WAS BUT FOR AN INSTANT THAT I SEEMED TO STRUGGLE WITH A THOUSAND MILL-WEIRS AND A THOUSAND FLASHES OF LIGHT;
THAT INSTANT PAST, I WAS TAKEN ON BOARD THE GALLEY. HERBERT WAS THERE, AND STARTOP WAS THERE; BUT OUR BOAT WAS GONE, AND THE TWO CONVICTS WERE GONE.
EVERY MAN LOOKED EAGERLY AT THE WATER.
PRESENTLY A DARK OBJECT WAS SEEN SWIMMING TOWARDS US. AS IT CAME NEARER, I SAW IT TO BE MAGWITCH. HE WAS TAKEN ON BOARD, AND INSTANTLY MANACLED.
GASP
SPLAASHH!
WE KEPT LOOK-OUT FOR THE OTHER CONVICT, BUT EVERYBODY KNEW THAT IT WAS HOPELESS. AT LENGTH WE GAVE IT UP.
WE PULLED UNDER THE SHORE TO THE TAVERN WE HAD LATELY LEFT. HERE I WAS ABLE TO GET SOME COMFORTS FOR MAGWITCH – PROVIS NO LONGER – WHO HAD RECEIVED SOME SEVERE INJURY IN THE CHEST, AND A DEEP CUT IN THE HEAD.
HE TOLD ME IN A WHISPER THAT HE AND COMPEYSON HAD GONE OVERBOARD TOGETHER. THERE HAD BEEN A STRUGGLE UNDERWATER, AND THEN HE HAD STRUCK OUT AND SWUM AWAY.
The SHIP
THE OFFICER GAVE ME LEAVE TO ACCOMPANY MAGWITCH TO LONDON. HERBERT AND STARTOP WERE TO RETURN BY LAND.
HIS BREATHING BECAME MORE DIFFICULT AND PAINFUL. I COULD NOT BE SORRY AT HEART FOR HIS BEING BADLY HURT, SINCE IT WAS UNQUESTIONABLY BEST THAT HE SHOULD DIE.
THAT HE WOULD BE LENIENTLY TREATED, I COULD NOT HOPE. HE WHO HAD RETURNED FROM TRANSPORTATION AND OCCASIONED THE DEATH OF THE MAN WHO WAS THE CAUSE OF HIS ARREST.
MY REPUGNANCE TO HIM HAD ALL MELTED AWAY. IN THE WOUNDED, SHACKLED CREATURE, I ONLY SAW A MAN WHO HAD MEANT TO BE MY BENEFACTOR, AND HAD BEHAVED WITH GREAT CONSTANCY.
AS WE RETURNED TOWARDS THE SETTING SUN, I TOLD HIM HOW GRIEVED I WAS TO THINK THAT HE HAD COME HOME FOR MY SAKE.
DEAR BOY, I'M QUITE CONTENT TO TAKE MY CHANCE. BUT LOOK'EE HERE, IT'S BEST AS A GENTLEMAN SHOULD NOT BE KNOWED TO BELONG TO ME NOW.
ONLY COME TO SEE ME AS IF YOU COME BY CHANCE ALONGER WEMMICK.
I WILL NEVER STIR FROM YOUR SIDE WHEN I AM SUFFERED TO BE NEAR YOU.
PLEASE GOD, I WILL BE AS TRUE TO YOU AS YOU HAVE BEEN TO ME!
IT PUT INTO MY MIND A THOUGHT: THAT HE NEED NEVER KNOW HOW HIS HOPES OF ENRICHING ME HAD PERISHED.

HE WAS TAKEN TO THE POLICE COURT NEXT DAY. HE WOULD HAVE BEEN *IMMEDIATELY* COMMITTED FOR *TRIAL*, BUT THAT IT WAS NECESSARY TO SEND FOR AN OLD OFFICER OF THE PRISON-SHIP TO *IDENTIFY* HIM.

I WENT TO MR. JAGGERS TO RETAIN HIS ASSISTANCE, BUT HE TOLD ME THAT THE CASE WOULD BE *OVER* IN FIVE MINUTES WHEN THE *WITNESS* WAS THERE.

WHEN CONVICTED, MAGWITCH'S *POSSESSIONS* WOULD BE *FORFEITED* TO THE *CROWN*. BUT IN HIS IGNORANCE, POOR FELLOW, HE NEVER MISTRUSTED BUT THAT MY *INHERITANCE* WAS *SAFE*. I IMPARTED TO MR. JAGGERS MY DESIGN OF KEEPING HIM *IGNORANT* OF THE *FATE* OF HIS WEALTH.

AFTER THREE DAYS, THE WITNESS CAME, AND HE WAS COMMITTED TO TRIAL AT THE NEXT SESSIONS.

AT THIS *DARK* TIME, HERBERT RETURNED HOME ONE EVENING CAST *DOWN*.

MY DEAR HANDEL, I FEAR I SHALL SOON HAVE TO *LEAVE* YOU. WE SHALL LOSE A FINE *OPPORTUNITY* IF I PUT OFF GOING TO CAIRO, AND I AM AFRAID I *MUST* GO, WHEN YOU MOST *NEED* ME.

IN THIS BRANCH HOUSE OF OURS, HANDEL, WE MUST HAVE A – A *CLERK*. AND I HOPE IT IS NOT *UNLIKELY* THAT HE MAY EXPAND INTO A *PARTNER*. IN SHORT, MY DEAR BOY, WILL YOU *COME* TO ME?

IF YOU THOUGHT YOU COULD LEAVE THE QUESTION *OPEN* FOR A *LITTLE* WHILE...

FOR *ANY* WHILE – SIX MONTHS, A *YEAR!*

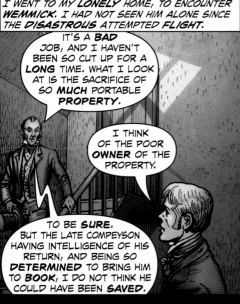

ON THE SATURDAY IN THAT SAME WEEK, I TOOK MY *LEAVE* OF HERBERT AS HE SAT ON ONE OF THE SEAPORT MAIL COACHES. I WENT TO MY *LONELY* HOME, TO ENCOUNTER *WEMMICK*. I HAD NOT SEEN HIM ALONE SINCE THE *DISASTROUS* ATTEMPTED *FLIGHT*.

IT'S A *BAD* JOB, AND I HAVEN'T BEEN SO CUT UP FOR A *LONG* TIME. WHAT I LOOK AT IS THE SACRIFICE OF SO *MUCH* PORTABLE *PROPERTY*.

I THINK OF THE POOR *OWNER* OF THE PROPERTY.

TO BE *SURE*. BUT THE LATE COMPEYSON HAVING INTELLIGENCE OF HIS RETURN, AND BEING SO *DETERMINED* TO BRING HIM TO *BOOK*, I DO NOT THINK HE COULD HAVE BEEN *SAVED*.

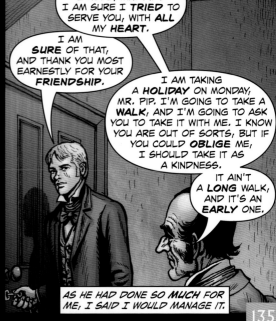

YOU DON'T BLAME *ME*, I HOPE, MR. PIP? I AM SURE I *TRIED* TO SERVE YOU, WITH *ALL* MY *HEART*.

I AM *SURE* OF THAT, AND THANK YOU MOST EARNESTLY FOR YOUR *FRIENDSHIP*.

I AM TAKING A *HOLIDAY* ON MONDAY, MR. PIP. I'M GOING TO TAKE A *WALK*, AND I'M GOING TO ASK YOU TO TAKE IT WITH ME. I KNOW YOU ARE OUT OF SORTS, BUT IF YOU COULD *OBLIGE* ME, I SHOULD TAKE IT AS A KINDNESS.

IT AIN'T A *LONG* WALK, AND IT'S AN *EARLY* ONE.

AS HE HAD DONE SO *MUCH* FOR ME, I SAID I WOULD MANAGE IT.

ON THE MONDAY MORNING, WHEN WE HAD **FORTIFIED** OURSELVES WITH RUM AND MILK AND BISCUITS, WE **SET OFF** TOWARDS CAMBERWELL GREEN.

HALLOA! HERE'S A **CHURCH!** LET'S GO IN!

HERE'S A COUPLE OF PAIR OF **GLOVES!** LET'S PUT 'EM ON!

AS THE GLOVES WERE WHITE KID GLOVES, AND AS HIS **POST-OFFICE** MOUTH WAS **WIDENED** TO ITS **UTMOST** EXTENT, I BEGAN TO HAVE STRONG **SUSPICIONS.**

THEY BECAME A CERTAINTY WHEN I BEHELD THE **AGED** ENTER AT A SIDE DOOR, ESCORTING **MISS SKIFFINS.**

HALLOA! HERE'S A **RING!** LET'S HAVE A **WEDDING.**

WHO GIVETH THIS **WOMAN** TO BE MARRIED TO THIS **MAN?**

NOW AGED P, WHO **GIVETH?**

ALL RIGHT, JOHN, ALL RIGHT, **MY BOY!**

WE HAD AN EXCELLENT **BREAKFAST** AT A PLEASANT LITTLE TAVERN. I DRANK TO THE NEW **COUPLE,** TO THE **AGED,** AND TO THE **CASTLE.**

I **SAY,** MR. PIP! THIS IS ALTOGETHER A **WALWORTH** SENTIMENT, PLEASE.

I UNDERSTAND. **NOT** TO BE MENTIONED IN LITTLE BRITAIN.

MR. JAGGERS MAY AS WELL NOT **KNOW** OF IT. HE MIGHT THINK MY BRAIN WAS **SOFTENING,** OR SOMETHING OF THE KIND.

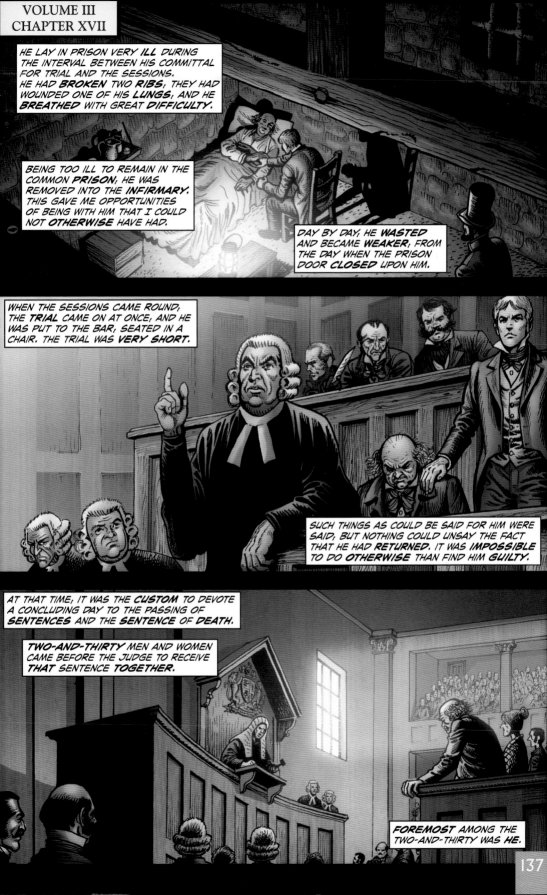

HE LAY IN PRISON VERY *ILL* DURING THE INTERVAL BETWEEN HIS COMMITTAL FOR TRIAL AND THE SESSIONS. HE HAD *BROKEN* TWO *RIBS*, THEY HAD WOUNDED ONE OF HIS *LUNGS*, AND HE *BREATHED* WITH GREAT *DIFFICULTY*.

BEING TOO ILL TO REMAIN IN THE COMMON *PRISON*, HE WAS REMOVED INTO THE *INFIRMARY*. THIS GAVE ME OPPORTUNITIES OF BEING WITH HIM THAT I COULD NOT *OTHERWISE* HAVE HAD.

DAY BY DAY, HE *WASTED* AND BECAME *WEAKER*, FROM THE DAY WHEN THE PRISON DOOR *CLOSED* UPON HIM.

WHEN THE SESSIONS CAME ROUND, THE *TRIAL* CAME ON AT ONCE, AND HE WAS PUT TO THE BAR, SEATED IN A CHAIR. THE TRIAL WAS *VERY SHORT*.

SUCH THINGS AS COULD BE SAID FOR HIM WERE SAID; BUT NOTHING COULD UNSAY THE FACT THAT HE HAD *RETURNED*. IT WAS *IMPOSSIBLE* TO DO *OTHERWISE* THAN FIND HIM *GUILTY*.

AT THAT TIME, IT WAS THE *CUSTOM* TO DEVOTE A CONCLUDING DAY TO THE PASSING OF *SENTENCES* AND THE *SENTENCE* OF *DEATH*.

TWO-AND-THIRTY MEN AND WOMEN CAME BEFORE THE JUDGE TO RECEIVE *THAT* SENTENCE *TOGETHER*.

FOREMOST AMONG THE TWO-AND-THIRTY WAS *HE*.

137

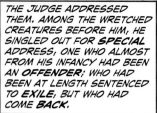

THE JUDGE ADDRESSED THEM. AMONG THE WRETCHED CREATURES BEFORE HIM, HE SINGLED OUT FOR **SPECIAL** ADDRESS, ONE WHO ALMOST FROM HIS INFANCY HAD BEEN AN **OFFENDER**; WHO HAD BEEN AT LENGTH SENTENCED TO **EXILE**; BUT WHO HAD COME **BACK**.

...THE APPOINTED **PUNISHMENT** BEING **DEATH**, YOU MUST PREPARE YOURSELF TO **DIE**.

MY LORD, I HAVE RECEIVED MY SENTENCE OF **DEATH** FROM THE **ALMIGHTY**; BUT I BOW TO **YOURS**.

FOR SEVERAL NIGHTS AFTER HE WAS SENTENCED I TOOK **NO** REST EXCEPT WHEN I FELL ASLEEP IN MY CHAIR. MY DAILY VISITS WERE **SHORTENED** NOW, AND HE WAS MORE STRICTLY KEPT; BUT NOBODY WAS HARD WITH HIM OR ME.

THE OFFICER ALWAYS GAVE ME THE ASSURANCE THAT HE WAS **WORSE**.

AS THE DAYS WENT ON, I NOTICED THAT HE WOULD LIE **PLACIDLY** LOOKING AT THE CEILING. TEN DAYS AFTER THE SENTENCE, I SAW A **GREATER** CHANGE IN HIM THAN I HAD SEEN YET.

Dear boy, I thought you was **late**. But I knowed you **couldn't** be that.

IT IS JUST THE **TIME**. I WAITED FOR IT AT THE GATE.

You always **waits** at the gate; don't you, dear boy?

God **bless** you! You've never **deserted** me, dear boy.

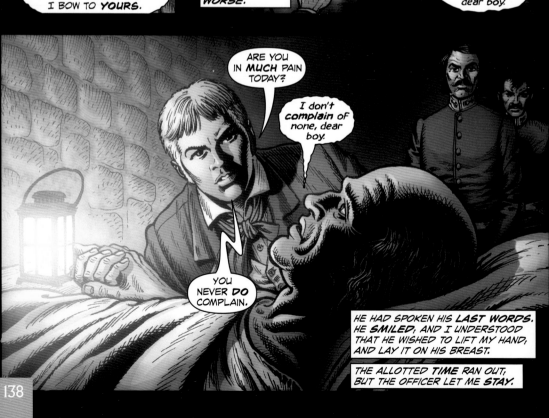

ARE YOU IN **MUCH** PAIN TODAY?

I don't **complain** of none, dear boy.

YOU NEVER **DO** COMPLAIN.

HE HAD SPOKEN HIS **LAST WORDS**. HE **SMILED**, AND I UNDERSTOOD THAT HE WISHED TO LIFT MY HAND, AND LAY IT ON HIS BREAST.

THE ALLOTTED **TIME** RAN OUT, BUT THE OFFICER LET ME **STAY**.

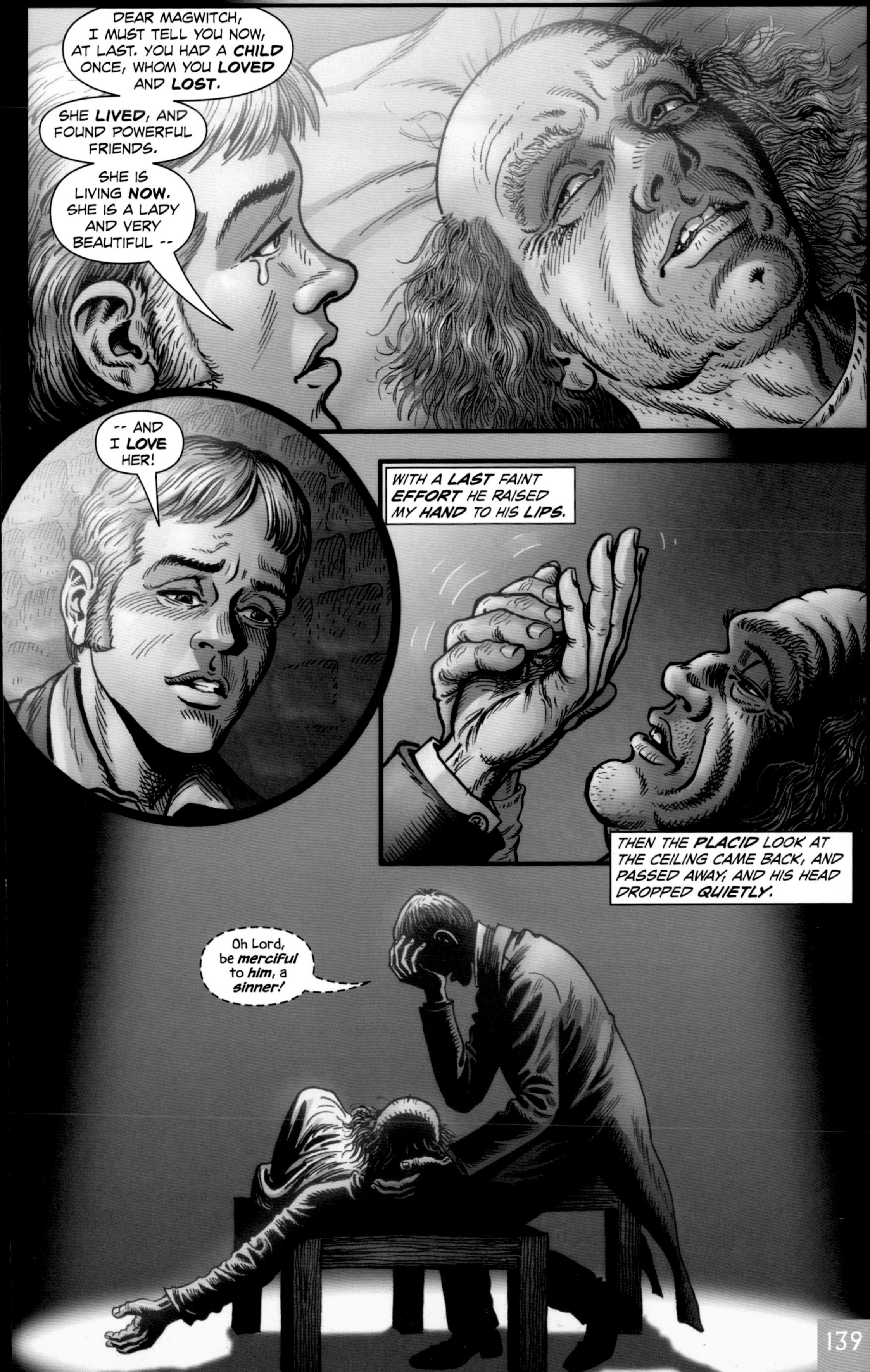
DEAR MAGWITCH, I MUST TELL YOU NOW, AT LAST. YOU HAD A **CHILD** ONCE, WHOM YOU **LOVED** AND **LOST**.
SHE **LIVED**, AND FOUND POWERFUL FRIENDS.
SHE IS LIVING **NOW**. SHE IS A LADY AND VERY BEAUTIFUL --
-- AND I **LOVE** HER!
*WITH A **LAST** FAINT **EFFORT** HE RAISED MY **HAND** TO HIS **LIPS**.*
*THEN THE **PLACID** LOOK AT THE CEILING CAME BACK, AND PASSED AWAY, AND HIS HEAD DROPPED **QUIETLY**.*
Oh Lord, be *merciful* to *him*, a *sinner!*

NOW THAT I WAS LEFT WHOLLY TO **MYSELF**, I GAVE NOTICE OF MY INTENTION TO **QUIT** THE CHAMBERS IN THE TEMPLE. I WAS IN **DEBT**, AND HAD SCARCELY ANY **MONEY**.

I SHOULD HAVE BEEN SERIOUSLY **ALARMED** BY THIS STATE OF AFFAIRS, BUT FOR THE FACT THAT I PERCEIVED THAT I WAS FALLING **VERY ILL**.

FOR A DAY OR TWO, I LAY ON THE **SOFA**, OR ON THE **FLOOR**, ACCORDING AS I HAPPENED TO SINK DOWN, WITH A HEAVY HEAD, ACHING LIMBS, AND NO **PURPOSE** OR **POWER**.

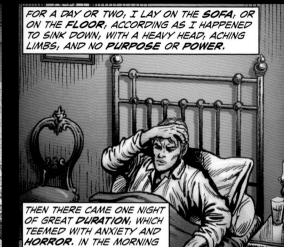

THEN THERE CAME ONE NIGHT OF GREAT **DURATION**, WHICH TEEMED WITH ANXIETY AND **HORROR**. IN THE MORNING WHEN I TRIED TO **SIT UP**, I FOUND I COULD **NOT DO SO**.

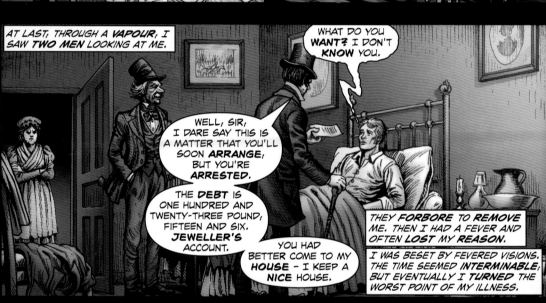

AT LAST, THROUGH A **VAPOUR**, I SAW **TWO MEN** LOOKING AT ME.

WHAT DO YOU **WANT?** I DON'T **KNOW** YOU.

WELL, SIR, I DARE SAY THIS IS A MATTER THAT YOU'LL SOON **ARRANGE**, BUT YOU'RE **ARRESTED**.

THE **DEBT** IS ONE HUNDRED AND TWENTY-THREE POUND, FIFTEEN AND SIX. **JEWELLER'S** ACCOUNT.

YOU HAD BETTER COME TO MY **HOUSE** – I KEEP A **NICE** HOUSE.

THEY **FORBORE** TO REMOVE ME. THEN I HAD A FEVER AND OFTEN **LOST MY REASON**.

I WAS BESET BY FEVERED VISIONS. THE TIME SEEMED **INTERMINABLE**, BUT EVENTUALLY I **TURNED** THE WORST POINT OF MY ILLNESS.

ONE DAY I **OPENED** MY EYES AND **SAW**, IN THE CHAIR AT THE BEDSIDE...

IS IT **JOE?**

WHICH IT **AIR**, OLD CHAP.

HOW **LONG**, DEAR JOE?

WHICH YOU MEANTERSAY, PIP, HOW LONG HAVE YOUR **ILLNESS** LASTED?

IT'S THE END OF **MAY**, OLD CHAP.

FOR, AS I SAYS TO BIDDY WHEN THE **NEWS** OF YOUR BEING ILL WERE BROUGHT BY **LETTER**, THAT HOW YOU MIGHT BE AMONGST **STRANGERS**, AND THAT A **WISIT** AT SUCH A MOMENT MIGHT NOT PROVE **UNACCEPTABOBBLE**. AND BIDDY, HER WORD WERE, "**GO TO HIM, WITHOUT LOSS OF TIME**."

NOT TO TALK TOO MUCH, I **DEFERRED** ASKING HIM ABOUT MISS HAVISHAM UNTIL NEXT DAY. HE SHOOK HIS HEAD WHEN I ASKED IF SHE HAD **RECOVERED**.

IS **SHE** DEAD, JOE?

WHY YOU SEE, OLD CHAP, I WOULDN'T GO SO **FAR** AS TO SAY **THAT**; BUT SHE **AIN'T** LIVING.

DEAR JOE, HAVE YOU HEARD WHAT BECOMES OF HER **PROPERTY?**

WELL, OLD CHAP, IT DO **APPEAR** THAT SHE HAD SETTLED THE **MOST** OF IT ON MISS **ESTELLA**. BUT SHE HAD WROTE OUT A LITTLE CODDLESHELL IN HER OWN HAND A DAY OR TWO AFORE THE ACCIDENT, LEAVING A COOL **FOUR THOUSAND** TO MR. **MATTHEW POCKET**, *"BECAUSE OF PIP'S ACCOUNT OF HIM."*

AND OLD **ORLICK**, HE'S BEEN A BUSTIN' OPEN PUMBLECHOOK'S DWELLING-OUSE AND HE'S IN THE COUNTY **JAIL!**

BY THESE APPROACHES WE ARRIVED AT **UNRESTRICTED** CONVERSATION. I SLOWLY BECAME LESS **WEAK**. JOE STAYED WITH ME, AND I WAS LIKE A **CHILD** IN HIS HANDS.

HE WOULD SIT AND TALK TO ME WITH THE **OLD** SIMPLICITY.

HE DID **EVERYTHING** FOR ME EXCEPT THE HOUSEHOLD WORK, FOR WHICH HE HAD ENGAGED A VERY DECENT WOMAN, AFTER **PAYING OFF** THE LAUNDRESS.

WE LOOKED FORWARD TO THE DAY WHEN I SHOULD GO OUT FOR A **RIDE**. WHEN THE DAY CAME, AN OPEN CARRIAGE WAS GOT INTO THE LANE. JOE TOOK ME IN HIS **ARMS** AND **CARRIED** ME DOWN TO IT.

THEN WE DROVE AWAY INTO THE **COUNTRY**, WHERE THE RICH SUMMER GROWTH WAS ALREADY ON THE **TREES**.

I FEEL **THANKFUL** THAT I HAVE BEEN **ILL**, JOE.

DEAR OLD PIP, OLD CHAP, YOU'RE A'MOST COME ROUND, SIR.

WE HAVE HAD A **TIME** TOGETHER THAT I CAN **NEVER** FORGET. THERE WERE DAYS ONCE, I KNOW, THAT I **DID** FORGET; BUT I NEVER SHALL FORGET **THESE**.

THAT NIGHT, JOE CAME INTO MY ROOM. HE **ASKED** ME IF I FELT **SURE** THAT I WAS AS **WELL** AS IN THE MORNING. I **ASSENTED**.

WHEN I GOT UP IN THE MORNING, I WENT TO JOE'S ROOM, BUT HE WAS **NOT** THERE, AND HIS BOX WAS **GONE**.

THERE WAS A BRIEF LETTER.

not Wishful to intrude you are well again Dear Pip and will do better without Jo.
p.s. Ever the best of friends.

AND THERE WAS A **RECEIPT** FOR MY **DEBT** AND **COSTS**, WHICH JOE HAD **PAID**.

WHAT REMAINED FOR ME NOW, BUT TO FOLLOW HIM TO THE DEAR OLD **FORGE**? THE PURPOSE WAS, THAT I WOULD GO TO **BIDDY**, AND SHOW HER HOW **HUMBLED** AND **REPENTANT** I CAME BACK. THEN I WOULD SAY TO HER:

BIDDY, I THINK YOU **ONCE** LIKED ME VERY **WELL**, WITH MY ERRANT HEART. IF YOU CAN LIKE ME ONLY **HALF** AS WELL ONCE MORE, I HOPE I AM A LITTLE WORTHIER OF YOU.

WILL YOU GO THROUGH THE **WORLD** WITH ME, AND I WILL TRY HARD TO MAKE IT A **BETTER** WORLD FOR YOU?

THE TIDINGS OF MY **FORTUNES** HAVING HAD A HEAVY **FALL** HAD GOT DOWN TO MY NATIVE PLACE **BEFORE** I GOT THERE.

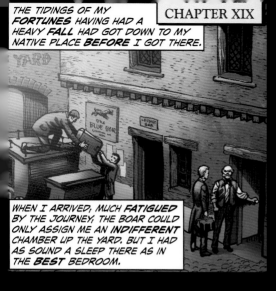

WHEN I ARRIVED, MUCH **FATIGUED** BY THE JOURNEY, THE BOAR COULD ONLY ASSIGN ME AN **INDIFFERENT** CHAMBER UP THE YARD. BUT I HAD AS SOUND A SLEEP THERE AS IN THE **BEST** BEDROOM.

EARLY IN THE MORNING, BEFORE BREAKFAST, I STROLLED ROUND BY SATIS HOUSE. THERE WERE PRINTED **BILLS** ON THE GATE, ANNOUNCING A **SALE** BY AUCTION OF THE HOUSEHOLD FURNITURE AND EFFECTS NEXT WEEK.

Saturday 3ʳᵈ May

FOR SALE BY PUBLIC

AUCTION

SATIS HOUSE

THE HOUSE **ITSELF** WAS TO BE **SOLD** AND **PULLED DOWN**

WHEN I GOT **BACK** TO MY BREAKFAST, I FOUND **MR. PUMBLECHOOK** CONVERSING WITH THE LANDLORD.

YOUNG MAN, I AM **SORRY** TO SEE YOU BROUGHT LOW. BUT WHAT **ELSE** COULD BE EXPECTED! AND HAS IT COME TO **THIS!**

AND AIR YOU A GOING TO **JOSEPH?**

IN HEAVEN'S NAME, WHAT DOES IT **MATTER** TO **YOU** WHERE I AM **GOING?**

FOR ONCE YOU ARE **RIGHT.** I **FORGIT** MYSELF WHEN I TAKE SUCH AN **INTEREST.** AND YET, THIS IS **HIM** AS I EVER SPORTED WITH IN HIS DAYS OF HAPPY **INFANCY!**

THIS IS **HIM** AS I HAVE SEEN BROUGHT UP BY **HAND**, LET HIM **DENY** IT IF HE CAN!

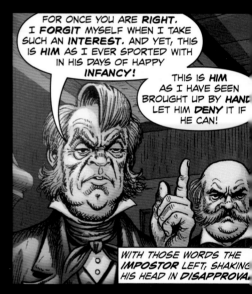

WITH THOSE WORDS THE **IMPOSTOR** LEFT, SHAKING HIS HEAD IN **DISAPPROVAL.**

I WENT **SOFTLY** TOWARDS THE FORGE, MEANING TO PEEP OVER THE FLOWERS, WHEN JOE AND BIDDY STOOD BEFORE ME, **ARM IN ARM.**
BIDDY GAVE A **CRY**, AND IN ANOTHER **MOMENT** SHE WAS IN MY **EMBRACE.**

BUT DEAR **BIDDY,** HOW **SMART** YOU ARE! AND JOE, HOW SMART **YOU** ARE!

YES, DEAR PIP.

IT'S MY **WEDDING DAY,** AND I AM **MARRIED** TO **JOE!**

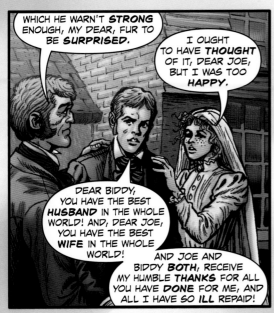

WHICH HE WARN'T **STRONG** ENOUGH, MY DEAR, FUR TO BE **SURPRISED**.

I OUGHT TO HAVE **THOUGHT** OF IT, DEAR JOE, BUT I WAS TOO **HAPPY**.

DEAR BIDDY, YOU HAVE THE BEST **HUSBAND** IN THE WHOLE WORLD! AND, DEAR JOE, YOU HAVE THE BEST **WIFE** IN THE WHOLE WORLD!

AND JOE AND BIDDY **BOTH**, RECEIVE MY HUMBLE **THANKS** FOR ALL YOU HAVE **DONE** FOR ME, AND ALL I HAVE SO **ILL** REPAID!

I AM SOON GOING **ABROAD**, AND SHALL NEVER **REST** UNTIL I HAVE WORKED FOR THE **MONEY** WITH WHICH YOU HAVE KEPT ME OUT OF **PRISON**.

BUT I MUST SAY **MORE**. DEAR JOE, I HOPE YOU WILL HAVE **CHILDREN** TO LOVE, AND THAT SOME LITTLE FELLOW WILL SIT IN THIS CHIMNEY-CORNER OF A WINTER NIGHT, WHO MAY **REMIND** YOU OF ANOTHER LITTLE FELLOW GONE **FOR EVER**.

DON'T **TELL** HIM, JOE, THAT I WAS **THANKLESS**. DON'T TELL HIM, BIDDY; THAT I WAS **UNGENEROUS** AND **UNJUST**.

ONLY TELL HIM THAT I **HONOURED** YOU **BOTH** BECAUSE YOU WERE SO GOOD AND **TRUE**.

AND NOW, PRAY TELL ME, BOTH, THAT YOU **FORGIVE** ME, THAT I MAY CARRY THE SOUND **AWAY** WITH ME!

O DEAR OLD **PIP**, GOD **KNOWS** AS I **FORGIVE** YOU, IF I HAVE **ANYTHINK** TO FORGIVE!

AMEN! GOD KNOWS I **DO!**

I SOLD **ALL** I HAD FOR A **COMPOSITION** WITH MY CREDITORS. WITHIN A MONTH, I HAD **QUITTED** ENGLAND, AND WITHIN TWO MONTHS I WAS CLERK TO CLARRIKER AND Cº.

SOON I ASSUMED MY FIRST **RESPONSIBILITY**, FOR THE PARLOUR CEILING AT MILL POND BANK HAD CEASED TO **TREMBLE** UNDER BILL BARLEY'S **GROWLS**, AND FOR HERBERT WENT AWAY TO **MARRY** CLARA. I WAS LEFT IN **CHARGE** OF THE EASTERN BRANCH UNTIL HE CAME BACK.

MANY A **YEAR** WENT ROUND BEFORE I WAS A PARTNER IN THE HOUSE; BUT I LIVED **HAPPILY** WITH HERBERT AND HIS WIFE. I LIVED **FRUGALLY**, AND MAINTAINED A CORRESPONDENCE WITH BIDDY AND JOE.

WHEN I BECAME **THIRD** IN THE FIRM, CLARRIKER BETRAYED MY **SECRET** TO HERBERT, AND HERBERT WAS AS MUCH **MOVED** AS **AMAZED**.

WE WERE NEVER A **GREAT** HOUSE, BUT WE WORKED FOR OUR **PROFITS**, AND DID VERY **WELL**.

FOR **ELEVEN** YEARS, I HAD NOT SEEN JOE NOR BIDDY, WHEN, ONE EVENING IN DECEMBER, I RAISED THE **LATCH OF THE KITCHEN DOOR,** AND LOOKED IN **UNSEEN.**

THERE, IN THE OLD PLACE BY THE FIRE SAT JOE; AND THERE, SITTING ON MY **OWN** LITTLE STOOL WAS – I AGAIN!

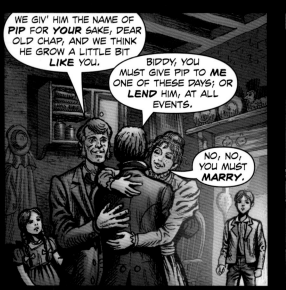

WE GIV' HIM THE NAME OF **PIP** FOR **YOUR** SAKE, DEAR OLD CHAP, AND WE THINK HE GROW A LITTLE BIT **LIKE** YOU.

BIDDY, YOU MUST GIVE PIP TO **ME** ONE OF THESE DAYS; OR **LEND** HIM, AT ALL EVENTS.

NO, NO, YOU MUST **MARRY.**

SO HERBERT AND CLARA SAY, BUT I DON'T THINK I **SHALL,** BIDDY. I HAVE SO **SETTLED DOWN** IN THEIR HOME, AND AM **ALREADY** QUITE AN OLD **BACHELOR.**

DEAR PIP. YOU ARE **SURE** YOU DON'T **FRET** FOR HER?

O NO – I THINK **NOT,** BIDDY.

TELL ME AS AN OLD **FRIEND.** HAVE YOU QUITE **FORGOTTEN** HER?

DEAR BIDDY, I HAVE FORGOTTEN **NOTHING** IN MY LIFE THAT EVER HAD A **FOREMOST** PLACE THERE. BUT THAT **POOR DREAM,** AS I ONCE USED TO CALL IT, HAS **ALL** GONE BY.

NEVERTHELESS, I KNEW, WHILE I **SAID** THOSE WORDS, THAT I INTENDED TO **REVISIT** THE SITE OF THE OLD HOUSE THAT EVENING FOR **HER** SAKE. YES, FOR **ESTELLA'S** SAKE.

I HAD HEARD OF ESTELLA AS LEADING A MOST **UNHAPPY** LIFE, AND AS BEING **SEPARATED** FROM HER HUSBAND, WHO HAD USED HER WITH GREAT **CRUELTY.** HE WAS QUITE **RENOWNED** AS A COMPOUND OF PRIDE, AVARICE, BRUTALITY, AND MEANNESS.

AND I HAD HEARD OF HIS **DEATH,** FROM AN ACCIDENT CONSEQUENT ON HIS **ILL-TREATMENT** OF A **HORSE.**

THIS RELEASE HAD **BEFALLEN** SOME TWO YEARS BEFORE; FOR ANYTHING I KNEW, SHE WAS **MARRIED** AGAIN.

IN THE **COLD** SHIVERY MIST, I BEHELD A **SOLITARY** FIGURE...

PIP!

ESTELLA!

I AM GREATLY **CHANGED.** I WONDER YOU **KNOW** ME.

THE **FRESHNESS** OF HER BEAUTY WAS INDEED **GONE,** BUT ITS **CHARM** REMAINED.

WHAT I HAD **NEVER** SEEN BEFORE, WAS THE **SADDENED,** SOFTENED LIGHT OF THE ONCE **PROUD** EYES.

AFTER SO MANY YEARS, IT IS **STRANGE** THAT WE SHOULD THUS MEET AGAIN, ESTELLA! DO YOU **OFTEN** COME BACK?

I HAVE **NEVER** BEEN HERE SINCE.

I HAVE VERY OFTEN **HOPED** TO COME BACK, BUT HAVE BEEN PREVENTED BY MANY CIRCUMSTANCES. **POOR, POOR OLD PLACE!** WERE YOU WONDERING HOW IT CAME TO BE LEFT IN THIS **CONDITION?** THE **GROUND** BELONGS TO **ME.**

IT IS THE **ONLY** POSSESSION I HAVE NOT **RELINQUISHED.** IT WAS THE SUBJECT OF THE ONLY DETERMINED **RESISTANCE** I MADE IN ALL THE **WRETCHED** YEARS.

I HAVE OFTEN **THOUGHT** OF YOU, OF LATE, **VERY** OFTEN. THERE WAS A LONG, HARD TIME WHEN I KEPT FROM ME THE REMEMBRANCE OF WHAT I HAD **THROWN AWAY** WHEN I WAS **IGNORANT** OF ITS **WORTH.**

BUT SINCE MY **DUTY** HAS NOT BEEN INCOMPATIBLE WITH THAT **REMEMBRANCE** --

-- I HAVE GIVEN IT A **PLACE IN MY HEART.**

YOU HAVE **ALWAYS** HELD YOUR **PLACE** IN **MY** HEART.

145

I LITTLE THOUGHT, THAT I SHOULD TAKE LEAVE OF **YOU** IN TAKING **LEAVE** OF THIS **SPOT**. I AM VERY **GLAD** TO DO SO.

GLAD TO PART **AGAIN**, ESTELLA?

TO ME, PARTING IS A **PAINFUL** THING. TO ME, THE REMEMBRANCE OF OUR LAST PARTING HAS BEEN **EVER** PAINFUL.

BUT **YOU** SAID TO **ME**, *"GOD **BLESS** YOU, GOD **FORGIVE** YOU!"* --

-- AND IF YOU COULD SAY THAT TO ME **THEN**, YOU WILL NOT HESITATE TO SAY IT **NOW**, WHEN SUFFERING HAS TAUGHT ME TO **UNDERSTAND** WHAT YOUR HEART USED TO BE.

I HAVE BEEN **BENT** AND **BROKEN**, BUT – I HOPE – INTO A **BETTER** SHAPE. BE AS GOOD TO ME AS YOU **WERE**, AND TELL ME WE ARE **FRIENDS**.

WE **ARE** FRIENDS.

AND WILL **CONTINUE** FRIENDS APART.

I TOOK HER HAND IN **MINE**, AND WE WENT **OUT** OF THE RUINED PLACE.

THE EVENING **MISTS** WERE RISING NOW, AND IN ALL THE BROAD EXPANSE OF TRANQUIL LIGHT, I SAW NO **SHADOW** OF ANOTHER **PARTING** FROM HER.

GREAT EXPECTATIONS

The End

Editor's Note:
The last phrase is taken from the revised ending that Dickens wrote for the first single-volume edition of 1862. It is intentionally ambiguous — probably more so than the previously published version of the phrase, which was, "I saw the shadow of no parting from her." However, because Dickens himself obviously felt that the 1862 ending was an improvement, we felt justified to use that phrase for this adaptation.

Charles Dickens

(1812 - 1870)

Charles Dickens was born was born in Landport, Portsmouth, on 7th February 1812. He was the second of eight children born to John and Elizabeth Dickens. Financially, the Dickens family were comfortable, and when they moved to Chatham, Kent in 1817 they sent Charles to the fee paying William Giles' school in the area.

By the time he was ten, the family had moved again; this time to London following the career of his father, John, who was a clerk in the Naval Pay Office. John got into debt and was eventually sent to Marshalsea Prison in 1824. His wife and most of the children joined him there (a common occurrence in those days); Charles, however, was put to work at Warren's Blacking Factory, where he labelled jars of boot polish.

When John's mother died soon after, she left enough money to pay off the debts and reunite the family. Although brief, Charles's time at the factory haunted him for the rest of his life:

> "For many years, when I came near to Robert Warren's, in the Strand, I crossed over to the opposite side of the way, to avoid a certain smell of the cement they put upon the blacking corks, which reminded me of what I once was. My old way home by the borough made me cry, after my oldest child could speak."

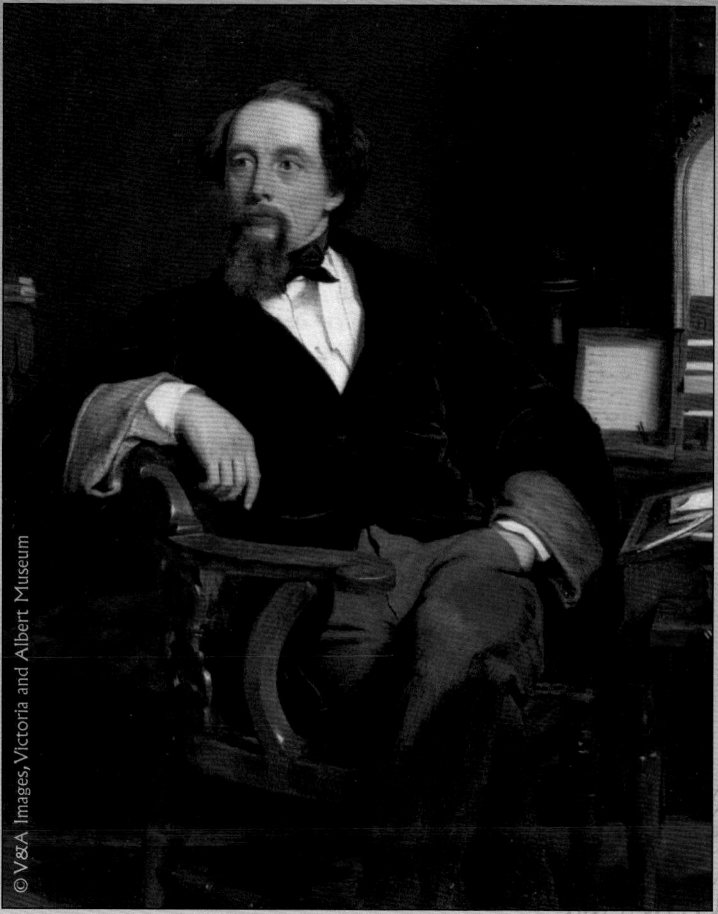
© V&A Images, Victoria and Albert Museum

Charles Dickens

Charles left school at fifteen and worked as an office boy with a Mr. Molloy of Lincoln's Inn. It was here that Charles made the decision to become a journalist. He studied shorthand at night, and went on to spend two years as a shorthand reporter at the Doctors' Commons Courts.

From 1830 to 1836 he wrote for a number of newspapers; he also started to achieve recognition for his own written work. In December 1833 his first published (but unpaid for) story, *A Dinner at Poplar Walk*, appeared in *The Old Monthly* magazine. About seeing his first work in print, Dickens wrote:

> "On which occasion I walked down to Westminster-hall, and turned into it for half an hour, because my eyes were so dimmed with joy and pride, that they could not bear the street, and were not fit to be seen there".

He wrote further stories for *The Old Monthly*; but when the magazine could not pay for them, Dickens began to write his "series" for *The Chronicle* at the request of the editor, George Hogarth.

In 1835, Charles got engaged to George Hogarth's eldest daughter, Catherine. They married on 2nd April 1836 and went on to have ten children (seven boys and three girls). Biographers have long suspected that Charles preferred Catherine's sister, Mary, who lived with the Dickens family and died in his arms in 1837 at the age of seventeen. Dickens had asked to be buried next to her; but when her brother died in 1841, Dickens's "place" was taken. He wrote to his great friend and biographer John Forster:

> "It is a great trial for me to give up Mary's grave... the desire to be buried next to her is as strong upon me now, as it was five years ago... And I know...that it will never diminish...I cannot bear the thought of being excluded from her dust".

The first series of *Sketches by Boz* was published in 1836 ("Boz" was an early pen name used by Dickens). Shortly afterwards, with the success of *Pickwick Papers* in 1837, Dickens was at last a full-time novelist. He produced works at an incredible rate; and at the start of his writing career, also managed to continue his work as a journalist and editor. He began his next book, *Oliver Twist*, in 1837 and continued it in monthly parts until April 1839.

Dickens visited Canada and the United States in 1842. During that visit he talked on the need for international copyright, because some American publishers were printing his books without his permission and without making any payment; he also talked about the need to end slavery. His visit and his opinions were recorded and published as *American Notes* in October of that year, causing quite a stir.

On 17th December 1843 his much-loved Christmas tale, *A Christmas Carol* (also available as a Classical Comics graphic novel) was published. It was so popular that it sold five-thousand copies by Christmas Eve — and has never been out of print since.

From childhood, Dickens had loved the stage and enjoyed the attention and applause he received. He performed in amateur theatre throughout the 1840s and 50s, and formed his own amateur theatrical company in 1845, which occupied much of his time.

Dickens became something of an international celebrity. In 1853 he toured Italy, and on his return to England, he gave the first of many public readings from his own works. At first he did these for charity, but before long he demanded payment.

By 1856, Dickens had made enough money to purchase a fine country house: Gads Hill in Kent. Although he had admired this place ever since his arrival to the area as a child, it was not to be a happy family home. A year later, Charles met a young actress called Ellen Lawless Ternan who went on to join his theatre company; and they began a relationship that was to last until his death.

Charles separated from his wife Catherine in 1858. The event was talked about in the newspapers, and Dickens publicly denied rumours of an affair. He was morally trapped – he was deeply in love with Ellen, but his writing career was based on promoting family values and being a good person; he felt that if he admitted his relationship with Ellen, it would put an end to his career.

Catherine moved to a house in London with their eldest son Charles, and Dickens remained at Gads Hill with the rest of the children and Catherine's sister, Georgina (there were rumours of Charles and Georgina having a relationship, too).

The more he tried to hide his personal life, the more it came out in his writing. *Great Expectations* was written around this time (1860) and includes elements of all the emotions he was experiencing: imprisonment, love that can never be, people living in isolation, and the compulsion to better oneself. He continued to look after Ellen

and made regular secret journeys to see her – not easy for the local celebrity that Dickens had become. He went to incredible lengths to keep his secret safe, including renting houses under different names and setting up offices for his business in places that made it easy for him to visit her.

In 1865, Dickens was involved in the Staplehurst Rail Crash: an incident which disturbed him greatly. He was travelling with Ellen and her mother, most likely returning from a secret holiday in France. The train left the track, resulting in the deaths of ten people and injuries to forty more. It is reported that Dickens tended to some of the wounded.

By 1867 Dickens's health was getting worse. His doctor advised him to rest, but he carried on with his busy schedule, which included a second tour of America.

He returned to England and, despite his bad health, continued his work and his public reading appearances. In April 1869, he collapsed during a reading at

Preston, and he was again advised to rest. Dickens didn't listen. He continued to give performances in London and he even started work on a new novel, *The Mystery of Edwin Drood*. This novel was never finished: he suffered a stroke and died suddenly at Gads Hill on 9th June 1870. He had asked to be buried "in an inexpensive, unostentatious, and strictly private manner" but public opinion, led by *The Times* newspaper, insisted that he should be buried in keeping with his status as a great writer. He was buried at Westminster Abbey on 14th June 1870.

His funeral was a private affair, attended by just twelve mourners. After the service, his grave was left open and thousands of people from all walks of life came to pay their respects and throw flowers onto the coffin. Today, a small stone with a simple inscription marks his grave:

"CHARLES DICKENS
BORN 7th FEBRUARY 1812
DIED 9th JUNE 1870"

The Dickens Family Tree

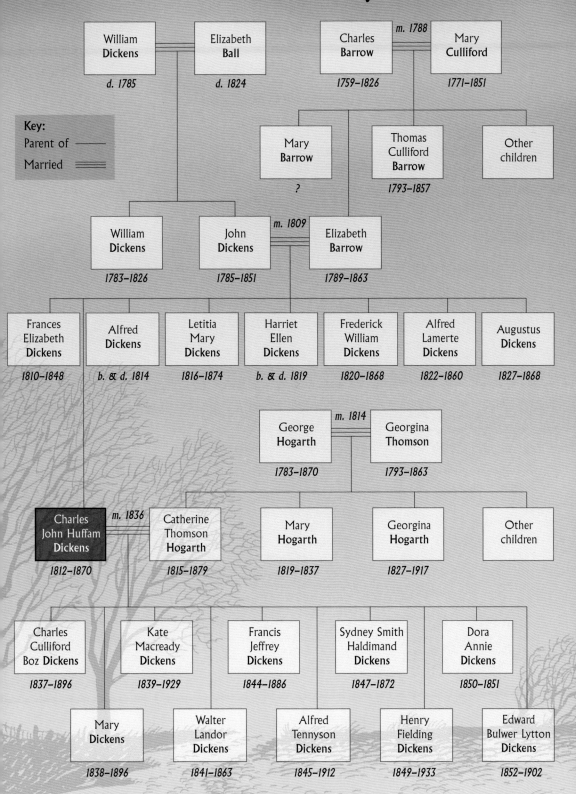

Key:
Parent of ——
Married ===

William Dickens d. 1785
Elizabeth Ball d. 1824

Charles Barrow 1759–1826 — m. 1788 — **Mary Culliford** 1771–1851

Mary Barrow ?
Thomas Culliford Barrow 1793–1857
Other children

William Dickens 1783–1826
John Dickens 1785–1851 — m. 1809 — **Elizabeth Barrow** 1789–1863

Frances Elizabeth Dickens 1810–1848
Alfred Dickens b. & d. 1814
Letitia Mary Dickens 1816–1874
Harriet Ellen Dickens b. & d. 1819
Frederick William Dickens 1820–1868
Alfred Lamerte Dickens 1822–1860
Augustus Dickens 1827–1868

George Hogarth 1783–1870 — m. 1814 — **Georgina Thomson** 1793–1863

Charles John Huffam Dickens 1812–1870 — m. 1836 — **Catherine Thomson Hogarth** 1815–1879
Mary Hogarth 1819–1837
Georgina Hogarth 1827–1917
Other children

Charles Culliford Boz Dickens 1837–1896
Kate Macready Dickens 1839–1929
Francis Jeffrey Dickens 1844–1886
Sydney Smith Haldimand Dickens 1847–1872
Dora Annie Dickens 1850–1851

Mary Dickens 1838–1896
Walter Landor Dickens 1841–1863
Alfred Tennyson Dickens 1845–1912
Henry Fielding Dickens 1849–1933
Edward Bulwer Lytton Dickens 1852–1902

Due to the lack of official records of births, deaths and marriages within this period, the above information is derived from extensive research and is as accurate as possible from the limited sources available.

Crime and Punishment

A strong thread of criminality runs throughout *Great Expectations*, much as it did in everyday Victorian London. Dickens himself was of course no stranger to the "wrong side of the law". As a young man, his father served time as an insolvent debtor in Marshalsea Prison, and for a while Charles worked as a court reporter. He also lived in a time of great social change, brought about by the increase in population, the impact of technological advances, the rise of industry, and the development of travel and transportation; but unfortunately also an increase in crime.

Elizabeth Fry

The most notable prison reformer of the nineteenth century was Elizabeth Fry. Born in Norwich in 1780, she decided while still a teenager to devote her life to helping people in need. At first, she did this by giving clothes to the poor, visiting the sick, and running a Sunday School in her house where she taught children to read. Then, she received her life's calling when she heard reports from a friend about the conditions in Newgate Prison (see opposite). Visiting the prison for herself in 1813, she found around three hundred women and their children huddled together in two wards and two cells. They were forced to sleep on the floor without any nightclothes or bedding; and some of them were still awaiting their trial (and therefore may well have been innocent).

She visited Newgate on a regular basis, supplying clothing and establishing a school and a chapel there. She also made sure that the women were kept occupied with sewing duties and Bible reading to help in their reformation.

In 1818, she was invited to speak to a House of Commons Committee on London Prisons. She told them how women slept thirty to a room in Newgate, where there were:

> "old and young, hardened offenders with those who had committed only a minor offence or their first crime; the lowest of women with respectable married women and maid-servants".

The committee was impressed with her work, but they disapproved of her views on capital punishment, which she said was "evil and produced evil results". Consequently, little was done.

However, in 1823 the new Home Secretary Sir Robert Peel (most famous for the introduction of the Metropolitan Police Force, also called "Peelers", and later "Bobbies") introduced *The Gaols Act*, which put some of Fry's recommendations into effect; but her work didn't stop there. The Act did not apply to local town gaols (jails) or debtors' prisons (like the one Dickens's father was sent to) and in 1820, Fry published a book which detailed the ongoing problems.

Although she was mostly concerned with prison reform she also campaigned to help the homeless, to improve the conditions in hospitals and mental asylums, and called for reforms to the workhouses. Elizabeth Fry's training school for nurses was a big influence on Florence Nightingale's work, and she even met with Queen Victoria on several occasions. Elizabeth Fry died in 1845.

Newgate Prison

Newgate Prison features heavily in *Great Expectations*; not only because it was the principle prison in London but also because it was regarded as the symbol of crime itself.

The term "Newgate" stems from the days when London was a Roman walled city with eight entrance gates, which also included Ludgate, Bishopsgate and Aldgate – names which have survived in street names to the present day. There had been a prison on the site since the twelfth century. The Great Fire of 1667 destroyed the prison building there at the time, and a new one "of great magnificence" was built in its place. This itself was destroyed by the anti-Catholic "Gordon Rioters" in 1780, when they attacked buildings that represented law and order, and in the process freed around four hundred prisoners. The prison was rebuilt straight away to a new design that incorporated three areas, one for each group of prisoners: debtors, male felons and female felons. Debtors were effectively the only long-term inmates at the prison; the male and female felons were only held there while awaiting trial, execution or transportation to the colonies. As detailed overleaf, prisoners awaiting transportation were mostly held in Prison Hulks that were moored on the River Thames until they received a place on a ship bound for Australia.

The population was increasing, especially in the cities, and this led to extreme poverty; forcing many into a life of crime. In an effort to control the rising crime figures, the government decided to strengthen the law, making many crimes punishable by death (see next page).

As a further deterrent and as a reminder of the law to others, condemned prisoners were hanged in public. Hangings took place at Tyburn, which is near where Marble Arch stands today. "Hanging Days", or "Tyburn Fairs" as they became known, were a renowned, gruesome spectacle. There were eight of them each year, and they were treated as public holidays. Crowds would gather outside Newgate Prison while a bell rang out. Carts would then take the condemned to Saint Sepulchre's Church so that they could be given their "last rites"; and from there they would be taken to Tyburn to be hanged from the gallows. The public would follow them, and become more rowdy and riotous as the journey progressed, rising to a fever pitch when they finally reached the scaffold.

These "Hanging Day" processions themselves posed a threat to law and order; so in 1783 when the Newgate Prison rebuild was completed, it was decided that public hangings would take place in the street outside the prison to avoid having to move the prisoners and incite the public (the Newgate Prison gallows are mentioned in Volume II, Chapter XIII of *Great Expectations*, and appear on page 79 of this book).

Hangings remained public events until 1868, when protests by many, including Dickens, put a halt to these terrible spectacles. Newgate Prison remained in operation until the turn of the century. In 1902, along with the nearby court rooms, it was finally demolished to make way for the Old Bailey. In all, 1120 men and 49 women were hanged there, mostly for burglary, forgery or murder.

The Death Penalty

With the rising crime figures that were a consequence of the abject poverty, the government decided to increase the severity of the law — and particularly the punishment for petty crimes such as theft.

Theft of property under the value of forty shillings (two pre-decimal pounds) carried a seven year prison sentence; theft over that amount was punishable by hanging.

However, not everyone who received the death penalty was executed. Hangings took place in public and were attended by hundreds of people; but before long, the public started to view the condemned as heroic martyrs instead of criminals.

Consequently, the number of hangings had to be reduced.

After receiving the death sentence in the courts, the Court Recorder would prepare his report to the King and Privy Council. In that report, he would indicate which prisoners should hang and which should be granted reprieve. Murderers were hanged within two days of sentencing; but other

criminals had to wait in prison for up to four months to hear their fate. It was quote common for female prisoners to claim that they were pregnant (which they often were!) and force a reprieve that way. Instead of being hanged, prisoners who were granted reprieve were selected for transportation (see below).

Transportation

The idea to ship criminals out of Britain started life nearly two hundred years before Dickens was born (and while Shakespeare was still alive). In 1597, an act was passed to "banish dangerous criminals from the Kingdom"; but it took until 1615 for the first convict ships to leave England. Back then, they were sent to America. This continued for over a hundred and fifty years; but with the War of Independence in 1775, the American colonies closed their ports to British prison ships, and a new destination had to be found. The government decided upon New South Wales (Australia) and the first 778 convicts (586 male, 192 female) left Britain in 1777.

The area formally became a British Colony in 1788, and from then until 1868 when transportation ended, 165,000 convicts were sent there, with only one-in-eight of these being female.

Surprisingly, despite the incredibly long journey of six to twelve months on crowded ships, few prisoners (less than one-in-twenty) died during the voyage. In fact, like Abel Magwitch in this book, many prisoners endured only a short period of confinement or labour, after which they were released "on licence". Although they could not return to Britain, many went on to prosper in their new home.

Prison Hulks

When transportation to America came to an abrupt halt in 1775, and before New South Wales became the replacement destination, a solution had to be found to house the growing number of convicts awaiting deportation. As a temporary solution, they decided to warehouse these convicts in old warships moored in the River Thames. Bought by the prison authorities after the Royal Navy had taken them out of service, these Prison Hulks went on to become long-term fixtures where convicts were held as they waited for the next voyage that would take them away.

Hulks were soon treated as the answer to the generally overcrowded prisons, and were used to detain many prisoners who were not even due to be transported abroad; at one point, over two-thirds of all prisoners were held on hulks. Conditions on these floating prisons were even worse than those on land. One famous hulk, *The Warrior*, comprised three decks, each holding 150 to 200 convicts. The decks were divided into caged cells on both sides of the hull, with a walkway down the middle. Each cell housed eight to ten men, with only the old gun ports in the sides of the hull for ventilation.

Prisoners were forced to sleep with chains around their waists and ankles to prevent them from escaping at night. Any that were found to have made an attempt to file away or otherwise remove them were either flogged, secured with extra irons, or put in solitary confinement.

The hulks were terribly unsanitary. Not only were there problems caused by the overcrowded living conditions, but all water was taken from the polluted Thames; and this gave rise to outbreaks of many diseases, such as cholera, "Gaol Fever" (a form of typhus spread by vermin) and dysentery. Large numbers of prisoners died from these diseases.

By 1850, the use of hulks was in decline; and in 1857, the last hulk was destroyed. Although hulks were no longer in use when Dickens started to write *Great Expectations* (1860), their presence in the book is not an error. The hulks appear at the start of the book, which is set in 1812 – a time when the use of hulks was probably at their peak.

Page Creation

1. Script

The first stage is to adapt the entire story into comic book panels, describing the images to be drawn as well as the dialogue and captions. The challenge that Jen Green faced with *Great Expectations* was how to condense a 400+ page Dickens novel into 140 pages of graphic novel and still retain all the events, details, plot twists and connections. There are two versions of the dialogue and captions: Original Text and Quick Text. Both versions use the same artwork.

Page 19 from the script of *Great Expectations* showing 2 text versions.

2. Character Sheets

Before the script was completed, John Stokes began work on visualising the characters and important scenes. Here you see his sketches of Pip and Miss Havisham. This pre-production is an important stage because it sets the tone for the whole book and enables the artist to develop the final look of the artwork.

3. Rough Sketch

Once the artist receives the script, he takes his character designs and creates rough layouts. John's "roughs" are very detailed. He is considering many things at this stage, including pacing of the action, emphasis of certain elements to tell the story in the best way, lettering space and even lighting of the scene. If any changes need to be made, then it is far easier to make them at this stage, before the page is drawn.

The rough sketch created from the script.

4. Pencils

The process to create the finished artwork begins as soon as the rough sketch is agreed with the editor. The artwork is drawn on A3 art board at approximately 150% of the finished printed size. Because John's roughs are so detailed, very few changes are made when the page is pencilled.

You can see that the tablet has been added in the first panel as a continuity from the previous page, and more lettering space was allowed for in panel 6.

Interestingly, the rough sketch details some artistic elements that won't be tackled until the colouring stage. For example, the last panel shows some night clouds in the rough, but a clear sky in the pencilled page.

The pencil drawing of page 19.